Solving Your Child's Reading Problems

Solving Your Child's Reading Problems

Ricki Linksman

A CITADEL PRESS BOOK
Published by Carol Publishing Group

A Citadel Press Book
Published by Carol Publishing Group
Citadel Press is a registered trademark of Carol Communications, Inc.
Editorial Offices: 600 Madison Avenue, New York, N.Y. 10022
Sales and Distribution Offices: 120 Enterprise Avenue, Secaucus, N.J. 07094
In Canada: Canadian Manda Group, One Atlantic Avenue, Suite 105,
    Toronto, Ontario M6K 3E7
Queries regarding rights and permissions should be addressed to Carol
Publishing Group, 600 Madison Avenue, New York, N.Y. 10022

Carol Publishing Group books are available at special discounts for bulk
purchases, sales promotion, fund-raising, or educational purposes. Special
editions can be created to specifications. For details, contact: Special Sales
Department, Carol Publishing Group, 120 Enterprise Avenue, Secaucus,
N.J. 07094

Manufactured in the United States of America
10 9 8 7 6 5 4 3 2 1

Library of Congress Cataloging-in-Publication Data
Linksman, Ricki, 1952–
    How to solve your child's reading problems / by Ricki Linksman
        p.   cm.
    "A Citadel Press book."
    ISBN 0-8065-1618-6 (pbk.)
    1. Reading—Parent participation.   I. Title.
LB1050.2.L56   1995
649'.58—dc20
                                                94-44300
                                                  CIP

Dedication

Dedicated to children all over the world
who have the right to reach their fullest
potential in all spheres of life,
to my own teachers and mentors who
have inspired and guided me,
to my parents who were my first teachers,
to my husband who encouraged me,
and to God for His many gifts.

Contents

Acknowledgments   ix

Introduction   xi

Part 1: Causes of Reading Problems

1. Five Main Causes of Reading Problems   3
2. Missing a Step in the Reading Process   6
3. Differences in Learning Styles   17
4. Self-Esteem and School Success   31
5. Motivation and Success in Reading   49
6. Reading Problems Caused by a Learning Disability   56
7. Why Schools Need Your Help   68

Part 2: Solutions for Reading Problems

8. What You Can Do to Help Your Child Read Better   81
9. How Reading Is Learned   83
10. Why You Need to Know How to Diagnose Your Child's Problem   90
11. What Is Your Child's Best Learning Style?   93
12. How to Diagnose Problems in Letter-Sound Relationships   115
13. How to Remedy Problems in Letter-Sound Relationships   129
14. How to Diagnose Problems With Vocabulary Skills   172

15. Remedies for Problems With Vocabulary
    Skills   178
16. How to Diagnose Comprehension Problems   195
17. Remedies for Comprehension Problems   202
18. How to Diagnose Problems With
    Independent Reading Strategies   229
19. Remedy for Problems With Independent
    Reading Strategies   233
20. Reading as a Pleasurable Activity   238
21. Hope for Your Child's Progress   258

    The Vowel and Consonant Guide   261

    Index   337

Acknowledgments

I would like to acknowledge all the students I have ever taught for they have been my best teachers. It was through my students that I learned how children and teenagers think and learn and what we as parents and teachers need to do to help them reach their highest potential.

Special thanks to my publisher, Steven Schragis, my editors, Hillel Black, Bruce Shostak, and Marcy Swingle, and copyeditor Deborah Dwyer for their vision and forsight in making this book available to the world so that all children have an opportunity to be successful readers.

Introduction

"Oh, No! My Child Has a Problem in Reading!"

You come home from a hard day's work, kick off your shoes, settle down in your favorite chair with a nice cool soft drink, and try to unwind. Your calm reverie is broken by the ringing of the telephone. Your neighbor is calling.

"Did you see your daughter's report card yet?" A knot of dread hits you in the stomach.

Your friend continues, "I just saw my son's, and he's failing reading. I called his teacher and she says I need to hire a tutor. If he fails one more quarter, he's at risk for being retained in the same grade next year." Report card day. You know that you are not ready to deal with this. Your daughter has had similar problems this year. You are hoping her report card has improved, but a sinking feeling tells you it will be just as poor. You call your daughter from her room and ask to see her report card. Hesitatingly she walks toward you with her head down and hands you the envelope. Your worst fears have come true. She too has failed reading. You tell yourself, "I am an educated person, a college graduate, who loves to read. How could my child be doing so poorly in reading?"

Many parents at one time or another must face the problem of children developing reading difficulties. It is not a problem limited to students with special learning needs. It can happen to any student at any time. In fact, a September 1993 study conducted by the United States Department of Education found that two-thirds of the nation's students struggle with reading.

One of the reasons this crisis has reached such large proportions is that reading problems are not remedied at the time they first surface. For every year the child does not receive help, the problem increases and the student lags further and further behind. This is one of the reasons many high school students are still reading at an elementary school level.

Can this problem be rectified? What can parents do about it? Fortunately, reading problems are not like terminal diseases. They can be solved. How do I know? Over the last twenty years I have solved the reading problems of elementary, middle, and high school students, as well as college students and adults. I have helped students who were below average, average, and gifted, as well as students who were challenged by learning disabilities, mental retardation, attention-deficit disorder, behavioral and emotional disorders, and physical handicaps. Every one of them learned to read and improved their reading with the simple techniques I present in this book. Although I was trained in diagnosing and remediating reading problems, I have developed techniques that can simplify the process. I have trained parents who have various levels of education, and they have all used this technique successfully with their children to bring their reading skills back up to grade level.

The book is written in a simple, step-by-step manner. So, parents, relax, sit back, and have confidence in yourself. By the time you have finished reading this book, you will have all the tools you need to solve your child's reading difficulties and replace them with the joys of success.

Part 1

Causes of
Reading Problems

Chapter 1

Five Main Causes of Reading Problems

Reading is a complex process. It is a form of communication between the writer and the reader. The writer converts his or her thoughts into symbols that appear on a page. The reader must look at these symbols and change them back into words. Reading is more complicated than speech. When a person speaks, the listener hears the words and interprets the message. Reading adds a step to the process by turning the speaker's message into symbols that the reader must decode and understand. In order to do that, the reader must know the language and the codes that symbolize the spoken word.

Each of us learns to recognize symbols. We understand that a red light means "stop" and a green light means "go." We recognize a stop sign, a danger sign, and a hospital sign. Our brains also interpret nonverbal communication. We understand a smile to mean that someone is happy and a frown to mean that someone is sad. As we grow up, we understand words that are spoken to us. We learn the meaning of "No," "I love you," and "Good night." By repetition of certain words and the actions associated with them, we begin to understand the language that those around us are speaking.

Besides associating certain words with particular actions in our culture, human beings can also learn to read symbols. Just

3

as children learn that a round object that bounces is called a ball, they learn that a circle drawn on paper is called the letter *o*. They begin to learn the alphabet and the names of all those strange shapes called letters. Later on, children learn the sounds of each of those letters. Building on that, they learn how letters are put together to form words. They have to learn how to pronounce the different combinations of letters. Besides pronouncing the words, they must form a picture or concept in order to make sense of the text. This process must be performed quickly and automatically in order for children to be able to read sentences and paragraphs. Readers must be able to form pictures and thoughts in their minds to receive the message intended by the writer. The text must speak to the reader so that he or she interacts with the material. By reading, one can expand one's horizons, gain knowledge, grow in awareness about oneself and the world, and form new ideas.

There are many components involved in the reading process. It is a joy to see a first grader who entered the school year as a nonreader complete the year reading aloud from a book. It is a constant source of marvel how in one year children learn the reading process!

By understanding the complexity of the reading process, it is easy to see how difficulties can arise. There are many rocks on which one can trip and fall. A child may have difficulties at any stage of reading development. If a child has problems in reading, it could be due to a variety of reasons. In order to simplify the process of identifying reading difficulties, we will look at five main causes of reading problems. They are:

1. missing a step in the reading process

2. differences in learning styles

3. low self-esteem

4. lack of motivation

5. a learning disability

The first part of this book will explain each of these five causes of reading difficulties. It will give you a yardstick to assess what your own child's problem is. You will learn how to pinpoint the cause of your child's problem. The second part of the book will then provide the solutions for your child's specific reading difficulty.

Chapter 2

Missing a Step in the Reading Process

There is no magic in reading instruction. Reading is like climbing a staircase. It is a developmental, step-by-step process. If one misses a step and slips back down, one cannot proceed to the next higher level without retracing one's steps.

How do students miss these steps in reading? Students may have been absent from school for a day, a week, or several weeks due to illness or an accident. If an important skill was taught during the time of their absence and it was not taught to them when they returned, they may have a gap in their learning. Although teachers attempt to make up missed work, sometimes a skill can slip through the cracks when there are many students absent and too many different skills to reteach. Sometimes the skill is retaught, but because the student missed the practice sessions, they are moved along to the next skill before they have enough opportunities to reinforce what they were taught.

A skill may have been missed because the student was not paying attention in school. Sometimes the student is still struggling with a previous skill and is not ready to attend to the next skill. At times, a student is taught a skill before he or she is developmentally ready for it. By the time the student is ready, maybe a few months or a half year later, the class has

6

already gone far beyond it and is working on the next higher-level skill. If the teacher does not backtrack and reteach the earlier skill, another possible gap is created in the child's skill base.

Reading instruction varies from school to school. In some schools, students move on based on their mastery of skills. Until they master the skill, they do not go to the next one. In other schools, when students complete one grade level and are promoted, they automatically go to the next higher reading book, which matches the grade in which they are placed. Thus, they skip the skills they did not master in the previous grade and move on to higher skills. This too can create a gap.

We live in a society in which people are constantly moving. When students change schools, they often face different reading textbook series or curriculum objectives. Each reading series teaches the skills in a different order. By changing schools, one also moves to a different reading series or a different curriculum, and it is likely that certain skills are missed in the process.

You may wonder why we don't have a skills chart that goes with the child from grade level to grade level or from school to school. Some school districts have developed such systems. I helped develop such a system for Palm Beach County schools in Florida. Each student had a record card of skills, and as one skill was mastered it was checked off. Thus, teachers could see what their incoming students had already mastered and what they still needed to learn. If your child's school does not have such a system, I suggest that you start keeping your own record of your child's skills so that you can ensure that there aren't any gaps. In this book, I have prepared a suggested chart (The Vowel and Consonant Guide: Part A) to help you keep a record of your child's skills. Just as you keep a record of your child's immunizations and health history, you can easily keep one of your child's reading skills.

After all, if your child moves to a different class, grade level, or school, you are the only one who will remain a constant in your child's life. You, as the parent, can ensure that your child is receiving the instruction that he or she needs.

Progress in reading is not determined by the number of hours one physically sits in reading class. It is dependent upon mastering each skill in the developmental process and being able to apply those reading skills to books, magazines, and newspapers. Good reading instructors know the developmental progression of those skills. If parents are aware of those skills, they can better understand what is happening to their children and can provide assistance.

FOUR MAIN CATEGORIES OF READING SKILLS

In the developmental process, there are four main categories of reading skills: (1) letter-sound relationships, (2) vocabulary, (3) comprehension, and (4) strategies for independent reading. Steps can be missed in a student's development along any of these lines.

Letter-Sound Relationships

The first of these four groups of skills is letter-sound relationships. It is also called word-attack skills or decoding skills, and each school district may have its own terminology for this category. Basically, it is the ability to know what sound or sounds each letter makes and how those sounds are combined to make words. In the English language this skill is more complicated than in some other languages in which one letter equals one sound. For example, in English the vowels, *a, e, i, o,* and *u,* and sometimes *y* can be pronounced at least two different ways—as a "long sound," which is the same as the letter name, or a "short sound." A long vowel sound is like *a* as in *cape*. A short vowel sound is like *a* as in *cat*.

Long and Short Vowel Sounds

Vowel	Short Sound	Long Sound
a	cat	cape
e	bed	meet
i	sit	bike
o	pot	rope
u	sun	flute

Some vowels have several other variations in pronunciation. For example, *o* is pronounced differently in the following words: *not, rope, cow, boy, book, boot, for, cough,* and *rough*.

A similar difficulty arises in learning consonants. A student may learn how to pronounce the consonants, but *c* can be pronounced as *s* or *k*, and *g* can be pronounced as a *j* as well. Consonants can also be combined to produce different sounds. Two or three consonants can be blended together to make what is called a consonant blend, like *tr* in *train*, *cl* in *class*, or *str* in *street*. If a student does not know how to combine *t* and *r*, they may end up reading *train* as "tuh-rain," or "tuh-ruh-ain."

Some consonants combine to make a totally new sound. These are called digraphs. For example, when *c* and *h* join together, they become *ch* as in *church*. *T* and *h* can combine and make two different sounds: *th* as in *think* and *th* as in *then*.

Thus, students need to learn not only the different sounds of a particular letter, but when to vary their pronunciation.

Usually, from kindergarten to third grade, students are taught the variety of ways each letter can be pronounced, and how to read a variety of words. This skill must be mastered or students will find themselves struggling to read the vocabulary words found in higher-level reading material.

Vocabulary

Vocabulary development is the second category of skills. Students need to learn the meaning of words to understand what they are reading. One of the biggest problems students face is that they do not know the meanings of the words, although they may have mastered the decoding skills and can "sound out," or pronounce, words correctly.

Learning how to find the meaning of words is a skill that must be taught. Meanings can be figured out from the context, that is, from the sentence or paragraph in which the word appears. One term for getting the meaning from the context is "using context clues." For example, take a look at the following sentences:

> Susan felt exhilarated when she won the award. It
> was the happiest moment she had ever experienced in
> her life.

Suppose you did not know what the word *exhilarated* means. By reading these two sentences, you could figure out that Susan was happy. Thus, you would get the idea that exhilarated had something to be do with happiness and how one feels when one wins an award. You might say it was a feeling of being extremely happy. This is using the context to get meanings of words.

Students need to be taught how to interpret context clues in order to figure out the meaning of a new word. If students do not know how to use context clues, the tendency is to skip over the hard words. They may sound as if they can read the words aloud, but meaning does not register in their minds.

Another skill students should learn in order to get word meaning is using a dictionary. If the meaning of a word is not clear from the context, students need to know how to look up words in a dictionary or a glossary. I remember taking a class of students to a library and assigning them the task of looking up words in a dictionary. I found one of my new students sitting with the dictionary but not writing anything.

"Why aren't you writing the definitions?" I asked.

The student replied, "I can't find the meaning."

"Where did you look?"

A blank stare was my reply.

"Have you looked at the book yet?"

The reply came, "I've been turning the pages but I don't see the answer."

It often seems as if students think answers come from the book by osmosis into the head just by holding the magical object or by flipping pages. They need to be taught how to find the word by using alphabetical order, by reading the guide words at the top of each page to locate the correct page, and by scanning the page for the right word. This is a skill that must be taught. If we find our children do not know how to look up a word in the dictionary, then we need to show them how to do so. Chapter 15 will show you how to teach this skill.

After figuring out the meaning, students need to know how to practice the new words so that they can remember them. Just looking them up and writing down definitions is not enough. Students need to learn practical strategies for using the words in their daily life in order to remember them.

Some students are never taught that if they do not know the meaning of each word in the sentence, they will not fully understand the sentence. These students merely skip over the hard words. As they move from grade level to grade level, the difficulty of the vocabulary increases. If students are in the habit of skipping difficult words, the number of words they are missing in any given reading will become so large that it will severely affect their ability to understand the passage.

Comprehension

Comprehension is the ability to understand what one is reading. Students may be able to sound out words and may know the meanings of many words, but they do not know what they are reading. How can this happen?

Comprehension must be taught. A shocking number of students, even at the high school level, have mastered the art of sounding out words, and when they read aloud they sound as if they can read. But ask them what they are reading and they have no idea. Somehow they were never taught the skill of comprehension. They never realized that reading was the process of making a mental connection between the words on the page and ideas and pictures in their heads. They were never taught that the words should create moving pictures or concepts in their mind, and that they should think about those ideas. Unless children form pictures, thoughts, images, and ideas in their head, they are only mechanically saying what their eyes see, and they are not really "reading."

True reading is comprehension, not saying sounds and words aloud in one's head or aloud without awareness of what they mean. It is a misconception that if a child does not comprehend, the child is "slow," "dumb," or "stupid." Often, lack of comprehension is due to the fact that the child was never taught this skill. One year while I was working with a class of high school students, I examined their standardized reading scores and saw how low they scored in comprehension. I decided to start a unit in which we focused on comprehension.

I handed them a short story to read, and after they read it silently, I began asking questions. Most students drew a total blank, or they gave me answers that had nothing to do with what they had read. I decided to start from scratch. "Read the first sentence," I told them. Continuing, I said, "Now tell me, if you were making a movie about this story, and you were the director, what would you have the actors and actresses do and say, and what would the movie set look like? Picture what you read like a movie."

Then I guided them. "Who is the sentence talking about?" They told me it was about a boy. "Picture what that boy looks like!" I told them. "What do you see?" Slowly students began to raise their hands and describe what the boy looked like to them. "Okay! What does the sentence say the boy is doing?" Then I guided them, saying, "The boy is driving his car. Picture that car and see the boy in the car. Do you see it yet? Raise your hands when you see this in your mind." Slowly the students raised their hands. "What do you see?" "A boy driving a car," they told me. Step by step I walked them through the paragraph until I was certain each had a visual image in his or her mind about what we read. Then I asked questions, and each one of them could recall the paragraph. Finally a student raised his hand and said, "This is fun, seeing the story like a movie. I never knew that that was what reading is about!" Others confirmed the same point of view. No one had ever taught them that they should "see" or "experience" the words on the page. They were so excited at this discovery. It was then that I realized that we cannot assume children know that reading is comprehending.

We assume that children will automatically do what we do when we read—form pictures and thoughts. But this process must be taught to them in order for them to be able to do it. Once they are taught how to make the connection between the words on the page and pictures or thoughts in their minds, those who we previously might have labeled as "slow" children come alive. They begin to grasp what reading really is and suddenly find new enjoyment in the process.

Strategies for Independent Reading

Readers also need to learn strategies to read independently. There is a set of skills or strategies that can be taught to children so that they can monitor their own reading habits. They need to learn to pull together all the other reading skills—letter-sound relationships, vocabulary, and comprehension—to read without someone else's help.

The first strategy is to learn a set of questions that a reader should be asking himself or herself while reading. These are self-checking questions to help the reader evaluate whether they are understanding what they are reading. These questions are:

a. Did what I just read make sense?

b. Did I picture or grasp everything I have read so far or have I missed a portion?

The reader needs to be aware of whether they are comprehending everything, or whether they are tuning in and out of the story or skipping over portions due to being inattentive or skipping hard words. If the child catches himself or herself skipping parts, he or she needs to be trained to go back and reread the missed portions. Many times, children just keep their eyes moving over the lines and keep their hands turning the pages without actually "reading." Their eyes are moving, but nothing is registering in their minds. They need to monitor or catch themselves when they find they are not registering so that they can go back to the last part they remember and reread from that point.

Children need to learn to be attentive to what they are reading and to stop when something is not making any sense. They need to understand that if it did not make sense, they might have made an error in letter-sound relationship, or they may not know the correct pronunciation of a word, or they may not know the meaning of a word. Children with poor independent reading strategies usually keep reading whether the sentences make sense or not. Good readers stop to figure out what the problem is. They check the words to make sure they are reading the letter-sound relationships correctly, or they check the meaning of the word in a dictionary. They know if they go on without making sense of what they just read, they will not understand the text properly. They also learn that the text builds on what they just read, and that if they did not understand one part, they may not understand what follows.

In school, students often do well with material the teacher has gone over with them. But without independent reading strategies, the same students may get stuck when they encounter new reading material such as those they check out of the library or those they buy from bookstores. They do not know how to use independent strategies to figure out words they have never seen before. By learning independent strategies, children can handle with ease any type of reading material.

Once parents are aware of these skills—letter-sound relationships, vocabulary, comprehension, and independent reading strategies—they can pinpoint where their child's difficulties lie. Diagnosis is the first step. If we know that the child's problem is in letter-sound relationships, we can teach or reteach the missing sounds. If we know that the problem is in vocabulary skills, we can teach children how to figure out new words. If the difficulty lies in comprehension, we can teach them how to picture what they read in their minds. If their problem is due to a lack of independent reading strategies, we can teach them how to be self-sufficient readers. There *is* a solution for each type of problem.

Chapter 3

Differences in Learning Styles

Human beings learn about the world around them through their five senses. We have the senses of sight, hearing, smell, taste, and touch. Research shows that each of us receives information in different ways. Those of us who learn better through our eyes are visual learners. Auditory learners learn better through their ears. Those who learn better through the sense of touch are called tactile learners. Some learn better through the sensations they receive through the movement of their large muscles. These people are called kinesthetic learners. Believe it or not, some people learn best through their sense of smell, making them olfactory learners. Finally, there are those who learn through their sense of taste, making them gustatory learners. If we look at infants, who must put everything in their mouths in order to learn what it is, we can get an idea of what a gustatory learner would be like. And we know that people who have lost their eyesight and their hearing may have to rely on their sense of smell, or their olfactory sense, to receive information about what is going on around them.

Each of us has a strength in one or more of the sensory modes. That strength is reflected in the way we prefer to receive information and how we communicate with others. If we are visual learners, then we connect better with information that is presented to us visually. We may also use language that describes visual impressions when trying to communicate with others. If we are not instructed in a way that matches our best learning style, we may have more difficulty learning the material than we would if the instruction were presented in our preferred learning style.

Let us see how this works and how it affects reading. We shall begin with this simple test of learning styles to get an idea of your own preference. Then you will understand how learning style preferences could affect your child's reading.

What Is Your Strongest Learning Style?

For each question, select one answer, either a, b, c, or d, and note it on a piece of paper.

1. When I am taking a course, a class, or a workshop, I prefer that
   a. the teacher writes the notes on the board or lets me read from a book.
   b. the teacher lectures, explaining the subject to me verbally.
   c. the teacher guides me through a demonstration in which I can touch and feel what is being taught, write notes, or draw pictures to remember the experience.
   d. the teacher involves me in some movement or activity in which I can experience what he or she is teaching.

2. When I have to drive to a new place, I prefer that
   a. someone writes the directions for me on paper or gives me a map showing me how to get there.
   b. someone explains the directions to me orally.
   c. I write the directions and make the map myself.
   d. someone actually navigates for me, because I need to experience going there once with someone before I can learn the way, or else as someone

explains the directions, I have to feel or experience in my mind the movements of turning at key landmarks before I am sure of where I am going.

3. When I meet people for the first time, one of the first things I notice about them is
   a. their appearance—how they look and what they are wearing.
   b. the way they talk, what they say, and the sound of their voice.
   c. how they make me feel.
   d. what they do and how they act.

4. After I meet people, I remember
   a. their face.
   b. their names or what they spoke about.
   c. how I felt being with them.
   d. what activity we did together.

5. When I enter a room for the first time, the main thing I notice is
   a. what the room looks like.
   b. the sounds in the room.
   c. how I feel at an emotional level being in the room.
   d. how physically comfortable I feel being in the room and the activity going on in the place.

6. In my spare time I prefer to
   a. read a book or look at magazines.
   b. listen to talk shows or talk to friends.
   c. do something that requires using my hands or that allows me to express my feelings.
   d. do an activity that requires movement such as sports or that allows me to try new things.

7. I feel happy being in a place that
   a. is visually attractive.
   b. has auditory stimulation.
   c. gives me good feelings.
   d. is physically comfortable and that gives me room to move around.

8. When I go into a restaurant, I notice
    a. the decor.
    b. the sounds.
    c. the mood and atmosphere.
    d. how comfortable I feel, the taste of the food, or the activity going on in the place.

9. I feel most uncomfortable
    a. in a messy, disorganized place.
    b. in a place that is too quiet.
    c. in a place where people do not like me.
    d. in a place where I am confined and cannot move around.

10. When I teach something to others
    a. I show them a picture, a written diagram, printed words, a map, or a chart.
    b. I tell it to them.
    c. I draw or write the instructions for them.
    d. I show them physically by demonstration or movement.

___

After answering the questions, total up the number of "a" answers, the number of "b" answers, the number of "c" answers, and the number of "d" answers. Do you have more of one type of answer? If you have more "a" answers, you may be a visual learner. If you have more "b" answers, you may be an auditory learner. If you have more "c" answers, you may be a tactile learner. And if you have more answers in the "d" category, you may be a kinesthetic learner. You may be tied for one answer, which may mean that you have strengths in two areas. You may have two scores that are close, showing a dominant sense and a secondary strength. You may find yourself tied in three areas. Some people have developed the ability to use several or all senses equally well.

Before we relate this information to your child's reading

habits, we must first understand the characteristics of each type of learner.

VISUAL LEARNERS

Visual learners receive most of their information from the world through their eyes. They notice visual detail more than the other types of learners. They notice how things look and observe colors, patterns, and designs. They prefer that their visual environment looks pleasing. When they meet people, they notice how they look. They observe their hairstyle, their clothes, their makeup or jewelry. In a room, they notice the interior decoration. These are the people who like everything to be visually in place.

Visual learners receive information from books, magazines, newspapers, charts, maps, diagrams, and pictures. If you try to explain information to a visual learner, they will tend to say, "Let me read it myself," or "show me a picture of what you are talking about." Information does not register with them unless they can see it.

AUDITORY LEARNERS

Auditory learners receive information through their ears. They enjoy listening, talking, and discussing. They process their thoughts by discussion to hear themselves think aloud as well. They learn best by listening to lectures, hearing information from radio and television, and having conversations with people. They like talk shows as well as music. If there are no sounds, they will create auditory stimulus by talking with other people, humming, singing, or talking to themselves out loud.

When they enter a place, they will notice the sounds, particularly the conversation. They will be quick to join into discussion. They are also easily distracted by noises, and when they are trying to read or study, they will have a hard time tuning out the auditory distractions. While visual learners can tune out the auditory stimulus and can read undisturbed while there is noise in the room, auditory learners need quiet for study.

Their best learning environment is one in which someone is lecturing or teaching through word of mouth or one in which they can discuss their ideas. They like to listen to audiotaped or videotaped lectures or readings. They like to debate, do public speaking, or oral presentations. While visual learners have to see the information written down, auditory learners prefer to hear it spoken to them.

TACTILE LEARNERS

Tactile learners receive information from their sense of touch and through their feelings. They learn best by using their hands and fingers. These are the people who learn by taking notes, writing information down, drawing or doodling, or by typing. If they read or hear something, they need to write it down to help them remember and learn it. If they want to remember a phone number, they need to touch the numbers on the telephone to remember them.

They also receive information through their feelings. The first thing they notice when they enter a room or meet someone is how that place or person makes them feel. They pick up the "vibrations" of a place or a person. They will remember whether they felt safe, happy, peaceful, or if they felt sad, upset, frightened, or unsafe in a place. They are sensitive to people's nonverbal messages conveyed by their tone of voice, facial expressions, gestures, and body language. While visual learners focus on how a person looks, and auditory learners focus on how a person talks, tactile learners focus on the feelings they get from being with a person. They will notice if someone is angry, sad, happy, upset, or agitated. Often they will "read" behind their words or "read between the lines" of what a person is saying, because they are perceiving their emotional state.

Tactile people learn best when they receive positive feelings from their mentor or teacher. If the atmosphere is negative, the tactile learner will be upset and will not focus on the information. They will remember best the information which was conveyed in a way that created an emotionally satisfying experience.

KINESTHETIC LEARNERS

Kinesthetic learners receive information from their large-muscle movements. They remember the sensation of their bodies moving. Thus, these learners learn best by doing, by movement, and by activity. They notice the activity level of a place and the actions that they performed. These types of learners need to learn by exploration, by experimentation, by active involvement, and by discovery. They have a difficult time sitting still. They have to be up and about in order to learn.

If you ask kinesthetic people to remember an incident from their life, they will recall their activity in those incidents. If they meet someone, they may not remember that person's name or face, but they remember what they did with that person. If you want kinesthetic people to remember what is taught, they have to be given the opportunity to perform an action associated with the information.

Kinesthetic people also notice their comfort level in a

place. They need the temperature to be just right for them. If they are too cold or too hot, they will not be able to concentrate until the environment is just right. If they are hungry, they must satisfy their hunger or they cannot focus on anything else. If the seat is too hard or too soft, they cannot function until they get their position just right. They also need to feel comfortable with the people around them. The smells in a place have to be to their liking or they will be disturbed. They are so focused on their own comfort level that they cannot tune into information until their environment is just right.

MATCHING LEARNING STYLE TO INSTRUCTION

We learn best when information presented to us matches our learning style. If we are visual learners, we learn best when data is presented to us visually. If we are auditory learners, we learn best when information is presented to us verbally. If we are tactile learners, we learn best when we can use our sense of touch or our feelings. If we are kinesthetic learners, we learn best by doing and moving.

If information taught to us comes from a different medium than one we are programmed to take in, we may tune it out. Just picture your own learning style. If you are visual, don't you have difficulty when someone is lecturing to you without visual images? If you are auditory, don't you become frustrated when someone is showing you something without explaining it verbally? If you are kinesthetic, aren't you frustrated when you have to sit still and listen to someone without doing any activity along with it? And if you are tactile, don't you have a hard time listening to someone without noticing their moods and emotional tone?

It is the same situation with your children. The method of teaching needs to match their best learning style. This leads us to another reason why some children have difficulty learning to read. If the method used to teach them reading did not match their best learning style, they may have tuned out much of the information. You will probably ask, can reading be taught visually, auditorially, tactilely, and kinesthetically? The answer is yes. Any subject can be taught in four different ways. The best instruction is that which matches the learner's style. Here are examples for each of the different types of learners and examples of what could happen in school that could cause a reading difficulty.

HOW A VISUAL LEARNER COULD DEVELOP READING PROBLEMS

Daniel is a visual learner. He needs information to be shown to him. He likes to see pictures and symbols when he learns. But when he learned to read, his teacher did a lot of talking. She talked about the sounds of the letters and did not always hold up a chart or picture of the letter. She would have them recite the alphabet or have them spell their new words out loud. He was not good at listening, and he had trouble remembering all the information she told them. She would have them recite the vowels, a, e, i, o, u, but did not write the letters on the chalkboard when she had them recite it. Without the visual stimulus, he could not remember what she had taught them, and he ended up confusing the vowels. When they started reading in their first readers, he could not remember which vowel was which, and he made many mistakes. He became frustrated because some of the children caught on and read very smoothly. He began to feel that he was stupid and did not like to read.

What was the problem? Daniel needed to see the letters each time they were spoken of or recited. Had he seen the letters, they would have registered in his mind, and he would have had the visual picture to go with the sound. He needed charts, pictures, and the written word in order to learn. He had the same ability to learn to read as the rest of the class, but he could not remember the auditory information.

If your child is a visual learner, it is important that the letters and words are shown to him or her in writing or with pictures and illustrations. Thus, when a visual child is learning the sound of *d*, he or she needs to see the letter *d* as well as a picture of a word beginning with *d*, such as *duck* or *dog*, in order to remember it.

HOW AN AUDITORY LEARNER COULD DEVELOP
A READING PROBLEM

Sally is an auditory learner. She needs to hear information in order to learn. When Sally was learning the letters, she was given many worksheets and had to circle pictures that began with the letter. Often the teacher gave out the worksheets and did not go over the letters orally. The teacher wrote the letters on the board and had the students copy them. There was little verbal discussion about the letters and the sounds. Sally needed to hear the sounds over and over in order to learn them. Because she did not have enough auditory stimulus, she confused many of the letters. When she was asked to read, she often guessed the sound of the letter and would get them wrong. No one knew that she needed to hear the sounds over and over. The teacher, who was a visual learner, taught mostly in a visual manner. Thus, Sally fell behind because she never mastered the sounds of each letter.

How could Sally's problem have been prevented? If the teacher had talked about the sounds and had spent more time having Sally repeat what she heard, Sally would have remembered the sounds each letter made. Sally's main strength, auditory learning, was not used, and she struggled with the visual approach to learning reading.

If your child is an auditory learner, it is important that the symbol be matched with the spoken sound. Oral repetition is important for auditory learners. These students need to hear the sounds and must be given an opportunity to say the sounds over and over to help them learn.

How Tactile Learners Can Develop Reading Problems

Peter is a tactile learner. He learns best through his sense of touch and his feelings. When he was learning the letters in school, the teacher would show the letter and say the sound. She did not have the students write down the letters they saw. She would just show it and talk about it. Peter was not given an opportunity to use his hands. There were no block letters or plastic letters for him to touch. There were no activities in which he could write the letters while he was learning them. Thus, Peter had no recollection of the letters. He drew a total blank when he was asked to read the words on the page. His teacher would become frustrated with him.

Peter felt that the teacher was annoyed with him, and he became upset. He felt his teacher did not like him because he could not read like the other children. He felt hurt. These feelings were so overwhelming that he dreaded each reading period. He tried to avoid reading at all costs because his feelings of being a failure were so strong. As time went on, he fell further and further behind and he developed a dislike for reading.

Peter's reading problem could have been prevented if he had been given an opportunity to use his hands to learn to read. He would have benefited from having plastic letters to touch. He needed to write and draw the letters over and over as he heard their sounds and saw them. He needed a variety of activities in which he could feel his fingers making the shapes of the letters or tracing the letters in order to learn. Had instruction been given to him through his sense of touch, he would have learned the letters very quickly. The success would have made him feel good about reading, and he would have enjoyed it more. The enjoyable feeling of success and the teacher's approval of him would have made reading an enjoyable experience that he would have wanted to continue.

How a Kinesthetic Learner Develops Reading Problems

Mindy is a kinesthetic learner. She needs to learn by moving around and remembering the sensation of her muscles in motion. When she learned reading, she had to sit still in her seat, look at the letters on a chart, and recite after the teacher. She was not allowed to move around or do anything active with the letters. Mindy was restless. She would wiggle in her seat, tap her fingers, lay her head down on her desk, or jump out of her chair. Her teacher was always reprimanding her for her misbehavior. Mindy would tap her pencil on the desk or tap her feet, which disrupted the quiet of the class. Mindy's teacher did not see these movements as signs of Mindy trying to internalize the letters through movement. The more she tried to make Mindy sit still, the less Mindy learned. Mindy could not learn any of the letters. By midyear Mindy was still unable to read the books. The teacher was going to recommend Mindy for a special reading class, thinking that she was either a slow learner or challenged by a learning disability.

Mindy needed to internalize the letters by movement. She needed to act out words that began with the letter she was learning. She needed to use her entire arm movement by writing the letters in large size on the chalkboard or on paper hung from a bulletin board. She would have learned better if she could have walked the shape and direction of the letters. She needed to jump rope as she spelled the words aloud. Had she been allowed to jump on a hopscotch board to spell the letters of her new words, she would have internalized them and remembered them. She needed to make the letters out of clay or play dough in large sizes. She needed to build the words out of large letter blocks. She needed to trace the letters in large size in the sandbox or in the air. If Mindy had been able to do activities with the letters and sounds, she would have learned them very quickly. By tapping into her strength, which was body movement, Mindy would have been recognized as a quick learner and would have been reading at the same level as the rest of the class.

THE IMPORTANCE OF IDENTIFYING YOUR CHILD'S LEARNING STYLE

As you can see from these examples, matching the method of instruction to your child's learning style makes a big difference in the ease with which your child learns. If the correct learning style is not used, will the child learn? Yes, ultimately he or she will, but the process will take longer and be more painful. The difficulty may cause the child to give up in frustration or tune out along the way. The child may not want to stick with reading long enough to master it. If you look at yourself and the way you prefer to learn, you may realize the level of discomfort and frustration you feel when information is presented to you in your weakest learning style! It is the same with your child. They may ultimately learn, but there will be more of a struggle, the process will not be enjoyable, and he or she may want to give up along the way.

In Part 2 of the book, you will learn how to identify your child's best learning style and adapt instruction to match his or her preference.

Chapter 4

Self-Esteem and School Success

Traditionally, when people look for the cause of a child's reading problems, they focus on instructional steps that were missed along the way and try to remediate them. Although information on learning styles has been around for many years, it has not yet been applied in every school. Sometimes one teacher in a school has been trained to teach to different learning styles and uses those methods in that class. In some schools all the teachers use those techniques. In some schools no one has used them, let alone heard of them. Again, teaching to various learning styles offers a way of presenting material to fit the learner.

There is another factor that plays a major role in preventing or causing reading problems, and that is self-esteem. In solving your child's reading problem, this area cannot be overlooked. In fact, it is the key element in reversing the cycle of failure and in bringing about your child's success.

If we have good self-esteem, we have confidence that we can succeed. We are proud of ourselves and our achievements. We believe in our capability to do well.

If we have low self-esteem, we lack confidence that we can do well. We are ashamed of ourselves and do not feel we have any achievements we can be proud of. We do not believe we are capable of doing well.

In order to understand the role self-esteem can play in reading success and failure, we will explore how self-esteem develops and how it has affected us in our own lives. Once we understand it, we will then look at our own child's sense of self-esteem and the role it played in his or her achievement. Finally, we will learn how to help raise our child's self-esteem to bring about success.

How Self-Esteem Is Developed

Our sense of who we are comes from the people around us. We get our idea of who we are by what others tell us. If we are well liked and people feel or say good things about us, we start believing that we are good. If people around us do not like us, or tell us we are bad and not worthy, over time we start believing them and we feel bad about ourselves.

Our sense of self-esteem begins in infancy. We may think that the child is a little bundle of a person who is not aware of what is going on around him or her, but everything we do and say is picked up by the child. It registers in the child's mind and is not forgotten. If it is not remembered at the conscious level, it is stored at a subconscious level. It forms the foundation of the child's beliefs about himself or herself, the world, and the people around him or her.

Self-esteem is formed by the significant people in a child's life. It is formulated by the person the child relies upon for food, safety, warmth, and protection. It could be the child's natural parents, stepparents, adoptive parents, guardian, babysitter, child-care worker, grandparents, or older brother or sister. These people's feelings about the child will form the basis of the child's self-concept, or image of himself or herself. Here are two scenarios depicting how good and bad self-concepts can be formed.

Laura

Laura's birth was unplanned, and her parents were not financially able to provide for themselves, let alone a child. The father held two jobs. The mother had to supplement the income by working, but chose to work at night so that she should be with the baby during the day. In the evening, when Laura's mother went to work, a baby-sitter took over until the father returned from work.

Laura's mother was not prepared for motherhood and found it difficult to have to be a full-time mother and to work outside the home. She often became impatient with her infant. When Laura cried due to hunger or wet diapers, her mother would become annoyed and often say things like "You always bother me at the wrong time," or "Sometimes you are a pain." While Laura's mother loved her, these expressions of annoyance were a frequent part of her vocabulary. These outbursts and the irritated tone of voice and body language did not go unnoticed by the baby, even though she could not judge or evaluate what was happening. Laura's father would be tired when he came home from work, and although he too loved Laura, he would try to push Laura back to her mother whenever he could. "You take her" and "I'm too tired to deal with this" were frequent expressions Laura heard from her father.

As Laura grew up, a pattern of communication developed in which her parents were frequently irritable or did not give her the full attention or time she needed. Laura sometimes did not feel loved by her parents. She began to act out her unloved feelings by dramatizing irritable behavior to her dolls and later to her playmates. She would get annoyed with her friends and often push them away by her tone of voice or her gestures. This would result in them rejecting her and fighting with her. Soon Laura did not feel liked by her friends. She started feeling left out and rejected.

This sad spiral continued into her schoolwork. She developed a pattern of behavior that made her reject others as a way to protect herself from being hurt. She developed a negative attitude in school, and sometimes it upset her teachers. She was afraid to try new things or to learn new concepts because she feared being rejected. Thus, she resisted learning. She did not feel liked, and she withdrew into her own world. She did not like herself or feel good about herself. Laura did not have the confidence in herself to do well. Thus, when it came time to learn how to read, she did not want to try. She did not put her whole attention into learning, and as a result, she did not master all the skills. Over time she was looked upon as a poor reader. Her cycle of reading failure had begun.

Laura did not receive the positive support at home to make her feel good about herself or her capabilities to do well. In fact, whenever she missed anything in school, her parents would get annoyed with her. "What is wrong with you?" they would shout. Often their anger was not so much at her as it was at the extra time they had to put in helping her with her homework. But she could not understand that and interpreted their irritation as coming from her "stupidity." The more she failed in reading, the more she wanted to stop trying in order to avoid the pain and embarrassment of failure. She resisted reading work and fell further and further behind. If asked whether she liked to read, her response would be, "I hate to read." The worse she did in school, the more fights she had at home with her parents. This cycle continued and it affected all her other subjects that required reading textbooks, including science, social studies, and health. By the time she was in high school, Laura could not wait until she turned sixteen so that she could officially drop out of school.

Robert

Robert was also born to parents who had to struggle to make it financially. They too both had to work. But the time they spent with Robert was considered quality time. When his parents were with him, they gave him their full attention and showed him much love and care. His mother would hold him and talk to him lovingly during the time she was with him. She would show him things around the house and name the object. She would talk to him about how the object was used and what it did. She would look lovingly in the child's eyes, smile, and just prattle with the child about anything and everything. Whenever the child made a response, such as a sound or a smile, she would respond with a big smile and a hug and tell the child, "You are so smart," "You are so wonderful," and "I love you." When the father was with the child, he would hold the child, look into his eyes, and also talk to him. He would put objects into the child's hands and show him how to use them. He would put a ball into Robert's hands and help him throw it and say, "What a pitcher! Good job." He would hold the child, placing his feet on the ground, and help the child try to walk, praising the child for every step.

Robert picked up the smiles, the hugs, and the praise from his parents. Even though it looked as though he was not understanding, he was. He enjoyed the pleasurable responses of the smiles and hugs and warm words, so he would repeat those behaviors that would result in those responses. Thus, he learned quickly. Whatever his parents appreciated, he would repeat, and he began to learn everything they taught him.

Robert liked to try anything that resulted in his parents' pleasurable response to him. When he tried to do or say something new, they were delighted. He learned that it was acceptable to try new things. Thus, he was not afraid to learn. Whatever he tried was accepted, and he quickly stretched his abilities and talents beyond his limits.

When Robert went to school, he looked at reading as another challenge. It was something new he could learn. When he would bring his books home and read to his parents, they were so excited and praised him. Robert responded to their positive comments and, as a result, wanted to repeat the act of reading. It made him feel successful. Because reading was hard and the people around him told him how well he was doing, he felt good about himself and was proud of himself. He developed confidence to continue to learn new things, and his skills in reading developed. Since he did well in reading, he also did well in the other subjects that required reading, such as social studies and science. His grades in school were good, his parents were proud of him, and he continued to be an excellent student all through high school. He set his goals to go to college and take up a professional career.

LOOKING AT OUR OWN SELF-ESTEEM

The above composite examples of two fictitious children contain elements that many children have also faced in their lives and which we may have had to deal with in our own lives. Whether we were raised by two parents or one parent, whether our parents were at home or working, whether our parents were rich or poor, does not matter. It is the quality of the contact with our parents that makes the difference. We can look at someone like the motivational speaker Les Brown, who was adopted and raised by Mamie Brown, a single parent. Yet her love and belief in him were so strong, he not only grew up with belief in himself, but he has the power to help others believe in themselves! We need not blame our economic level or situation as being hindrances in our capability to be good parents. The key to being a good parent is providing children with love, care, and a belief in their goodness and abilities to succeed. Whether or not we ourselves were brought up in a positive way does not matter; it requires only a small adjustment in our thinking to provide a positive approach for our children. With a bit of guidance and some practice, we can demonstrate love and belief in the child so he or she receives the gift of good self-esteem which lays the foundation for all future success. Here are the steps:

✔ Develop positive facial expressions and body language.

✔ Learn how to use a positive and loving tone of voice.

✔ Learn how to say positive statements and affirmations to build your child's self-esteem.

Let us see how we can make each of the above behaviors a part of our interactions with our child.

POSITIVE FACIAL EXPRESSIONS AND BODY LANGUAGE

Former President George Bush made famous the phrase "Read my lips!" Let us keep in mind instead, "Read my face," and realize that whether we know it or not, that is what our children are doing when they look at us. Remember, a child's first communication with the world around him or her is not the spoken language, because they do not yet understand the words. But they are learning through the facial expression and body language of those around them. Remember the smiles Robert received from his parents and how positively he responded? Smiling is a universally accepted form of communication of pleasure. It is understood in all languages. Babies understand it as a positive, pleasurable experience. A smile costs nothing and takes less effort in terms of muscle movement than a frown. By smiling when your child is around, the child receives the message that you enjoy his or her company. Think about yourself: How do you feel when you are around someone who frowns? Do you start to wonder whether that person likes you or not? Think again about being around someone who smiles. Do you feel that he or she is enjoying your company?

When a child is reading to you or showing you something he or she has done, you may not say anything at all, but the child is reading your face. Does it have an expression of approval? Or are you furrowing your eyebrows in a look of annoyance or discontent? Look in the mirror to see your face. Keep a mirror handy so that when you are working with your child, you can glance into it and observe your facial expression. What you see is what your child will see. Would you want someone to be looking at you like that when you are learning something new? If the answer is yes, then your facial expression is probably positive and loving. Keep it up. Your child needs to see that! If it is not a positive expression, wipe it off and replace it with a smile. Even if you do not really mean it at first, get in the habit of smiling. The habit will ultimately become part of your nature, and you will automatically smile. Over time and with practice, you will also smile on the inside. Cultivate a sense of joy and happiness when you are around your child. You know you love them; you know how painful it would be if anything happened to them; so show your love with a smile from the inside and the outside.

Body language is also perceived by your child. Positive body language can be reflected in hugs, putting your arm around your child, patting the child's shoulder or head, or physically drawing your child close to you. It is also expressed by holding open your palm or your hand as a welcoming gesture or inviting your child to share with you.

Negative body language consists of gestures that push your child away from you, or those in which you close up and withdraw from contact with your child. Negativity is expressed in gestures such as crossing one's arm across one's chest in a defiant, angry stance. How many of you have shrunk from someone who was pointing their finger at you in an accusatory way? How do you feel when someone raises a hand in a motion as if he or she were going to hit you? Can you recall a time as a child when a parent struck you in anger? Negative body language can be conveyed by people standing in an aggressive way, tapping their hands on a table, or shaking their fist at someone. All these gestures are perceived by a child as unloving and threatening. The result is that the child feels fearful and unloved.

Take a glance at yourself in the mirror when you are communicating with your child. Gauge whether your body language is positive or negative. If it is positive, it will reinforce your child's good feelings about himself or herself. If it is negative, it has the power to send a strong message to your child that you are unhappy with him or her and that he or she is not good or worthy.

POSITIVE TONE OF VOICE

We may not realize the power that our tone of voice has on a child. Again, it may not be what we say, but how we say it that gives the child the message that he or she is considered worthy or unworthy, loved or unloved.

Tone of voice is conveyed by whether we speak with loving, caring tones or harsh, irritated tones. Positive tones express warmth, happiness, joy, smiles, and love. In the way we speak, we show that we care about others. Conversely, negative tones express anger, irritation, resentment, frustration, and even hatred. Sometimes our tone of voice can even contain biting sarcasm and harsh criticism. Even if we do not say anything harmful, our tone of voice can communicate our true feelings, and children will pick them right up.

Leave a tape recorder running one day, of course letting everyone in the household know what you are doing, and record some typical home conversations between you and your children. Play it back later and listen for the tone of voice you use. Is it cheerful, warm, and caring? Or is it harsh and biting? This can help you gauge what your children hear when you speak to them.

If we realize that self-esteem is the basis for success in reading, and self-esteem develops by the way we speak to our children and the way we present our facial gestures and body language, then it is worth our while to adjust our gestures and our tone of voice. The small adjustments we make will save us years of grief later in trying to remediate our children's academic problems.

How can we develop a positive tone of voice? Think about how we speak to our boss, who holds our career in his or her hands. Don't we hide our feelings and put on a cheery, happy voice when we speak to him or her? Think about how we speak when we are with those we love, our family and our good friends. Think about how courteously we speak to strangers or employees in a store in which we shop. Sometimes we speak in nicer tones to people we do not know than we do to our own families. Sometimes our families see our worst side due to the pressures of life that we let loose at home. But the tone of voice we use has a powerful effect on our children. Those of us who are trying to help our children do well in school may wish to consider making an adjustment in our tone of voice in order to bring about long-term successful gains for our children. After all, we are forming the basis of their identity for the rest of their lives. It is as important as the nutritious food we make sure they eat in order to ensure a healthy physical development. Our positive tone of voice can ensure a healthy mental, emotional, and academic development as well.

POSITIVE STATEMENTS OR AFFIRMATIONS

A popular phrase amongst educators today is "the self-fulfilling prophecy." It is interpreted in the field of education as becoming that which we believe we can become. How do we get our beliefs? It comes from what others believe about us. If someone feels we will fail, we *will* actually fail. If someone believes we can succeed, we *will* truly succeed. Experiments have been performed in schools in which a group of children were assigned to a teacher. The teacher was led to believe that the children were gifted and talented. With that belief, the teacher taught them as if they were gifted. By the end of the year, the children performed exceptionally well. The teacher later learned that they were not gifted at all. Her belief in their giftedness, however, had translated into the way she spoke to them and how she taught them, and they ended up achieving more than they had ever done before. On the other hand, a group of extremely bright students were assigned to a teacher who was led to believe that they were a group of failing students. She talked to them and taught to them with the expectation that they were difficult, unsuccessful students. At the end of the year, many of the students, who had never failed before, began to fail academically. Why does this happen? It is the phenomenon of the self-fulfilling prophecy. The teacher's expectations of the children's capabilities became what the children expected of themselves. If the teacher expected them to fail, the children began believing they were failures and began acting according to those expectations. If the teacher expected them to succeed, the children believed they would succeed and began acting according to the expectation to do well.

This phenomenon has powerful implications for parents. The same principle that applies to teachers and students also applies to parent and child. Our child will become that which we expect of him or her. Our child will achieve that which we believe the child is capable of doing or achieving. It is a principle that cannot be ignored. Thus, if we want our child to succeed, we need to build the belief in the child that he or she *can* succeed. Ultimately, that will become fact, and our child *will* do well.

How can we build the child's belief in his or her ability to succeed? This can be conveyed by positive statements or affirmations that we make to the child. Tell a child, "I know you can do it!" and observe the results. But if you tell a child, "You'll never make it," we have sealed the child's fate for failure. We are not merely talking about one statement made at one time. These statements cover the entire period of a child's lifetime, from birth to adulthood. If the child continually hears positive statements about his or her capabilities, day after day, month after month, year after year, it will become so firmly embedded in the child's belief system, nothing will shatter their faith in themselves. If they continually hear they will never become anything, or that they are dumb or stupid, what do you think they will eventually become? They will believe they are dumb, stupid, or a failure and will begin to act that way.

What do psychologists do when someone comes to them with problems with low self-esteem? In some therapies the psychologist will provide positive affirmations to their patient. Whether the patient improves through undergoing hypnosis, speaking to the psychologist, or listening to positive affirmation tapes, the underlying principle is the same. It is an attempt to rescript or rewrite the person's belief system. The patient, due to years of hearing that they are a failure, believes it. Thus, they act like failures in various spheres of their lives. If the patient can listen to positive statements that they can succeed, it can erase the old programs they carry around within them. Over time they start believing the new statements about themselves, that they can succeed and are capable. They begin to act upon their beliefs and behave like winners.

As parents, we can choose whether we want to raise children who believe and act like winners, or whether we want to provide future patients for the psychologists of the next generation. You have the power to create winners or losers. The choice is yours. If you wish to create winners, the method is simple. Act as though your child is a winner, treat him or her like a winner, and tell the child frequently that you know that he or she can make it, or that you know that he or she will be successful. Not only say it, but back it up with positive facial expressions, encouraging tones of voice, and loving and caring gestures.

You may think, "I know my child is a failure in reading. How can I act like he or she is a winner? Isn't that deceitful? Isn't that faking it? Won't my child see through it?" All I can say is try it—the magic works. How do I know? I have witnessed the power of positive affirmations and statements in reversing the cycle of failure in hundreds of children I have taught over the past twenty years. If there is one key element in reversing failure in reading, it is the teacher or parent believing in the child's ability to succeed.

Here is a typical scenario based on a composite of many situations I have witnessed over the years. A student comes to me. The student knows that I know their past record and the student knows that I know that they can't read. But that doesn't stop me from believing in the child's capabilities to overcome these difficulties. The very first thing I establish in the relationship with the child is that I believe the child is going to make it this year. I talk to the child and say, "I know things have been difficult in the past, but you are smart, you are capable, and I am going to show you how you can learn to read. This is the year that you are going to be reading, and you will be reading so well that no one will ever know that you ever had a problem in the past." Like magic, the child is spell-bound, hanging on to every word I say. From that point on, the child seeks me out every chance he or she gets. Even when class is over, I cannot get these children to leave me to go to their next teacher. Why? It may have been the first time someone ever believed in them and told them they could make it. It may have been the first time someone ever told them they were smart or capable. And they want to hear more of it. The result is that they develop a respect and trust in me because they know I sincerely believe in them. They know that I care about them and their future. This respect builds a trust that I am out for their best interest. As a result, they will do whatever work I give them—even if they never did a stitch of work for anyone else before in their lives. They start working hard. They start putting in the effort. I continue to affirm them and their abilities. And as they work and pay attention to the lessons, they *do* start achieving. They see the fruits of their work. They prove the truth of my belief that they will make it. The more proof they see of this, the harder they work. And every single one of them learns to read. This principle has worked for primary grade students, intermediary students, middle school students, and high school students. It has worked for students who were considered gifted, average, or below average. It has even worked for students who are challenged by a learning disability, mental retardation, or emotional disorders. It has worked for college students and adult learners. It even works in the work place, when we believe in the capabilities of our coworkers and they rise to the occasion. They fulfill our expectations of them.

If that power can work between a teacher who sees the students for a period of one hour or six hours a day for one hundred eighty days—the length of an average school year—and can bring about such a powerful transformation in students in a large classroom setting, imagine the power you have when you have your child every day for eighteen years on a one-on-one basis! You have the power to make your child a grand success in any area you wish. It all lies in the positive statements you make to your child. Does it cost anything? Not a penny. Does it depend on your economic background? No. Does it depend on whether you are considered to be a minority group in society, whether it be of religion, nationality, or skin color? No. Every parent, regardless of their outer conditions, can make their child a winner by believing the child is a winner and telling the child he or she is a winner.

I see these success stories every day. I see children who walk around as if they could take on the world, and when you listen to their parents speak of them, their parents believe their child is top banana. I see children who feel they are total wipe-outs, and when you see them with their parents, you hear the parents telling them they are dumb, stupid, or total embarrassments.

If you leave with nothing else from this book but the fact that you have the power to make your child a winner, then no matter what else is happening in your child's life, he or she will overcome any obstacle and become a winner.

Forget the past. Forget what your children's previous

records are. Start today and tell them you know they are capable of becoming good readers, and you now have the tools to help them succeed. Let them know whatever has happened to them in the past may have been due to something they missed or an approach that didn't work. But now you have some new techniques, and you know they are going to work. Tell your children you know they are smart and capable, and it has only been the previous techniques that caused the problem. Do not blame the school or the teachers, because the last thing you want to do is ruin a child's respect for the teachers and schools. Do not blame anyone. Instead, place the blame on some nonhuman cause such as a technique. Tell your child that you are going to start afresh. Since they have learned so many things in this short life, you know with some new methods they will learn to read and will become great at it. Say it with conviction. Start believing it yourself. I can give you examples of hundreds of cases of nonreaders for whom everyone had lost all hope. These were students no one wanted to even attempt to teach anymore. Some of them were average learners who had become hopeless cases. Some were even challenged by learning disabilities or mental retardation. But every single one of them learned to read. And your children will learn to read and reverse the failure cycle as well by your positive belief in them and use of techniques that will work for your child.

The first thing you must do is to eliminate from your vocabulary all negativity toward your children's abilities. Think twice and thrice before you speak to your children, and filter out any comments that would make them feel you think they are dumb, stupid, inferior, incapable, or inadequate in any way. Next, weed out all comments that compare them with their older or younger brothers and sisters who are doing so well. Eliminate comparisons altogether. Even if your children make negative comments about themselves, counter them with positive statements. If they say, "I am so stupid," tell them, "You are not. You are good at so many things, and you can be good at whatever you want to be good at. We just need to try some different techniques and you will see how good at this skill you can be." No matter how many times they argue with you that they cannot do it, continue to repeat to them your belief that they can do it. Their arguments, based on years of previous conditioning, will begin to lose strength. When they see that you are not buying into their failure belief, they will eventually give up saying negative things about themselves. They will start quietly listening to the good things you have to say about their capabilities. Their negative comments are merely a way of testing the waters to see how firm you are in your beliefs. Do not give in to their negativity. Keep being positive and they will ultimately begin to believe it about themselves as well.

Here are some positive statements you can use as a base. Adapt them to phrases and words with which you feel comfortable. Add to the list by finding all the things your children do well, and remind them of their accomplishments so that they will continue to do well. If they are good at sports, tell them they are good at sports. If they are good at math, tell them how smart they are in math. If they are good at drawing, praise their talent for drawing. Here are some more statements you can add to the list:

You are wonderful.

You are smart.

You are capable.

You can do it.

You can succeed.

You can be anything you want to be.

You are a real winner!

You can make it.

You are bright and intelligent.

You are talented.

If you want to confirm for yourself the power these statements have, think back over your life. Think of a person who believed in you. It could be a teacher, a coach, an instructor in one of the arts, a parent, a friend, anyone. Now, try to remember how the person treated you. Can you recall some of the statements that they made to you? Can you recall their attitude toward you? Did they believe in you? Did you succeed because of their belief in you? Now apply that recollection to your own child's life. Don't *you* want to be the one on whom your child can look back as an adult and say, "My parents believed in me, and I attribute my success in life to them!"

Chapter 5

Motivation and Success in Reading

Close your eyes and recall a time when you tried hard to do something and you failed. It could have been a school assignment or project. It could have been in the field of sports. Maybe it was a craft you tried but could not produce properly. It could be a failure in any area. Think about how you felt at the time. Were you embarrassed? Frustrated? Ashamed? Did you worry about what others would think of you? Finally, did you feel like attempting that task again? Or did you give up and wish you would never be put in that spot again?

Now recall a time when you were successful at some task or activity. Again, it could have been in a school subject. It may have been a sports activity. Maybe it was an activity in one of the arts. Remember your most successful moment. Think about how you felt. Were you proud? Ecstatic? Excited? Confident? Were you boosted up by the praise and approval of others? Finally, did you feel like attempting that task again? Did you continue to improve your abilities in that area?

Now relate your feelings about success and failure to what your own child may be feeling. Do you wish to continue in activities in which you keep failing? Or do you try to avoid those activities? How about successful experiences? Do you wish to continue doing those activities in which you are successful?

Success in reading requires continued practice. The connection between the words on a page and understanding in the mind can be made only through repeatedly seeing those words over and over again. The speed at which we recognize words increases as the same nerve passageways are used over and over again. Think how slowly we read unfamiliar words or even words in another language. But as we read the same materials over and over again, we recognize them instantaneously and automatically. It is like any skill involving our muscles. At first when we exercise, our muscles ache. But as we do the same exercise daily, over and over, the muscles get used to the movements and no longer take as long to work and no longer ache.

Studies have indicated that the habits of good readers develop by reading fifteen minutes a day. That amount of practice increases one's ability to read fluently. Without that amount of practice, it will be harder for a student to read fluently. If a student continues to fail in reading, the student will want to avoid the task, just as we wanted to avoid any activity at which we kept failing. In order to spend enough time to gain proficiency in reading, a student must desire to keep reading. That can happen only when a child has successful experiences in reading. If the child experiences success, the child will feel good about himself or herself. He or she will feel capable. The child will gain the approval and appreciation of others for the success. The result will be that the child enjoys the feeling of success and wants to repeat the activity and the pleasurable results it brings. Thus, the child will read more and more. But if the child does not experience success and instead feels like a failure, with the attendant embarrassment and frustration, the child will avoid reading. Thus, the child will not spend enough time in practicing so as to become proficient.

It is important for parents to understand this cycle of success and motivation. People are motivated by the pleasure they receive from having the approval of others and the pride and enjoyment of being successful. How can we make our child feel successful? We must provide learning activities at which the child will ultimately succeed. This does not mean giving easy work. It means giving work which will lead to success. We need to keep in mind that the end result should be that the child accomplishes the task successfully. This means that the task must not be impossible. It may be a bit hard, but it must be such that the child has the tools and the method by which to accomplish it. That is what we must teach the child. If the child lacks the tools and method to succeed, we must teach them to the child or guide the child along with models and examples so that the child will learn the method. Our aim must be the child's success at the task.

For a toddler learning to walk, the goal may be for the child to take several steps forward with the parent's support. When the child does that, everyone applauds, smiles, and shows approval with hugs and loving gestures. The child will want to repeat that activity. The child will continue those early steps until he or she can take a step forward on his or her own. We would never expect the child to walk upright fully across the room on the first day and withhold approval if he or she could not do it. The goal must be realistic.

Similarly, if the child is learning to read, we set the goal of reading simple books with assistance. Whatever new step the child takes, we show our approval and appreciation. This will make the child feel good and wish to continue the reading task. Our next step will go to a slightly more challenging book, but not one that is so far advanced, the child will fail. When we go to the slightly more challenging reading material, we provide support by helping the child with new words or new skills so the child will read the new book successfully. We make the work harder only in small steps and give the child whatever skills are needed to accomplish the task. This is how we keep the child's motivation high.

Young children are highly motivated to involve themselves in learning. Watch babies and young children at play. They find enjoyment in almost any task they attempt. Our own exhaustion from keeping up with them can attest to the high energy level they have. There is no sense of failure for young children. They keep trying things until they master the activity. When they cannot do something, an adult shows them how and guides their hands until they can do it themselves. But as children get older, we assume they can do anything we tell them to do the first time and get it right. We stop providing them support and guidance. Have you ever seen a child learn a math skill, have a practice sheet to do, and then get a grade on their sheet even though they are just learning it? Practice means practice. It means doing something over and over again until it is mastered. But often we make the child feel like a failure for not succeeding on a practice sheet—a worksheet which was originally designed to allow the student to make mistakes. Mistakes are a necessary part of learning. Each time we make a mistake, we learn not to repeat the wrong practice. The more mistakes we make, the more sure we are of how to arrive at the right answer. If we are put in a maze, it is only by trying all the wrong doors that we ultimately know which is the right door.

We need to allow a child the safety of making mistakes, while guiding the child toward finding the right answer or method or solution. We must allow the child the discovery time to find out the wrong way of doing things, but must ultimately see that the child can learn the correct way. This requires our help, support, and instruction. When a child comes to us for help with homework, do we say, "Figure it out for yourself"? It is true that we do not want to do the child's homework for them. But if they need help, it means they are lacking some skill or methodology of doing it. Then it is time for us to step in and guide them to finding the right answer. We can model similar examples for them. We can explain the thinking process we use in arriving at the answer. We can ask them questions and give them hints or clues to think about in order to mold their thinking toward the thought process needed to arrive at the answer. We need to teach them how to think through the problem. It is only by putting into words what *we* think when *we* do the problem that they can learn how to think in a similar manner. They will not get it by reading minds.

Each time children have a successful experience, it ensures that they will attempt the task again. They will enjoy the feeling of accomplishment and the sense that they are capable. They will enjoy the approval of others as a confirmation of their abilities. If we wish to make our children lifelong readers, we must select activities that will make them feel successful. If they bring home schoolwork that is beyond them, we must guide them through the process so that they can complete it successfully. If we feel the work is much too hard for them and the child continues to experience a sense of failure and frustration, it is essential that we talk to the teacher and find out what both of you can do to either help the child master the skill, or decrease the difficulty of the work so that it is at a level that the child can handle.

The power of motivation through successful experiences has worked for every child I have ever taught. Here is a typical scenario. A fourth grader has repeatedly failed reading. She does not want to try, and any attempt to help her is rebuffed by comments she makes about herself such as "I am too dumb," or "I can't do it!" That's the key phrase of children who have repeatedly failed: "I can't." After explaining that there are many things they can do, and giving them an easier developmental task, I prove to them that they *are* competent. I may give the fourth grader a reading skill that I know that they mastered in first grade. After working through some practice activity, the child exclaims, "This is easy!" I praise the child for having completed the task successfully. Since I had previously identified the skills the child knows and does not know, I spend a few weeks repeating the skills the child knows. This reestablishes the child's feelings of success. Remember, it has been so long that some of these children have felt successful that they have forgotten how it feels. All they remember and have come to know about themselves is that they "can't do it." After several weeks or a month of them doing "I can do it" activities, I slowly build in new skills, structured in a way that they will succeed. Because I have reestablished their confidence, they no longer resist the task. In fact, they enjoy the feeling of success so much that they look forward to the challenge and feel safe knowing I will help them until they succeed. Over the years, some of the most unmotivated children or teens have been assigned to me. But when I structured the work so that the child could ultimately succeed at the task, he or she became highly motivated, announced how much fun the task was, and wanted to do more and more of that task again. It has worked in every single case! And it can work for your child or teen as well.

If you work through this book, you will understand the steps involved in the reading process. You will know what steps came before your child's current level. You will know what steps come next. Thus, if your child is having difficulty with a particular work level, you can back up to an earlier level. You can find the point at which your child can do the task with ease. Then, after he or she masters it, move on to the next step, which is slightly harder. It will provide a challenge, but not so much of a challenge that the child will fail.

It should be a task at which the child will, with practice and guidance, succeed.

Another aspect of motivation is interest. We want to repeat those tasks at which we are successful. Over time we develop an interest in those activities. We want to spend our time in tasks we enjoy. If we want our children to love books, it is important that they be able to choose books in fields which interest them. Many parents provide their children with books they think the child should read, or books the parents read and enjoyed as a child. But your child may not have any interest in those subjects. They have their own preferences. Do you want someone telling you what you have to read during your free time? Similarly, your children want to read about fields they enjoy. If your child likes baseball, you can stimulate his or her interest in reading by pointing the child in the direction of books about baseball, baseball players, how to play better, or the history of baseball. If your child is interested in snakes, show him or her where to find books about these reptiles. If dogs are of interest to your child, he or she may wish to find books about how to take care of dogs, fiction stories about dogs, or factual books about the characteristics and habits of dogs. Find out your child's interests and provide the reading materials along those lines. Present the child with many choices and guide him or her to make the selection.

Many people think motivation depends upon providing rewards and prizes. But motivation to succeed is inherent in all human beings. If the child can experience success, that feeling of accomplishment is the reward in itself and will provide the motivation for him or her to continue repeating the reading practice.

Chapter 6

Reading Problems Caused by a Learning Disability

Over the years, there has been much confusion about the meaning of the phrase "learning disability." Many people lump all reading problems under the term "learning disability," while others call a reading difficulty "dyslexia." There are vast differences between a reading problem, a learning disability, and dyslexia.

A learning disability is a specific dysfunction of the central nervous system. In current terminology (which may change each year!) a learning disability is a problem in the transmittal of sensory information to the brain and back to the senses. Like a short circuit in the central nervous system, it causes unclear communication between the organs of the senses and the brain. We can think of the human information system as a machine consisting of input and output. Information on the world around us comes through our senses. Sight depends upon input through our eyes; hearing upon input through our ears. We also receive information through our senses of smell, taste, and touch. The input is sent from our eyes, ears, nose, tongue, and skin to the brain, which then interprets the information. After the brain interprets these messages, it sends signals back to a part of the body in response. The brain may instruct a body part to move, or our vocal cords and mouth to speak, or our hands to write something. It may direct our body or face to make certain gestures as a nonverbal way of communication. In a learning disability these messages cannot get through properly due to a dysfunction. It could be thought of as crossed wires, jumbled information, or reversed messages. Any number of difficulties could be taking place in the central nervous system to distort, confuse, or mix up the message.

There are a variety of ways this dysfunction manifests. The disability could be related to receiving visual input or auditory input, or to output through speaking or writing. Here are some examples of each type of dysfunction.

Disability of Visual Input

When a child reads, the message from letters or words the child sees is not properly received by the brain. Either the letters are interpreted as mixed up, reversed, backwards, or double, or they do not register at all. The nervous system's inability to transmit the words the child sees is dyslexia. The child may know what the sounds are, but the brain may not be getting the correct message from the eye. Thus, it is a physiological problem, or a problem in the body. Not knowing the correct pronunciation of a vowel is just a difficulty that can be rectified. A problem with the central nervous system cannot be solved with more practice. It is a condition the child has and must learn to compensate for by getting the information in another way, or by learning how to make sense out of the distorted messages. For example, if the child sees all words backwards, the child needs to learn how to interpret the words in a backwards manner. So if *cat* is always seen as *tac*, the child needs to know to read all words from right to left instead of left to right. If the child sees all words as double, the child needs to learn techniques for reading words in that manner. It is not impossible to learn to read, but special techniques must be used. We cannot just give them repeated practice using standard techniques to get them to read better. Those methods will not work. Methods dealing with their disability must be used as alternative ways of learning to read.

A good special education program will teach students how to compensate and find alternative ways to learn. Learning disabilities are diagnosed by special tests usually performed by a psychologist. These tests will determine whether the child has a true learning disability, or whether the child has a reading problem caused by lack of understanding or knowledge of letter-sound relationships, lack of vocabulary skills, or comprehension problems. Here are two composite studies to show the difference between a visual input learning disability and a reading problem:

Anna

Anna looks at the word *cat* but reads it as *cup*. Upon evaluation it is determined that Anna can see the letters as *c*, *a*, and *t*, but she has not been taught how to pronounce an *a*. Instead, she reads *a* as *u*. Anna also has read *t* as *p* because she has not been taught to look at the end of the word, and after seeing the beginning *c*, she guessed the rest of the word. Upon instruction, Anna learns the sound of *a* and she learns to look at the ending, and she begins to read *cat* correctly. Anna's problem was not due to a learning disability. Rather, it was a reading problem rectified by better instructions.

George

George looks at the word *cat*, but says "boy." It appears he is guessing at the word. The teacher goes over the sound of *c*, then the *at* pattern, but George still cannot read *cat* each time he sees it. She teaches him how to look at the beginning, middle, and end of a word. After much work, George still cannot read the word *cat*. This happens with all the words he reads. She works with him for six months and there is no improvement. George is finally tested by a school psychologist, who discovers that although George's vision according to an eye test is perfect, he is unable to recognize the letters *c*, *a*, or *t*; his brain is not registering them as those letters. He cannot get it because the central nervous system is not sending those letters to his brain properly, or his brain is not interpreting the message of those letters properly. Thus, George is one who has a learning disability.

Disability of Auditory Input

The same mix-up can occur with information coming in through the ears. Even though sounds are picked up by the ears, they do not get sent properly to the brain and they may come out as distorted, mixed up, or jumbled. It has nothing to do with an inability to hear. The child may have perfect hearing. It is the distortion or jumbling of the message to the brain that causes the learning disability. Thus, instead of a child hearing the word "cat," the child may hear the word "tac" or "act" or "rob," or any number of words. Again, tests performed by a psychologist can determine whether the child is properly receiving auditory information.

Disability Due to Aural Output

Aural refers to speaking. A child may have a disability because the brain is unable to correctly send the response to the vocal cords and mouth. The child may have read the right word silently, but says the wrong word when asked to read aloud. The child may understand in his or her mind what was seen, but the mix-up happens on the way from the brain to the mouth. The child cannot understand why he or she has made a mistake, because in the child's mind the word is correct. The child is having the trouble in saying the word correctly. The word could come out backwards or jumbled, or a wrong letter substituted for the correct one. The child sees *cat*, sends the message of *cat* to the brain, but says "tac," "act," or "dog," or any other word.

Through testing, a psychologist can determine whether the learning disability is in the aural output system. Once it is determined that this is the problem, special education methods need to be used to help the child compensate for this mix-up in his or her central nervous system.

Disability Due to Written Output

The brain may be unable to send a message to the hand in order to write properly. The child may see the word correctly and say the word correctly, but the message becomes garbled when the child has to write it on paper. The letters may get mixed up, they may be written backwards, reversed, or upside down, or they may be altogether incorrect. Psychological testing can determine whether the child's problem is in writing output.

How Can You Tell If Your Child Has a Learning Disability?

Diagnosing a learning disability is a difficult process. It is hard to determine because there are many factors that can make a reading problem look like a learning disability, as well as many factors that make a learning disability look like a mere reading problem. At first glance, a child may simply have a reading problem due to a missed step, a lack of understanding of the letter-sound relationships, a small vocabulary, or a lack of comprehension. Some parents may panic and think the child has a learning disability. The first step in making the determination is teaching the child all the different reading skills appropriate for his or her reading level. The skills should be taught in a manner that matches the child's learning style. The child needs to develop good self-esteem and have motivation to learn and be successful. If all these variables are in place and the child still cannot read the words, then the parent must talk to the child's teacher, principal, or school psychologist about the possibility of testing to see if the problem is a true learning disability.

On the other hand, there are children who may have a true learning disability but no one picks up on it. Why? Some children have learned how to compensate on their own. They find other ways of getting information from the book. They may have asked their friend to help them. They may listen to and memorize what the other children read so that when they are asked to read, the teacher does not know the child has copied someone else. There are cases of children "faking it" for years before anyone finally catches that they cannot read for themselves at all. In some cases a child gets good grades because he or she is getting help from other students or has a good memory. But on a standardized test the child scores in the lowest percentile for reading because the child cannot talk to anyone else to ask for help during the test.

Here are several things to watch for in determining whether your child should be tested for a learning disability:

1. You or the teacher have tried all the steps described in this book to help the child. You have taught or retaught all the letter-sound relationships, you have taught the child how to get the meaning of vocabulary words, you have taught the child comprehension strategies, and

you have taught the child in a way that matches his or her learning style. You have built up the child's self-esteem, making him or her feel safe in taking risks and in trying to read. The material is presented in a way that helps increase the child's motivation and interest. You have spent enough time on each skill with the child. If you have tried all these things over a period of many months and the child shows no sign of grasping any of it, then it may be time to recommend that the child be tested to see if he or she has a learning disability.

2. If your child's scores on standardized tests show up in the lowest stanines or percentiles, such as 1, 2, or 3 out of 9, or 0–35 percent out of 100 percent, or in the bottom third, and you are sure the child has gone through all the steps described in this book, then the test may be an indicator of a problem that needs further investigation.

3. If your child can read aloud correctly but cannot write what he or she sees correctly, even after much help, then it may be time to have your child evaluated.

4. If your child correctly copies what he or she sees, but cannot read the word correctly, even after being taught those letters and sounds, then that is another sign to be on watch for a possible learning disability.

Parents need to know that the public school systems in the United States have their own rules and guidelines for having a child tested for a learning disability. There is a procedure that they must follow. Parents cannot just walk into their child's school and demand testing for a learning disability; schools are under legal constraints to follow certain guidelines. The general procedure for diagnosing a learning disability in a public school is as follows:

✔ The teacher observes that the child does not seem to be learning a skill. The teacher tries alternative methods of reteaching the skill to see if the child can grasp it another way. If, after trying all possible methods, the child still does not "get it," the teacher may bring up the problem with a committee of other teachers and specialists. The committee may consist of other teachers who have worked with the child, a reading teacher or reading specialist, a social worker, a guidance counselor, a school psychologist, a speech and language teacher or therapist, an administrator, a school nurse, a special education teacher with certification in specific learning disabilities or learning disability (SLD or LD) or in mental retardation (also called mentally handicapped or educable mentally handicapped [EMH], educable mentally retarded [EMR], or trainable mentally handicapped [TMH]), or in emotional or behavioral disorders (ED or BD). The team listens to the teacher describe the problem and all the "interventions," or methods used to remedy the problem. The team may make other recommendations for the teacher based on their own experience. The teacher is given a time limit to try the new teaching methods.

✔ After the teacher tries further methods, and the team also observes the child, the team meets again. At this time they may decide to recommend the school psychologist test the child. At this point, the parents need to sign permission for testing. A meeting is scheduled with the parents to discuss any concerns and explain why the team feels testing is necessary.

✔ If the parent signs a consent form, the child is placed on a waiting list for the test. The psychologist often has a long list of students to test for a variety of reasons.

Due to the long list, it may be a long wait for testing. Then, after testing, a detailed report must be written.

✔ After the results of the test are prepared by the psychologist, the team meets again to go over the results. Based on the test and their experience, the team makes a recommendation to the parents to either place or not place the child in a special education program.

Sometimes there are students who are diagnosed as having an actual learning disability, but their parents won't put them in a program because they do not like the "label." It is true that it is difficult to have your child "labeled" with a learning disability, but the child needs special education services in order to learn. Repeating a grade or receiving continual practice in the same skill is not going to help a student challenged by a learning disability. They can only learn using different methods. If no one uses these different methods to instruct your child, he or she is just passing time in that particular subject without learning the material or performing according to the expected standards for his or her age level. Every year the child is not taught using techniques suited for his or her learning disability is another frustrating, painful year he or she will lag further behind. Parents need to weigh the alternatives if their child is diagnosed with a learning disability. They should decide whether it does more harm to the child to receive special help even if it means having a "label," or whether it does more harm to have the child continue to fail in the regular classroom because the parents did not consent to the services their child needed. Are the parents prepared to learn those special techniques and work with the child at home? If so, the child will have a chance. But if no one works with them using the method suited to their particular disability, the child is missing much of his or her instruction and will fall further and further behind each year.

One way to understand a learning disability is by imagining a blind person. No matter how many times one flashes words before the blind person's eyes, he or she will not learn to read. Only when we teach the person to read by listening to books read aloud or by touching braille can they learn to read. If a child has a visual learning disability, they need to compensate by using their other senses such as touch or hearing to learn to read. Parents should know this in order to make the best possible choice for their child's education.

IS THERE HOPE FOR A CHILD CHALLENGED BY A LEARNING DISABILITY?

To answer this, let us look at the example of Helen Keller. She was blind and deaf. Yet her teacher, Annie Sullivan, found a way to communicate to her so that she learned to feel the letters formed by the fingers as sign language and later by braille. If a child who is blind and deaf can learn to read, there is hope for every person who has a learning disability as well.

NIP THE PROBLEM IN THE BUD

The sooner you catch your child's reading problem, the easier it will be to resolve it. It is important to stay on top of your child's progress from kindergarten and first grade on, closely monitoring any difficulties that arise. What happens if you don't? Your child could become a statistic, one of the millions of students with reading problems reported by government studies. It is hard to believe that there are middle school, high school, and college students who are still taking remedial reading courses in an advanced nation such as the United States. Even businesses are frustrated by the reading level of recently graduated students they hire. How could such a situation develop?

When a reading problem is not caught, children find themselves missing more of the readings. Either they are too shy to ask for help, or they are afraid of admitting they do not know what the rest of the class seems to know, but continue on silently in their confusion. As the class progresses, children become stuck on some portions of the work. They begin to skip over difficult words, and as a result their comprehension of the passage worsens. If they cannot master their current grade level work, how can they be expected to master the work at the higher grade level? By the time the child is in middle school, he or she may still be reading at a second- or third-grade level.

As children move to higher grades, less time is spent on reading. Teachers in grades four, five, and six traditionally have not taught letter-sound relationships; they are more concerned with teaching literature and comprehension. Thus, the child who enters these upper grades without all the letter-sound relationship skills in place will not receive much instruction in these skills. Thus, they stay at the same level. As the work grows harder each year and the child moves into high school, he or she does not have any chance to make up the missed skills. Middle and high school teachers are trained to teach a particular subject and do not expect to be teaching second- and third-grade reading skills. If these children are placed in a remedial reading class, they have so many years to make up that it seems they will always be behind the other students.

It is frightening to see the number of students in some high schools who are still reading at second- and third-grade level. They do not know the meaning of basic vocabulary words, how to get meaning from what they read, or how to read independently. One wonders at the fate of this country when these students join the work force in several years. But more heartbreaking is seeing these children speak about themselves as "stupid" or "dumb." They have such a low self-concept that they feel like failures in all areas of life. Can you imagine a student saying, "I got an A on the test! I got an A! That never happened to me before!" These children are so used to failure that they are shocked when they actually succeed at something. Many are so used to failing, they no longer wish to try any work. Had their reading problems been caught and solved when they were still in elementary school, they would not have to suffer today.

One common complaint I hear from parents is that they would like to help their child but they do not have the time. I tell them, "You can take a few moments to work with your child every day now to prevent problems in the future, or you can choose not to spend time with them now, and when they fail in the upper grades you will have to spend hours with them to get them through middle and high school. Furthermore, if they continue to struggle in school, the chances of them dropping out increase." We need not extrapolate further where they may go from there! An ounce of prevention is worth tons of cure.

Chapter 7

Why Schools Need Your Help

If you have ever worked with your child in the area of reading, you have seen what an intricate process reading is. Think about the time you may have spent teaching the alphabet, helping the child read words, guiding the child through the process of figuring out new words, and then helping the child understand what he or she read. It requires continual attention, constant nurturing and care, like nourishing a seedling until it grows into a full-fledged plant. Think of the time and attention one child alone needs. Now multiply your child by twenty-five (and in some schools, thirty), and you will have a sense of what it would be like to be a teacher responsible for all twenty-five children learning to read! It is a job worthy of appreciation and admiration.

Elementary school teachers are usually given one or two hours a day to spend in reading period. Within that time, he or she has to see that all twenty-five children are moving along at a steady pace. But the reality is, not all students move at the same rate. First, not all students entered the class at the same level. Some came into the class reading below grade level, some were on grade level, and others were ahead of grade level. Thus, within that class period, many teachers must divide the students into groups according to their reading level. Instead of spending one or two hours on the same skill with all students, the teacher must divide the time three ways (and in some schools, four or more ways), depending upon the number of reading groups there are. Within each reading group, there are variations in students' needs. Some students require more help from the teacher, others less. The teacher has to be aware of each student's needs and continually adjust and readjust his or her strategy for that child. If one student falls behind and the teacher has to give more help, the other students receive less time.

If you picture yourself teaching reading not only to your own child, but to twenty-five other students with as strong a desire for your help as your child, you can see why teachers need all the help they can get from parents.

What happens to children or teens in school when they have a reading problem? There are several avenues that schools take when they find students with reading problems. Before providing an overview of some of these possibilities, it is important to have an idea of how reading is taught in the schools.

There is no one method of teaching reading. There are a variety of ways in which reading is taught. The skills present-ed in this book form the basis that underlies a good reading program. Every successful reading program must teach the skills of letter-sound relationships, vocabulary, comprehension, and strategies to be an independent reader and thinker. Teach-ing methods vary from school to school and even from class to class. In some programs, students pass through a continu-um of skills step-by-step and cannot go to the next step until they demonstrate mastery of the previous one. Programs on the other end of the spectrum require children to read books of their choice. Skills are taught as the children show a need for them. For example, the child may not learn how to read an *ea* vowel pattern until he or she comes across a new word with that pattern. At that moment the teacher decides to teach the sound of *ea*. Between these two ends of the spectrum are a variety of programs. Some schools mandate the use of a particular program, while others let each teacher decide which program to use.

Curriculum is continually changing in the field of education. A school district may adopt a textbook series and build the entire curriculum around that. Two or three years later the district may decide to adopt a different series. The entire curriculum is then revamped. As new findings in the field of education are popularized, educators change their views on the best way to teach. This brings about further changes in the way reading is taught. The pendulum may swing back and forth from one view of teaching to another one. For example, at one time phonics instruction was popular in which *only* the letter-sound relationships were taught using workbooks, programmed or basal readers, and practice sheet. The children never had a chance to apply the skills in reading "real" literature in books. In some whole language programs, whereby children read from any books of their choice or read from their own writings and self-made books, phonics or letter-sound relationships are not systematically taught unless a child shows the need for help with a word or sound. Some educators become very dogmatic about a particular method. Various camps form within the field of reading, with some educators waving the banner for phonics, and others advocating whole language. Then there are educators who take an eclectic approach and use each of these methods in the curriculum. Some believe that the method should be matched to the learner and use a combination of instructional techniques until they find the best one for each child. It is difficult for parents to keep up with the changes that take place in the curriculum, the school's philosophy, the method of instruction from one grade level to the next, or even from one teacher to the next. Although there are new trends in the field, teachers who received their education twenty years ago may continue to teach in the same manner they were taught. Teachers who have just graduated college may teach in the manner that their college instructors taught them, which may also be the methods used twenty years ago or which may be the newest methods. To keep abreast of the newest developments in the field, some teachers attend the latest conferences. There isn't any national standard for reading instruction. Teachers' instructional methods are as different from one another as snowflakes.

How can a parent make any sense out of the variety of methods taught? If you can absorb and understand the basics of reading as presented in this book, you will have a yardstick to measure any reading program your child encounters. Whether your child is being taught in School District A or B, whether your child is in second grade or third grade, whether your child is in Mrs. B's class or Mr. C's class, you will know what basics your child should learn in reading instruction. As your child moves from teacher to teacher, grade level to grade level, school to school, or district to district, you can keep track of your child's knowledge base and skills to prevent any gaps in instruction. At the end of the book are two charts you can use (see The Vowel and Consonant Guide, Part A and Part B) to track your child's skills and stay on top of his or her educational career. The skills chart (Part A) lists the skills your child should be learning, and the second chart (Part B, which is identical to Part A) provides places for you to write on and check off as you diagnose the skills your child does not yet know. Keeping a chart of your child's reading skills will also give you a tool for communicating with your child's teacher if your child receives a low grade or fails in reading. You can then ask specific questions to find out what your child's difficulties are so that you can do something about the situation.

One note of caution, though. When approaching educators, keep in mind that some are very dogmatic about their method and do not want to hear about any other technique. You may have experienced this if you ever tried to help your child with math. Even though you may feel your child will "get it" if you show them your easy method, your child's teacher may have frowned upon you for using any other method than the ones they use in the classroom. It is true that we do not want to confuse the child, but if one is open-minded and realizes that all children are different, then we can accept a variety of techniques in the quest for one that works best for a particular learner.

If you know the basics of reading—letter-sound relationships, vocabulary, comprehension, and independent reading and thinking strategies—you can ensure that your child receives coverage in all of these no matter what reading program is taught in the schools. Trends may change, new approaches may be developed, but the bottom line is, the child has to convert all those strange symbols into meaning and personally interact with those ideas.

Just as reading programs differ throughout schools, so do methods of solving reading problems. There are thousands of different ways schools deal with reading problems. There are a multitude of textbooks, learning materials, curricula, and programs for those who have trouble with reading. Listed below are some of the possible steps that schools take when they discover a child has a reading problem. It is important to know what steps your own child's school uses to deal with the problem so that you know what further support you need to provide as a parent.

> ✔ Some schools do nothing. The child is expected to keep up with the rest of the class, and since the child's

problem is not being addressed, he or she continues to fail and falls further and further behind.

✔ The teacher tries to repeat the work over and over until the child gets it. The teacher uses the same method that did not work the first time and finds that the method does not work the second or third time either. The teacher may just give up because he or she has already spent a lot of extra time with the child and cannot shortchange the rest of the class anymore. The child receives a failing grade, and the teacher goes on with the next skill, hoping with time the child will pick up the missed skill.

✔ The teacher tries to repeat the skill over and over and tries a variety of methods. The child responds to different methods and ultimately learns the skill. This process is also difficult in a school setting because the teacher has to plan different lessons for a variety of student needs. The teacher has to find time to instruct many students in these different techniques. In a large class it is not always possible to take time from the large group to work with individuals. Even if an excellent teacher does have a variety of techniques to match the students' needs, extended time is not available to provide consistent individualized help. There are too many other requirements that must be addressed and too many other students with competing needs.

✔ A reading aide, parent volunteer, or another student is assigned to work with the child to help him or her with the skill until the child masters it. Every class does not always have the luxury of an additional person to help the teacher. Having other students work with the child is also time-consuming since the teacher has to guide the other child becoming a helper. Also, the teacher needs to take time training the aide or parent volunteer, and the schools do not always provide teachers with enough planning time to meet with these assistants. Because the child's needs and skills change daily, teachers have to meet with assistants daily to keep them up-to-date on the next step.

✔ If the child has repeated failures in reading, the teacher may recommend him or her for a special reading program. Some schools have remedial reading classes and others do not. In some schools the remedial reading class is limited to a set number of students, and your child may have to be on a waiting list to be admitted. Some schools qualify for federal assistance in the area of remedial reading. These classes are called Title I (formerly known as Chapter I) reading classes, which also vary from school to school. In some programs, the child is pulled out of the regular class to work in the reading class with a small group. The group can vary from two or three students to as many as fifteen students at a time. It is very rare that the child receives one-on-one help in these remedial classes. Within the setting of a group, the teacher may spend some individualized time with your child, but generally not for the entire duration of the pull-out period. In Chapter I or remedial reading classes, the teachers, who should be certified in reading, teach students a variety of skills so that they can read on grade level. These skills can be taught separately from the student's regular class work or can be integrated with skills from the regular class. Progress in these classes is usually measured by performance on standardized reading tests. The methods used in these classes vary widely. Skills are taught in isolation, as whole language skills, or in a combination of skills and the whole-language approach. In a good reading program the teacher will find out what steps the child has missed along the way. An excellent reading program will find out the child's best learning style and match instruction to that. Remember, the best reading program is one that matches your child's needs. The best programs will also make the child an independent reader and develop self-esteem and motivation to encourage him or her to be a lifelong learner who derives pleasure and joy from reading. Successful experiences will help the child find reading positive and enjoyable. The teacher will be supportive, care about the child, and provide appreciation and specific praise for the child. Since the child will be pulled out of class two, three, four, or five times a week for a half hour or longer, maximum time is spent in activities that target the child's specific needs.

✔ A reading teacher or specialist goes into the class to work with your child or a group of children with reading problems. This system, often termed "inclusion," or the "regular education initiative" or "REI," has become more popular in the 1990s. In this process, students are not pulled out for special programs. Rather, a specialist comes into the classroom to work with the child. One plus is that the child is not separated from the class. Ideally, the reading teacher works with the child on skills that the regular classroom teacher is presenting so that there is more correlation between the special reading teacher and the classroom teacher. On the down side, the schedule often does not allow the specialist to work in each classroom during the reading period, since many classes have reading at the same time.

Thus, the specialist may enter the class during another subject such as math or science or art, and the child receives reading help while the rest of the class is working on something else. Also, the specialist must go to students in their own individual classes rather than pull out many students in a group, so the logistics may not allow the teacher to be with each child for as much time as necessary. Rather than spending a half hour with three fifth graders, the teacher may have to spend ten minutes apiece visiting three fifth-grade rooms in the same half hour. In some schools other students who do not need reading help may be grouped with your child so that the child does not feel singled out. While the child may feel better, the reading teacher who has come for your child must also work with other students, giving your child less individualized time.

Although the amount and the quality of reading assistance varies from school to school and classroom to classroom, one fact remains constant—the child receives little one-on-one time. The most any child can receive is a few minutes with the teacher at his or her desk going over some work, or a few minutes when the teacher circulates around the room, stopping to help students individually. It takes a highly skilled, experienced, and trained teacher to help solve students' reading problems in a classroom setting. Reading specialists and teachers can do it, but without some level of specialized reading training, regular classroom teachers have a difficult time diagnosing every child's problem and coming up with an individualized plan and matching the learning style to meet students' special needs. The resources and training are not always there to provide classroom teachers with the support they need to do that job. We cannot blame the teachers, because much of what happens to them is based on school or district policy. The school systems need to provide students with experienced reading teachers who are given the time and the resources to meet the children's needs. This is one of the reasons parental support is important. You can provide the one-on-one assistance critical to your child's success.

Part 2

Solutions for
Reading Problems

Chapter 8

What You Can Do to Help Your Child Read Better

After looking at the difficulties school systems have in providing enough one-on-one instruction to help your child read better, we can see that more support is needed. Parents provide the most valuable resources—time, attention, and love. Although the child is in school for six hours a day, the parent is responsible for the child for the remaining eighteen hours, five days a week, as well as all day on weekends, holidays, and school vacations. No teacher, aide, or reading specialist can provide that amount of time to your child on a one-on-one basis. That alone is a factor that can lead to reading success. You are already attentive to your child's needs. You have watched your child grow up from infancy and know your child better than anyone else does. You are more attuned to your child's needs and can better meet them. You have an abundance of love and concern for your child. That love drives you to provide your child with the best you can give. All you need is the skill and know-how to effectively target your child's problem, which is the purpose of this book. By working through the rest of the book, you will have all the tools necessary to make your child a successful reader. The time, the attention, the love, and the know-how are the key ingredients to help your child be successful.

Are you having doubts that you can actually help your child in reading? If you doubt your ability, go through your closet and dig out your child's baby picture. Find the earliest one possible. Now dig out a recent picture of your child. Think about what your child was like as an infant. The baby could not walk or talk or eat by himself or herself. Think about your child now. Hear your child talk. Think about all the skills and talents your child has. Listen to how the child expresses his or her thoughts. All that your child is today is due to *you*, the parent. If the child is walking, talking, thinking, and doing a variety of activities, it is all due to you, the parent, and the instruction you gave your child. You were the child's first teacher. That power and influence that you have on the child does not end when the child begins elementary school. It is said that children learn more in the first seven years of life than they will learn throughout the rest of their lives. You need to remember that you were your child's first teacher and that the great quantity the child learned in the first few years was due to *your* efforts.

You are capable of continuing to instruct the child. All you need is a willingness to learn. You hold the key to your child's future. You can provide the support the child needs in order to be successful not only in school but in life. The experience of success in early years lays the foundation for future successes.

Chapter 9

How Reading Is Learned

Did you ever stare at the words in a book and marvel at how those words create pictures, movies, and thoughts in your head? It seems almost miraculous. How does reading take place, and how can one learn it? If we understand how reading is learned, we can help our child learn the process better.

Before one learns to read, one needs to understand language. In the first few years of life, the child develops the ability to speak and understand what is being spoken to him or her. The child develops a vocabulary of hundreds of words that continues to increase each year. The more words a child is exposed to in the early years, the richer the vocabulary. This will provide the base for a larger reading vocabulary in later years.

Either in preschool or in kindergarten the child learns the alphabet, which he or she sees as assorted shapes—some with lines, some with circles, some with squiggles, and some with a combination of shapes. Each shape has its own name. Thus, they learn that each letter has a name. They learn how to make the sound of the letter's name.

In kindergarten or first grade, students learn that if they put these alphabet letters together they get a word they already know. They learn that c, a, t spells cat. Some may learn to put these letters together phonetically by saying each sound, "c," "a," "t"—"c-a-t"—"cat." Others learn to read the word by patterns, by learning that *a-t* is *at*, and if you put a *c* at the beginning, *at* becomes *cat*. Others learn by sight words in which they see the word *cat*, are told it is *cat*, and they just memorize the word. Others see a picture of a cat, with the word underneath, and have the ability to memorize the word. Generally, during kindergarten or first grade, the child develops the concept that alphabet letters make sounds, and those sounds form words. Once they grasp this, they can look at letters and ask what word it is. If the words they see in print are words they have in their speaking vocabulary, they will begin to form pictures of the word in their minds, which is the basis of comprehension in reading.

In many schools the child begins to read simple books, called preprimers and primers, in first grade. The first ones that a child reads have only a few words on each page. They may hear the teacher read aloud from the page, and the children mimic it. They begin to learn that there is a space between each word and start making associations between the written word and the spoken word. The teacher may teach the new words in advance so that the children will know those words while reading aloud. In another approach, the teacher will not tell what the word is, but has the child figure out the word by using their knowledge of letter sounds. The more work the child does in letter-sound relationships at that stage, the more experienced the child will be in figuring out words. In some programs the students discuss what is happening in the picture, look at the first letter of each word under the picture, and use thinking skills to figure out what word would make sense. Whatever method is taught, students learn in first grade that letters form words and that words are put together in sentences to convey an idea.

Throughout first and second grade the child learns the short and long vowel sounds as well as the consonant sounds that appear at the beginning and end of the word. They gain the ability to read three- and four-letter words. In either first or second grade they learn blends (*bl*, *cr*, *dr*, *tr*, etc.) and digraphs (*ch*, *sh*, *th*, *wh*) and some of the irregular vowel patterns such as *ai*, *oe*, *au*, etc. They learn some of the unusual patterns of the language, such as when a *c* sounds like *s* as in the word *city*, and when it sound like *k* as in the word *cat*. They learn when a *g* sounds like *g* as in the word *go*, and when it sounds like *j* as in the word *gem*.

By third grade, most of the basic letter-sound patterns have been covered. They learn some of the ending markers that are added to words, such as *ed*, *ing*, *s*, *es*, *er*, or *est* and other endings such as *ly*, *ily*, *gle*, *le*, etc. Throughout third and fourth grade, they continue to learn about prefixes (word parts that go at the beginning of a word) and suffixes (word parts that go at the end of the word) and how to read compound words (two words combined to make one word).

By fourth grade, they are able to figure out two-, three-, and four-syllable words. They learn how to break up words so they can read longer words and new vocabulary words.

Along with learning letter-sound relationships, their vocabulary continues to expand. Each time they read a new story or a new chapter in one of their content-area textbooks, they learn the meanings of new words. They also learn how to use context clues, which is the process of using the context or the meaning of the passage in which the word appears to figure out what the word means. Dictionary and glossary skills are also taught.

At the same time as letter-sound relationships and vocabulary skills are developed, students learn comprehension skills. Each time they read from their books, the teacher asks questions to find out if the students understand what they are reading. Students are asked to answer questions about the main idea and details of the story. They often must determine which events happen first, second, third, and fourth in a story. They must infer or use clues to figure out what is happening in the story or what the characters are thinking or feeling. They must predict or think about what will happen next in a story. They must evaluate the story and form judgments.

Finally, students learn independent reading strategies. They learn to monitor their reading so that they notice when the material does not make sense. They learn skills to correct themselves so that the sentences make sense. They learn to check the sounds with the letters of the word to see whether they have read the word correctly. They learn to check whether they are paying attention to what they are reading or whether they have drifted off into a daydream, even though their hands keep turning the pages. They learn how to attack a new word by figuring out how to pronounce it, then figuring out what it could mean using the context clues in the rest of the paragraph or by looking up the words in a dictionary.

Students should be reading independently by the time they reach fifth and sixth grade, if not earlier. There are some students who grasp reading so quickly, they can read independently even in the lower grades.

As they get to middle school or junior high school, they may have classes called Reading, Language Arts, or English. In these classes, time is devoted to studying different types of literature, analyzing it, and discussing the plot, the theme, and the ideas. They relate the themes in literature to issues in their own lives. Students also learn about the writer's craft and the elements that constitute good writing. They also should be expanding their vocabulary skills. Comprehension activities become more advanced as students must not only answer simple questions about what they read, but analyze, evaluate, contrast, compare, and apply the ideas in the piece. They may have to respond either in class discussions or by writing their responses.

In high school, "reading classes" refer to either remedial reading classes, enrichment classes for study skills, or reading in the content areas of science or social studies. What was referred to as Reading, Language Arts, or English in middle school is referred to mostly as English or Literature in high school. Students will most likely have one year of English Literature, one year of American Literature, one year of World Literature, and a variety of elective courses on different types of literature or themes. At this stage, students are analyzing and discussing the literature for plot, theme, character development, conflict, and the use of language and literary techniques. Some high schools have remedial reading and others do not. If your child's high school does not, then children who do not grasp reading in elementary school or middle school will have a hard time receiving help after that. High school teachers are trained to teach literature, not basic reading skills. Unless a teacher has had that training in reading, they do not have the same ability to teach reading as an elementary school teacher. The learning facilities for reading are strongest in elementary school. Over the past decade, middle schools, faced with many students who still cannot read after elementary school, have increased their ability to teach remedial reading by hiring teachers trained in that field and by developing reading labs to teach students the skills. More and more high schools are offering a remedial reading class, but they may have room for only a small amount of students, and when there are budget cuts, sometimes the reading classes are the first to be eliminated.

The federal government provides funds to school districts that have a certain number of students below a particular income level. The district uses those funds to establish Chapter I classes, which help students who have a low reading level or math level. Again, they can only provide services to a fixed number of students, and not everyone who needs the help can get into the class. Some districts budget their own money for remedial reading classes. In some schools a reading specialist works with the teachers to help them improve reading instruction. But the greatest opportunity a student has to learn reading is in the early years.

The above process describes the average progression of reading skills in public and private schools. There are many variations. Some children go through the progression more quickly and start reading independently earlier; others go through the progression more slowly and start reading independently later. But in order to read, students must master all these skills and processes.

As you read this book, you need to evaluate where your own child stands in the progression. Once you can determine what he or she knows and does not know, you can pick up the skills from that point and move ahead. Your child may be behind the rest of his or her class, at the same point as a majority of the class, or ahead of most of the students in the class. Wherever your child is, you have the power and ability to move him or her forward. If your child is behind, you can help him or her catch up. If he or she is on the same level as the rest of the class, you can move your child ahead of the class. And if your child is already ahead, you can advance him or her further.

Why would you want to advance your child further? If your child can read at a higher reading level, he or she can read more advanced books. By reading higher-level books, your child will be exposed to more challenging ideas and concepts that will stimulate his or her thinking. Your child's mental abilities will reach higher levels, and he or she will be better equipped to deal with material at higher grade levels. By mastering the reading skills of the next grade level in advance, your child will not have to concentrate on the basic skills, but can spend more time on higher-level thinking and more challenging content. Your child's improved skills can be applied to reading materials in science and social studies classes. Reading ability helps students do better on tests that require reading. With stiff competition to gain acceptance into good colleges and to win scholarships, the head start you give your child in the early years will give him or her a better chance of becoming a top student later. The better one does in one's higher education, the more opportunities one has for a better career in life.

If your child is an infant, toddler, or preschooler, this knowledge can also help you prepare your child for school. If you know the progression of reading skills, you can guide your child to develop the skills that will make him or her a successful reader when he or she enters school.

You cannot gauge your child's reading ability by report card grades that are often a subjective grade based on the teacher's own standards, or by standardized test scores that only report where your child stands in relation to other children of the same age across the nation. The rest of the book will help you determine what your child's current reading skills are and show you how to move him or her forward. By knowing how reading is learned, you can take your child from whatever point he or she is now and move them to the final goal of successful reading.

Chapter 10

Why You Need to Know How to Diagnose Your Child's Problem

A good reading instructor should be able to diagnose your child's problems, but unfortunately, not every school has a trained reading specialist. There is a difference between the training of a regular classroom teacher and that of a reading specialist. A regular classroom teacher in an elementary school has a degree in "elementary education." This degree requires the teacher to have taken only one or two courses in each elementary school subject, such as reading, language arts, science, social studies, math, art, music, health, and physical education. This gives the teacher a broad but general knowledge of all the subjects. Whereas a teacher with an elementary education degree has taken one or two courses in reading, a reading specialist has had anywhere from six to ten courses in reading. They have more extensive knowledge of diagnosing and remediating reading problems and are more familiar with the developmental process in reading.

Teachers at the high school level receive courses in the subject area they will teach, such as science, social studies, or math, but do not necessarily receive instruction in teaching reading.

For many regular classroom teachers, when faced with their first teaching job, their on-the-job training in reading instruction consists of the principal or curriculum coordinator handing them a reading textbook series with the instructions to take their students through it page by page. How do I know this? That is what I was asked to do when I took my first teaching job and was still asked to do in public schools in two other states over the next twenty years!

As a teacher trainer and consultant, I see the same situation going on in many classrooms today. Few regular classroom teachers are trained to diagnose a child's reading problem or rectify the difficulty. I had to go through special courses and undergo years of experience and training to become a reading specialist equipped to diagnose reading problems. That training made me realize the vast difference between the training I had as a regular classroom teacher and that which I received as a reading teacher. It is like the difference between a general medical practitioner and a brain surgeon. It is not that the regular teacher is not excellent, or lacks the skills to teach, any more than a general practitioner lacks the skill to treat patients. The difference lies in the degree of specialization.

Over time, classroom teachers usually gain more experience in teaching reading to the students of their own particular grade level. The difficulty arises when all the students are not working at that grade level. Some are above grade level and some are below. Teachers often are prepared to teach to students on their current grade level, but may not be trained or lack the support or materials to teach students at a different grade level. In many cases a teacher may have students functioning on two, three, four, five, and even six different levels in a class of thirty. It is difficult to find enough time in the curriculum to address so many varying levels.

With the large number of students in each classroom, and a small amount of time at the teacher's disposal to work with students on an individual basis, a parent is the child's best coach. You can provide support to the classroom teacher by working with your child at home. You are there for your child every evening and can give your child individualized attention. Your love and concern for your child, coupled with the skill to guide your child, can be a powerful influence on your child's ability to succeed. Parents need to be aware of the basic steps in reading development so that they can step in and troubleshoot when their child is having problems. This information can also help you better communicate with the child's teacher to get assistance.

What do you do when your child gets sick? You may not be a medical doctor, but you quickly learn what disease your child has, what its symptoms are, and what the best treatments are. You learn how to administer the treatments or remedies at home. You can see how effectively you have worked as a doctor and a nurse over the years without a medical degree! You can empower yourself with the same ability to help your child with school problems as well. This section of the book will serve as your guide and training manual so that you can supply the support your child needs to overcome reading difficulties.

What I have done is to condense my years of experience as a reading teacher and specialist into its simplest steps so that you will not need years of experience to be able to work with your child. No matter what your level of education, if you can read this book, you can teach your child to be a better reader. This book is written so that even those who have had no training can use it. You will be able to apply these simple steps to help your own child.

Chapter 11

What Is Your Child's Best Learning Style?

Before diagnosing your child's ability level in the different skills, it is important to identify your child's best learning style. Why? As reading skills are presented, we want to match the instruction in each skill with your child's preferred learning style so that he or she grasps it quickly. In each section, there will be some suggestions for presenting the same material four different ways: visually, auditorily, kinesthetically, and tactilely. It is important that you choose the method that matches your child's learning style for quicker results. You can see for yourself which methods work by trying several of them. You may see a blank stare when you use the wrong method or a spark in your child's eyes when you use the correct one. The following section will help you figure out your child's best learning style.

If your child is having a reading problem, it may be due to missed steps, or instruction given in a way that did not match your child's learning strengths. Thus, when you go back to reteach the missed skills, it must be done in a way that matches his or her learning style.

Before determining what skills your child needs and beginning instruction, you must find out your child's learning style so that you can match instruction to it. There are four ways to do this. The first is asking your child the questions given in the learning style questionnaire you took in Chapter 3 to see how many answers he or she chooses in each catetory: visual, auditory, tactile, and kinesthetic. If your child is too young to answer these questions, observe your child's behavior and try to answer the questions yourself. The second method is looking for clues according to the Observation Checklist given below. The third method is speaking to your child using certain verbs and noting the ones to which he or she best responds. There are verbs that match each learning style. By observing the verbs to which your child responds more positively, you can gain clues to his or her preferred learning style. The fourth method is teaching your child something new using a visual, auditory, tactile, or kinesthetic approach and observing the method to which he or she best responds.

Method 1: Questionnaire (see Chapter 3)

Method 2: Observation Checklist

Your child is *visual* if he or she:

- ✔ looks at books and pictures for long periods of time
- ✔ likes to look at mobiles or at pictures hanging on the wall
- ✔ likes to point out things they *see* that are interesting to them
- ✔ notices what people wear or how people look
- ✔ notices objects, cars, signs, or people as you drive
- ✔ notices colors and designs
- ✔ likes to keep things in a certain visual order

✔ responds to pictures or charts that you show him or her

✔ is particular about how his or her belongings are visually arranged

✔ maintains good eye focus on the person who is talking to him or her

Your child is *auditory* if he or she:

✔ talks a lot

✔ sings or hums a lot

✔ makes noise when everything becomes too quiet

✔ likes to listen to tapes, CDs, or the radio

✔ seems to remember what he or she hears people say

✔ memorizes and can recite back stories or poems that someone else has read to him or her

✔ memorizes what people talk about

✔ talks to himself or herself out loud

✔ reads aloud or whispers the words when asked to read silently

✔ cannot sleep if there is noise or sounds in the room

✔ becomes distracted by extraneous sounds

✔ moves his or her eyes back and forth from left to right when thinking or talking to people rather than looking straight ahead or up or down

Your child is *tactile* if she or he:

✔ is always touching something

✔ likes to draw, doodle, or write when people talk to him or her or while talking on the phone

✔ can spend a long time working on an arts and crafts activity

✔ likes to make things with clay or play dough.

✔ is sensitive to touch: either likes people to hug and be affectionate, or dislikes them to touch him or her (can be either of these, depending upon the person touching him or her or the circumstance)

✔ is emotional

✔ is sensitive to people's moods

✔ is always checking on how everyone feels

✔ notices people's emotions

✔ responds to nonverbal cues, facial expressions, gestures, and tone of voice

✔ has mood swings based on other people's reactions

✔ cries easily at sad endings of movies or books

✔ likes to type or use fingers to play an instrument

✔ sometimes looks down when thinking or answering questions

Your child is *kinesthetic* if he or she:

✔ is always in motion

✔ has a lot of energy and seems to be bouncing off the walls

✔ enjoys sports and physical activity

✔ moves from one activity to another frequently

✔ is restless

✔ cannot sit still

✔ wiggles in the chair, or slides in and out of the chair

✔ likes to explore

✔ complains about being too hot, too cold, or uncomfortable

✔ needs his or her bed or chair to be comfortable

✔ is not concerned about his or her appearance as long as he or she is comfortable

✔ sits in a slouched or comfortable position and sometimes puts his or her head on the desk when writing or studying

✔ likes to sprawl out on the floor to do homework or to read

✔ looks down or away when someone speaks to him or her

METHOD 3: SPEAK TO YOUR CHILD USING VERBS THAT MATCH HIS OR HER LEARNING STYLE

There are certain verbs or action words that match different types of learners. Visual learners respond to verbs that have to do with seeing and showing. Auditory learners respond to verbs that relate to hearing, listening, or "tuning in." Tactile learners respond to verbs that have to do with feeling and touching. Kinesthetic learners respond to verbs that have to do with moving and action. Try talking to your child using the different lists. When you use a verb that matches his or her learning style, you will see a flash of recognition in your child's eyes. His or her face will light up. You will see an immediate response. When you use a verb that does not match the learning style, there will be a dead response or a blank look. You may have seen this look when you have told your visual child to pick up his or her toys. Telling is not enough. You have to visually show him or her what you are talking about. You may have seen the blank state when you have left a note for your auditory child instructing him or her what chores to do. They do not want to read it; they want the instructions to be told to them. If you did not tie your instructions to your tactile child into words that express the sense of touch or of feeling, he or she may have ignored you. If you did not use action words with your kinesthetic child for whatever task you wanted him or her to do, forget about a response!

Here are some word lists that match the different types of learners. Try using different verbs and see which result in that desired flash of understanding from your child.

For *visual* learners, use:

   See
   Show
   Look at
   Watch
   Point to
   Observe
   Notice
   Find
   Look for
   Locate

Example sentences:

   "*See* the letters on the page."
   "*Look* at this word."
   "*Find* the right answer."

For *auditory* learners, use:

   Listen
   Hear

Tune in
Tell me
Talk to me
Speak
Say
Sing
Explain
Talk about
Discuss

Example sentences:

"*Listen* to the *sound* of this letter."
"*Hear* the words."
"*Tell* me the right answer."

For *tactile* learners, use:

Feel
Touch
Play with
Make
Draw
Design
Illustrate
Write
Type
Sculpt
Construct
Build

Example sentences:

"*Feel* the shape of the plastic letters."
"*Make* a design out of the words."
"*Write* the correct answer."

For *kinesthetic* learners, use:

Move
Jump
Run
Play
Exercise
Feel
Act
Do
Explore
Discover
Experiment
Bring back
Carry
Climb

Example sentences:

"*Move* the plastic letters around until you spell the word."
"*Do jumping jacks* to spell the word."
"*Discover* the correct answer."

METHOD 4: TRY DIFFERENT TEACHING METHODS

Take a skill that your child needs to learn. It could be learning the letters, or it could be comprehending high school level reading material. It could be learning what a noun is. Try teaching it using a visual, auditory, tactile, or kinesthetic approach. Observe which method works best for your child. Also ask your child which method he or she liked best. This method will probably match his or her learning style. Try this experiment several times to confirm that the child chooses the same style.

Here are some sample lessons taught four different ways. One lesson will be for an elementary school student. The other would be applicable for a middle or high school student.

Elementary School Student

As an example, we will use the skill of teaching the vowel sound of short *a* as in *cat*, to demonstrate how it can be taught four different ways to match the child's learning style. (If your child already knows this skill, then select a skill at your child's grade level that he or she does not yet know and use the same methods to teach it in these four different ways. For example, you may teach a vowel combination such as *au* or the prefix *mis* or the suffix *able*.)

Visual Approach

Write the letter *a* on a large piece of paper. Draw a picture of a word that starts with short *a* such as *apple*. Write the word *apple* under the picture of the apple. Then write a word containing short *a* such as *cat*. Draw a picture of a cat. Say the sound of short *a* as in *cat* while pointing to the letter on the chart. Have your child read the words *apple* and *cat* while pointing to the word and the picture. Write other words with a short *a* sound and draw a picture to go with each. For example, write *bat*, *hat*, *mat*, and *rat*.

Then have your child look in a book or on a worksheet to find pictures of the same objects. Have your child look at a book or worksheet with words and find and circle all the words that are the same as the ones you just taught him or her.

Give your child a storybook containing some of the words you just taught. Before attempting to read, ask your child to locate any of the words he or she just learned.

Auditory Approach

Write the letter *a* on a piece of paper and draw an apple. Have your child repeat the sound of *a* as in *apple* several times while looking at the letter. Have your child say the word "apple."

Say aloud a list of words and have your child raise his or her hand every time he or she hears a word with the short *a* sound in it. For example, say "boy," "alligator," "dog," "animal," "tiger," and "apple."

Write the word *cat* as an example of a word with a short *a* in the middle. Show your child a word list, read aloud the words, and have your child say the short *a* sound when he or she comes across a word with that sound in it. For example, write and say "cat," "doll," "bat," "cup," "sat," "big," etc. Your child should make the short *a* sound after hearing the words "cat," "bat," and "sat."

Have your child recite a list of rhyming words with short *a* in them: *bat*, *hat*, *cat*, *mat*, *rat*, etc.

Select a book to read which has words with the short *a* sound. Have your child read aloud the words with the short *a* sound.

Tactile Approach

Show your child the letter *a* and give your child a real or a toy apple to hold. Make a word card or flashcard with the word *apple* written below an outlined picture of an apple. Have your child color in the apple and trace over the word *apple*. Also give your child a flashcard with the word *cat* on it. Have an outlined picture of a cat on it over which your child can color. Have your child trace in crayon over the word *cat*. Then have your child trace over the word that was outlined in crayon and feel the shape of the letters with his or her fingers. Have your child draw his or her own picture of a cat on a new sheet of paper and write the word *cat* below it.

Cut out the letters c, a, and t in sandpaper. Guide your child to arrange the letters in correct order. Then have your child trace the word *cat* on the sandpaper with his or her fingers.

Buy plastic letters and have your child feel and trace over the letters c, a, and t while saying *cat*. Have your child trace *cat* in nontoxic glue. Then have your child glue dried elbow macaroni or sparkles to it to make an arts and crafts picture. Have your child make a picture of a cat to go with the word.

If you have a typewriter or computer, have your child type the word *cat*.

Repeat the activity with other words with short *a* in them such as *hat*, *bat*, *mat*, and *rat*.

Then have your child read a story with short *a* words. Have your child point to the words with the short *a* in them.

Kinesthetic Approach

Write on paper the letter *a*. Also have a large plastic letter or a block with the letter *a* raised on it for your child to hold. Place a real apple next to the picture and have your child play with it while saying short *a*.

Write the word *cat* and have a stuffed cat or toy cat (unless you have a real live cat, which is even better) to show your child. Have your child use plastic letters or blocks to spell the word *cat* while also playing with the toy cat.

Have your child write the word *cat* in extra large letters on a large sheet of paper attached to the wall. Have your child stand up while writing. Tell your child to close his or her eyes and trace the letters c, a, and t in the air with the entire arm, from the shoulders down to the hand. While tracing the letters in the air with closed eyes, have your child visualize the word in the mind and say it aloud at the same time. The large arm movements will help the child's body to remember the feeling of writing the word, and that will transfer to the fingers when they pick up a pencil to write.

Use masking tape to make a giant *c*, *a*, and *t* on the carpet. The letters should be about four or five feet long. Have your child walk along the letters in order, saying the letters as he or she walks. Have your child jump or hop along the letters. Have the child walk like a cat along the letters that spell *cat*, and say the letters and the entire word as he or she walks.

Have your child do jumping jacks while spelling the letters of the word *cat*. Have him or her do it with eyes closed, and picture the word while doing the jumping jacks.

Middle or High School Student

As an example, we can take the skill of learning a new vocabulary word to understand how it can be taught four different ways to a student in a middle school or high school.

Visual Approach

Select a new vocabulary word and have your child look it up in the dictionary.

Example: Protean

Definition: readily assuming different forms; changeable

Write the word on paper along with four different definitions, only one being the correct one. Have your child circle the correct definition.

Have your child make a chart for new words. The chart should have a column for each of the following: word, definition, part of speech, synonym, antonym, sentence, and picture. Have your child use a dictionary to look up the definition and part of speech. Your child can use a thesaurus to look up synonyms and antonyms. A synonym is another word having the same meaning. An antonym is the word's opposite. Then have your child make up an imaginative sentence for the word and write it in the appropriate column. Finally, have your child find a picture in a magazine to illustrate the word and cut it out to paste in the last column.

Have your child read a sentence or passage in which the word appears, point to the word, and say the definition.

Auditory Approach

Have your child look up the word in the dictionary and read its meaning aloud, then write the word and its meaning. Have your child read the word aloud and say its meaning once more. Discuss the meaning with the child. Talk about how the word could be used. Have your child make up several sentences in which the word could be used. You can also make up sentences and have your child tell you the meaning of the word in your sentence. Talk about the word's part of speech. Discuss words that would be synonyms for the word. Below is a sample dialogue you can have with your child to help him or her learn the word:

PARENT: *Let's look up the word* protean *in the dictionary. Read the word and meanings to me.*

CHILD: *"Protean": It says, "readily assuming different forms."*

PARENT: *Does it have any other meanings listed there?*

CHILD: *It also says, "changeable."*

PARENT: *Can you think of anything that could take on different forms or that would be changeable?*

CHILD: *In some movies the creature takes on the form of different people to confuse its enemies.*

PARENT: *Good example. Let's make up a sentence for that.*

CHILD: *The creature was protean.*

PARENT: *Let's say a little more about that sentence.
            The creature was protean because . . . ?*

CHILD: *The creature was protean because it took the
            form of a man we knew.*

PARENT: *Good. That will help you remember more
            clearly the word we are talking about. Now
            let's talk about how we can use the word in
            other ways. In what other situations would
            something be protean or changeable?*

CHILD: *One of my friends has a protean personality.
            He is always changing his behavior.*

PARENT: *Good example. Say the name of the person
            who is protean so that it will help give you an
            image when you hear the word again.*

CHILD: *Laramie is a protean guy who is always
            changing the way he acts.*

PARENT: *The sentence you just told me is a good, clear
            example.*

[Note to parents: Notice the use of specific praise in which you
not only say the child gave a good sentence, but you explain
why it was good. This gives your child a clear picture of what
behaviors or examples to repeat when doing this kind of work.
Also note the choice of words such as "talk," "say," etc.,
which are key words to use when speaking to an auditory
learner.]

PARENT: *What part of speech is the word* protean?

CHILD: *It is an adjective.*

PARENT: *When would you use* protean *in a sentence?*

CHILD: *You would use it as a describing word for a
            noun.*

PARENT: *Can you think of any synonyms for* protean?

CHILD: *Changeable.*

PARENT: *Good word. Sometimes the words used in the definitions are also synonyms. If you want to find more synonyms, where would you look?*

CHILD: *In a thesaurus.*

In the above example the parent is not only teaching the definition of the word, but is also giving the child strategies to use when learning other words. The child is learning the importance of looking up the definition, part of speech, and synonyms, as well as using the word in sentences and examples which will be meaningful to the child. The child, through this discussion, will remember not only the word, but the method used to learn a new word.

Tactile Approach

Have your child write the word *protean* with a colored marker or pen, then look up the word *protean* in the dictionary and write the meaning in a different color. Tell your child to draw or use clay to make something that illustrates *protean*. The child may draw a blobby shape in one picture and then a different shape in the next picture or make a shape with clay and change it. Have your child label the picture or sculpture with the word *protean* and write the word *changeable* next to it.

Ask your child to close his or her eyes and picture something or someone who is protean. Tell your child to make the image meaningful to him or her. Tactile children learn through their feelings, so the image should be something that makes an emotional impression on the child. For example, ask your child to think of a person they like who is changeable or protean. Have them visualize themselves with that person and see them change into another person or form they like. Or have the child picture an object they like, such as a souvenir, a baseball or football, or a favorite outfit. Have them see that object as protean, changing into another object they like. The memory of that object attached to a strong emotion will help the child remember the word. The child should draw or write the image they imagined, with the word and its definition below it. Writing and drawing are tactile experiences that will help the child recall the word.

Ask the child to name the part of speech for the word *protean*. After they look it up and find out that it is an adjective, have the child list other nouns (persons, places, or things) that could be protean. They can draw images to go with each phrase. For example:

protean child

protean jelly

protean sea

Since the sense of touch is a key strength for tactile learners, the images should be something they could touch or visualize themselves touching.

Follow these directions to have your child make a word map: Have your child write the word in a circle on the middle of a page. Extend five lines radiating from the circle. Attach a large circle to the end of each of the other lines. (See illustration below.) In one circle, have the child write the meaning in one color. In another circle, have the child write the part of speech in another color. Then, in third circle, the child should write a synonym for the word. In the fourth circle, have your child make up and write a sentence using the word. Then, in the fifth circle, have your child draw a picture of the word or action, or of a scene in which the word applies. Example of a word map:

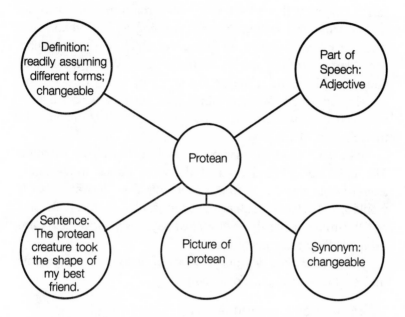

Note that the sentence and illustration should be imaginative to help establish a memorable picture in your child's mind. Then have your child reread the sentence and picture the meaning of the sentence.

Kinesthetic Approach

Kinesthetic learners have to experience what they want to learn through movement. Have your child look up the word *protean* in a dictionary, read the meaning aloud, and relate the word to an action. After the child defines *protean* as "changeable," have him or her describe nouns whose actions could be changeable. Talk about the motion of the ocean as protean. Have your child visualize himself or herself swimming in an ocean. The child should close his or her eyes and see himself or herself in the water, while saying, "I am swimming in a protean ocean, whose waters are changeable." The child can supplement this by acting out swimming motions with his or her arms and saying, "I am swimming in a protean sea." Another example would be giving the child clay and making some large protean shapes with the clay. While tactile students would use the clay for the sense of touch through the fingers, kinesthetic learners would need to make larger figures in which their whole arm and physical energy is engaged in the creation of the image.

Ask your child to imagine himself or herself as protean. The child could stand up and do some dance movements, exercise movements, or free movements that illustrate what it would be like to be protean or changeable. As the child acts out the movements, have the child say, "My movements are protean; they are rapidly changing."

Have your child describe a series of actions or movements that could be protean. For example:

✔ describe a protean dancer

✔ describe a protean creature and the different forms and movements it makes

A Child Who Has Several Preferences in Learning Styles

After using the above four methods, you may find your child has one learning style he or she consistently preferred. You may find that the child has two strong preferences or that the child can handle all types of methods. There are some children who have developed their ability to learn using any of the senses. If your child has a strong preference, then it is best to teach the child new material using that strength. If the child has two equally strong learning styles, then you can use both methods to teach the child. If the child handles all learning styles equally well, then you can use all the styles to teach the child, or you can use one or two at a time. The main point is to avoid teaching new material in your child's weakest learning style.

Anything Can Be Taught Using the Different Senses

The above two examples of learning the sound of a letter or a new vocabulary word can be adapted to any of the four types of learners. In the following chapters, as we discuss the different types of reading skills, we can apply the four different methods to the skill so that they match your child's best learning style. In some cases, when a child has two or three learning styles that are strong, a combination of the activities can be used. A child who is visual and kinesthetic can be taught by using the senses of the eyes and of movement. For optimum learning, we can incorporate all the senses. Combinations of activities can be used so that the child sees it, hears and says it, touches or feels it, and acts it out.

If the method of instruction in your child's school is not matching his or her best learning style, then teach your child these techniques. The child can learn how to "translate" or convert the school activity into one that uses his or her best sensory process. Here are some ways to teach your child to independently adapt the lesson into his or her best learning style.

Visual Adaptations

If the teacher is lecturing, teach your child to take notes to write down what the teacher says so that the child can look at the notes later. Teach him or her to illustrate the notes with pictures to help him or her remember the data. The child may also learn to be brave enough to ask the teacher to write the words or notes on the board, or ask to see a picture, map, or chart to illustrate the lecture. In conferences with the teacher, you can talk to the teacher about adding visuals to the lectures, or to provide written outlines on paper or the chalkboard to help your child grasp it more clearly.

Auditory Adaptations

If much of the class work is written in books or on the blackboard, have your child read it aloud softly to himself or herself so the hearing process can be activated. Have the child ask if he or she can take turns reading the material aloud in a group or with a partner. If the child feels comfortable, he or she can ask the teacher to go over the material orally or to have an oral review. In parent-teacher conferences, discuss your child's auditory strengths and see if the teacher can build in some more oral discussion or review to help your child process the information better.

Tactile Adaptations

A majority of schoolwork is presented auditorily or visually. Tactile learners can convert the material into writing and drawing, since the sense of touch helps them process the material. Whereas visual children need to see the written word or a picture, tactile learners need to do the writing and drawing themselves. Tactile learners can make their own charts, diagrams, maps, and illustrations to help them process the auditory or visual material the teacher presents. Wherever possible, the child can do projects to illustrate the ideas they learn. The projects can be sculptures, constructions, buildings, dioramas, arts and crafts, models, or any other hands-on activities. When feasible, the child should close his or her eyes and visualize the lesson so that he or she can experience the concepts in some way that ties into his or her emotions or sense of touch. You can talk to the teacher to discuss your child's needs to do hands-on activities related to the lesson.

Kinesthetic Adaptations

Since kinesthetic learners require movement and activity, this adaptation draws more attention to the student. Thus, is it preferable that the parent contact the teacher so that an acceptable strategy can be worked out. If the child acts out the material on his or her own, it could be perceived as disruptive behavior! With the teacher's input, come up with ways that the material can be converted into projects and activities. Making the material come to life with simulations, games, projects, and experiments will help your kinesthetic child process the information. When material is presented, your child can learn how to put the material into action in the form of projects and experiments. The child needs to ask the teacher for permission to do those projects as a way of learning the material. If the teacher has not presented any alternatives, the child should start thinking for himself or herself by offering suggestions for active projects. Teach your child to visualize himself or herself acting out the material. For example, if the child is learning about the Civil War, the child needs to visualize himself or herself acting out a scene from the Civil War. If it is a math problem such as $4 + 4 = 8$, the child should pretend to bounce four balls of one color, then four balls of another color. The child may tap his or her right foot four times and left foot four times to sense the movement of eight objects. When child comes home, help him or her convert the lesson into a "moving" experience.

What About the Sense of Taste and Smell?

There are children whose predominant sense may be taste or smell. If you find that your child is keenly attuned to what he or she tastes and smells, then add examples of flavors and odors to the learning experience whenever possible. When teaching a skill, use examples of food items your child can taste or items with strong odors your child can smell to make a lasting impression in the child's memory.

For example, when teaching the letter *b*, use foods that begin with letter *b* as teaching tools. You may have your child touch, smell, and taste bananas, blueberries, blackberries, or beets. If you were teaching the word *protean,* you could have your child "change" a banana into another shape.

For the sense of smell you may use flowers or foods that have strong odors as examples. Wherever possible, tie in tastes and smells to the lesson to reach your child who prefers the sense of taste and smell.

You Are Ready to Translate into Your Child's Best Learning Style

Now that you have found your child's best learning style and understand how to "translate" a lesson into the correct learning style language, you can now begin the process of pinpointing the skills your child needs to learn. As you work through the next section, continue to refer back to this chapter as a reminder to teach each new skill either visually, auditorily, tactilely, or kinesthetically.

Chapter 12

How to Diagnose Problems in Letter-Sound Relationships

The first place to look in pinpointing a reading problem is the child's knowledge of letter-sound relationships. The child must know the alphabet and how to read each letter. Then the child must know the sounds each letter makes. Problems with letter-sound relationships form the crux of many difficulties in reading. We generally think that "knowing the sounds" means the child can give one sound for each letter of the alphabet. When the child learns the alphabet, at home, in kindergarten, or in first grade, someone often asks the child, "What sound does this letter make?" The child gives a sound that is correct, and we feel satisfied that the child knows the sound of the alphabet letter. If the child can give a sound for each of the twenty-six letters, we feel confident that the child knows all the sounds.

But—and this is a big "but"—many letters have more than one sound! *A* is pronounced differently in *cat, rate, August, car,* etc. Vowels can be combined with other vowels to make different sounds. We think of *o* as the sound in *hot* or *rope.* But when combined with *i,* we get *oi* as in *boil.* When combined with *u,* we get *ou* as in *foul.* In other languages, one letter equals one sound, but English is more complicated.

As we can see, there is much for a reader to learn. Just knowing one pronunciation of each letter is not enough. One needs to learn all possible letter-sound relationships if one is going to become an independent reader.

Often parents feel their child is reading well in first grade and possibly through part of second grade. Then suddenly, in late second grade, third grade, and even fourth grade, the parent suddenly discovers that their child is having trouble in reading class. I see this all the time. A fourth grade parent will come to me and say, "My son loved to read and he read all the time in first grade. He always had a book in his hand. We never had any problems with him. But now that he's in fourth grade, he's getting low scores on his standardized tests, his teacher says he is having trouble, and he is frustrated when he reads. He seems to miss so many words. I wonder if he has a learning disability." Upon examination, in many cases I discover that the child is having trouble with vowel combinations or irregular patterns. He or she sees the word *rain* and does not know *ai* is like the *a* in *make*, so he or she reads it as *ran*. The child sees *boat* and wants to read the *o* and *a* as two different sounds and comes out with *bo-at*, or he or she is so confused that no attempt to read the word is made at all. I have found that with instruction in all possible vowel combinations, their problem is relieved.

Your next question may be, "Don't children learn these sounds in school?" Only you can find out the answer to that question, because each school and each class is different. Every reader needs to know the sounds, and if our child does not, how can we as parents diagnose what sounds our child is missing and how can we teach them to our child?

DIAGNOSING LETTER-SOUND RELATIONSHIPS

Here are some simple activities to help you determine if your child knows every sound each letter makes and every sound of the letters when they are combined.

There are two techniques for checking your child's knowledge of letter-sound relationships: listening to them read aloud to you from a book or textbook, and listening to them read word lists to you. I prefer to use both methods because one can get more information about the child's problem when he or she reads. When a child reads a passage, he or she may not know all the sounds, but might read some of the words correctly because it makes sense in the context of the sentence. For example, the sentence may be: "The boy fell on the ground." The child may not be able to read *ground* when the word is shown to him or her by itself. But the child may read *ground* correctly in the sentence, because the child knows that it starts with a *g* and it is one of the few words that would make sense in that context. "Where else would the boy fall?" the child asks mentally. Thus, in passage reading, we will find *some* of the letter-sound relationships with which the child is having difficulty, but not *all*, because the child may be guessing words that make sense.

In word lists the child does not have any frame of reference but must deal with the letters without any clues. The child may still try to take guesses or think of a word that has the same letters. They may come up with a word that contains the same letters jumbled up in a different order. A child may read *aware* as *area*, or *tracks* as *turkeys*, etc. When parents see this happen, they often panic and think their child has a learning disability. But if the child is doing this only on words he or she hasn't learned yet, most of the time it is a compensatory tactic the child uses to guess at the word.

In word lists that contain certain letter combinations repeated several times, we can see whether the child misses the pattern once or consistently misses each time. This will indicate which patterns continually give the child problems.

Checking Letter-Sound Relationships
by Passage Reading

1. Take any of the textbooks that your child is using in his or her current grade. It is best to use a reading textbook or novel from his or her current grade level. Select a chapter he or she has not yet read.

2. Mark off a passage of one hundred words. Copy, type, or write out the hundred-word passage so you have a copy of what your child will be reading.

3. Be prepared to time how long it takes your child to read the hundred words.

4. Have your child read the passage aloud. As the child reads, circle the missed words on your copy. If you can keep pace with your child's speed, try to write above the missed word the error that the child said in place of the correct word. (See below.) If the child skips a word, circle it but do not write anything above it.

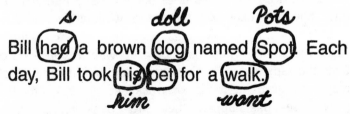

For example: If the sentence is, *I see a dog*, and the child reads, "I see a doll," circle *dog*, and above it write *doll*. Circle all the words that the child mispronounces or stumbles on.

Another time-saving way to mark your copy is to indicate which letter(s) in a word the child missed. For example, if the child reads *train* as *tain*, circle *train* and put a line through the *r* to show the child left that letter out. If the child reads *hat* as *hot*, circle *hat*, but put a line through *a*, writing *o* above it. This will remind you that the child mispronounced *a* as *o*. If the child reads *cat* as *sat*, circle *cat*, cross out the *c*, and put an *s* above it.

5. Stop the child after he or she has read the hundredth word and note how many minutes and seconds your child took to read the passage. Convert the time into seconds and divide into 6,000. This will tell you how many words the child read per minute.

For example:

1 min. 25 seconds = 85 seconds

6,000 divided by 85 = 70.5, which rounds off to 71

Thus, the child read that passage at 71 wpm (words per minute).

6. Count the number of mistakes.

7. Make a list of the mistakes your child made. You may see a pattern if the child misses the same letters over and over again. This process helps you see which letters the child still does not know. Did they miss vowels? Did they miss consonants? Did they have trouble with combinations of vowels, or combinations of consonants? Did they miss the longer words? This will give you some idea of the difficulties your child may be having with books for his or her grade level.

Analyzing Word Speed

Our reading rate varies according to the types of materials we read and the task. If we are reading a novel for pleasure, we may read it more rapidly than a technical scientific text. The reading rate varies from one child to the next. By figuring out the number of words read per minute, we can compare the child's original speed with his or her speed on texts for lower or higher grades. If the child is reading comfortably at grade level, the child may be reading from 40 to 60 wpm. The child may read 60 to 120 wpm, which is a quick pace. If the child is reading much below 40 wpm, then he or she may be struggling with words or not yet recognizing them automatically.

Reading too slowly may not be a problem if the child takes his or her time and reads accurately. It could be a problem if the child stops frequently and takes a long time to figure out many of the words. The child may be too busy trying to figure out the words to understand what he or she is reading. If this is the case, the material may be too hard. If the child is having so much trouble with one passage, you can multiply the length of time he or she would take in reading longer passages or entire stories or chapters.

Reading too quickly may also create problems. Often we feel happy when our child can read aloud quickly, but the child may be reading too quickly to comprehend what he or she is saying. Later, when we analyze comprehension problems, we may find that the rapid reader does not have a clue as to what he or she has just read. If that is the case, you will need to encourage your child to slow down.

If your child reads 38 wpm or 42 wpm, you should not panic. It is not the exact figure that matters, but whether they read very slowly or too quickly. Even without a timer, we can see whether the child is clipping along at a good pace or struggling in a word-by-word fashion.

If we find the child is reading too slowly at grade level, we can give the child a passage from an earlier grade level to see if the child reads more rapidly without struggling over the words.

ANALYZING THE NUMBER OF ERRORS IN PASSAGE READING

If your child scores 0–1 error, your child is reading comfortably at this grade level. In educational terminology, this is referred to as "reading at an independent level," which means the child has mastered the skills required to read the passage and can read by himself or herself.

If your child scores 2–4 errors, the child is reading at "instructional level." That means the child is still learning the skills at this particular grade level and must continue to be taught or practice those skills. This amount of errors is appropriate for the child's current grade level.

If your child scores 5 or more errors, he or she may be struggling. If the errors are in words that are important for understanding the story, it may affect the child's comprehension of the story. For example, if some of the key words in the story are *turtle*, *field*, and *farmer*, but your child read *tractor*, *fire*, and *fireman*, obviously he or she will not have a correct picture of the story. If your child makes little mistakes such as reading *a* as *an*, or *the* as *that*, then the story will not be altered. These small errors are just careless ones the child makes reading ahead and skimming the little words to get to the important ones. The child can correct this by simply slowing down a bit.

ANALYZING THE TYPES OF ERRORS IN PASSAGE READING

After you have listed the child's errors, you can use the checklist provided in the appendix called "Skills Checklist for Letter-Sound Relationships: Diagnosing Errors" (The Vowel and Consonant Guide: Part B) to note the frequency of errors in each category. For example, if the child read *hat* as *hut*, note a tally in the short *a* column and note that *a* was read as *u*. This will give you a profile of your child's difficulties. Sound too easy? It is easy. It is a simple diagnosis to spot repeated errors. This method indicates what skills your child needs to be taught.

You may find your child does not know one or more of the following:

consonant sounds

short vowel sounds

long vowel sounds

vowel combinations

consonant blends

consonant digraphs

r-controlled vowels

l-controlled vowels

silent letters and irregular consonant pronunciations

endings

doubling rule

prefixes

suffixes

compound words

two-syllable words

three-syllable words

words of more than three syllables

PULLING TOGETHER READING SPEED, NUMBER OF ERRORS, AND TYPES OF ERRORS

Several possible combinations can come out of your analysis of word rate and number of errors.

✔ **The child reads at 40 or more wpm with 0–4 errors.** Your child is reading comfortably at this grade

BELLOWS
(815) 943-0170
DAN MATTHEWS
(708) 520-4047

level.

higher

to see

with

child

✔ **You**
0-4

er

per

tha

bu

rel

m

m

silent reading will help the child increase his or her speed. The child may also be reading slowly to take a lot of time to figure out each word. Even though they get it right, the words do not come automatically, and the time they spend trying to "sound out" each word will distract them from understanding the material. Again, this indicates that the child needs more practice reading on a daily basis until it goes faster.

✔ **The child reads at 40 or more wpm but has made 5-10 errors.** Note the errors, and reteach (or teach for the first time) those letter-sound relationship skills. Give the child practice reading similar words.

✔ **The child reads at less than 40 wpm and makes 5-10 errors.** The material may be too hard for the child. Even though they are only missing five to ten words, they lack some of the skills to read smoothly. If the child reads slowly and makes mistakes, he or she is struggling with reading at this level. Reteach the skills so that the child does not make those errors. The child should practice reading material from the previous grade level.

✔ **The child reads at 40 or more words per minute and makes more than 10 errors.** The child is struggling with the material. His or her speed may be good, but he or she is skipping words, substituting words, or guessing the meaning of the words from the context. The child needs more instruction in letter-sound relationships. The child's speed shows that he or she does well in word patterns already mastered but gets stuck on letter-sound relationships he or she has not yet mastered or was never taught.

✔ **The child reads at less than 40 wpm and makes more than 10 errors.** The material at the current grade level is too difficult, and the child is probably frustrated. In educational terminology, this is called "reading at frustration level." The child has not yet reached a comfortable reading speed for this level and makes too many errors to adequately understand the passage. The child needs both reteaching of the missed letter-sound relationships and practice to improve.

A child should not be reading at frustration level. Why? Reading is a process in which the symbols on the page are converted to words, pictures, thoughts, and ideas in one's head. If a child is working at frustration level, he or she is so busy trying to figure out what words the letters make that he or she cannot concentrate on meaning. The child is merely converting letters into sounds and words. Although this is important when learning a new skill, there should be a balance between figuring out the words and getting meaning when the child is actually reading material. If too much time is spent figuring out the words, the child is not getting any meaning or pleasure from the act of reading. If the child is not getting meaning, he or she is not really reading. If the child is not getting pleasure, he or she will resist reading and will not want to practice, and practice is essential. If the child resists reading, he or she will not gain the fluency needed to be a good reader. Therefore, we want to avoid frustrating the child and prevent him or her from reading at frustration level. So what do we do? We need to drop back a grade level or more. We need to find the point at which the child reads at an independent or instructional level so that he or she can comprehend and enjoy the reading and want to keep practicing it.

While reading at instructional level, the child continues to learn new skills. But his or her reading should not fall below instructional level, in which he or she makes only 0–4 errors and reads about 40 wpm or more. (Again, 37–40 wpm is close enough; it is the range that matters, not the exact number!)

Diagnosing Letter-Sound Relationships With Patterned Word Lists

1. Use the word lists provided in The Vowel and Consonant Guide (Parts C through L) to help you diagnose the child's problems with different sound patterns. You should make one copy for your child to read aloud and one copy for you to mark. For younger children, your child's copy should have larger print than your copy so you should rewrite the words in larger size on paper or flashcards. Because these word lists will be used later for instruction, they contain more words than you need for the diagnosis. Select about five words from each category for your child to read.

2. As your child reads the words aloud, circle the ones they miss and write the word they read instead next to the missed word. If the word is *house* and they read "horse," circle *house* and write *horse* next to it. This will help you analyze the type of mistakes he or she is making.

3. Continue reading through each word list, noting the errors. It is not necessary to time this portion of the diagnosis. If you find your child is becoming tired or frustrated, take a break and continue when he or she is fresh. If your child is having difficulty with the short and long vowels and individual consonants and blends, it is pointless to go further to the irregular patterns and the multisyllable words. If he or she has trouble with the individual sounds of consonants and vowels, we know what skills they need without going further. It will only frustrate them to try reading the harder lists.

ANALYZING THE RESULTS OF THE PATTERNED WORD LISTS

It will be clear to you whether your child is having any trouble with letter-sound relationships. Note down all the lists with which your child had difficulty. Enter the number of errors and types of errors on the chart in Part B of The Vowel and Consonant Guide, "Skills Checklist for Letter-Sound Relationships: Diagnosing Errors." You already marked the errors from the passage reading on this list. This will complete the picture of your child's letter-sound relationship problems.

THE PROFILE PROVIDES A STARTING POINT FOR YOUR INSTRUCTION

You now have a profile of the skills you need to help your child learn and practice. You may find that younger children have trouble with the lists of consonants, short vowels, blends, and long vowels. If you find that your third, fourth, fifth, or sixth grader, or even middle school or high school student, has trouble with any of the lists, you have an indication of what their reading problems are. They may have been passed along from grade level to grade level without fully mastering the lower grade level skills. Each year, their reading difficulties increased as the vocabulary became harder. Had someone caught these problems in an earlier grade, it may have saved the child from years of frustration! But it is never too late to rectify the situation. At any age level, you can reteach the missed skills and provide time to practice so that they can make up the skills quickly and easily. In fact, in my experience, children have been so relieved that someone will teach them these letter-sound skills that they pay close attention and work hard to learn the skill.

AN OPPORTUNITY TO REBUILD SELF-ESTEEM

If your child has had trouble reading for more than a few months or for years, he or she may be wondering what is wrong with himself or herself. Most children blame themselves for their reading problems and start to feel that they are "dumb" or "stupid." It is such a relief for your child to learn that the cause of their problem may not be themselves, but the fact that they were not instructed in all the letter-sound relationships. Whether or not they received instruction, the parent can say to the child, "Your reading problem is due to not understanding all the letter-sound relationships. We are going to go over the ones causing you trouble. Once you learn them, you will be able to read much better." This is truly a relief for children who do not know why they are having trouble. It helps them see a light at the end of the tunnel—they feel there is hope to solve their problems. This motivates them to practice and pay more attention to the lessons you will teach them. You and the child will be amazed at the results. Once they learn all the short vowel patterns, they will be amazed to see how many more words they can read. If they are learning the irregular vowel patterns, they will suddenly be able to attack the words in their reading. It will help them gain a sense of accomplishment and will rebuild their confidence!

I have seen hundreds of students who were sinking in the depths of despair because they could not read well. When their problems were diagnosed as a lack of some of the letter-sound relationship skills and they began to receive instruction, these children blossomed. They felt like new people. They realized they were not as hopeless as they thought. They saw that they were able to learn and improve immediately. This renewed confidence changed their entire attitude and sense of self-worth. I along with their parents have seen incredible transformations in their self-esteem and attitudes when they were able to relearn the missed skills. Diagnosis is the first step. Next comes the cure.

Chapter 13

How to Remedy Problems in Letter-Sound Relationships

Once you establish the letters with which your child has trouble, you can begin to help him or her. You can also use this chapter as a guide for teaching your child the letter-sound relationships for the first time. You can move your child to the next higher level and advance him or her. Parents often ask me to explain the benefits of advancing children through reading skills. When I talk about advancing, I mean that when a child has mastered one skill, he or she should move on to the next, rather than stay at that skill waiting for the rest of the class to catch up. That valuable time when your child is treading water waiting for the others to reach him or her could be time that the child practices higher-level skills and moves ahead. The quicker they learn the letter-sound relationships, the more they are empowered to read higher-level books and more challenging materials. The higher the level of books they can read, the more their thinking processes develop. They will be exposed to more advanced words, and their thinking will develop. By interacting with more difficult material at a higher level, their minds will be challenged. This exposure to higher-level reading will help them sail through their grade-level schoolwork with more ease. The sooner they master all the letter-sound relationships, the more time they can spend in the

more enjoyable process of reading books rather than struggling with skills. By mastering reading, your child will gain positive self-esteem and confidence.

Whether you use this chapter as a tool to reteach missed
skills or to advance your child, the procedure will be basically
the same. Provided on the following pages are simple activities to help your child learn the letter-sound relationships. The
first part of this chapter provides activities to teach the consonant sounds, and the second part contains ideas to teach the
vowels.

How to Integrate Learning Styles With Instruction

Before beginning, we need to remember the importance of
matching instruction to the child's best learning style. You may
wish to review the chapter on learning styles (Chapter 11) to
refresh your memory of the techniques that will work best with
your child. For each skill, suggestions will be given on how to
teach each type of learner. Thus, if you are teaching the consonants to an auditory learner, you will follow directions for
the auditory learner. If you are teaching consonants to a kinesthetic learner, you will follow the directions specified for kinesthetic learners. Some activities are multisensory and will be
labeled "For all types of learners." There is no harm in using
all the techniques given, or using techniques that appeal to you
and your child from other categories of learners. Not everyone
is solely one type of learner; we may be a combination. By
experimentation you will find the techniques that work best for
you and your child. Remember, there is no hard-and-fast rule
for any learner. Each person is different. These techniques will
give you some ideas and a starting point. You may try some
of them or use all of them. You may even think of your own

techniques. The bottom line is finding what works best for you and your child.

ACTIVITIES TO LEARN THE ALPHABET AND THE SOUNDS OF EACH LETTER

Letter Fun

1. Choose a letter of the alphabet with which your child is having trouble.
2. Tell your child its sound.
3. Have your child write the letter and say its sound.
4. Do some of the activities given below which match the learning style of your child:

Visual

✔ Have your child write the word in his or her favorite colors.

✔ Have your child write the word in the warm colors of red, orange, and yellow.

✔ Have your child write the word in the cool colors of blue, green, and purple.

✔ Have your child find the letter in newspapers or magazines, cut them out, and glue them on colored paper to make a collage of that letter.

✔ Search through the food cabinets to find food labels with that letter.

Auditory

Some children learn better by hearing and saying the letters. Here are some auditory activities to learn the sounds of a letter.

✔ Have your child make up a song using the letter and words that begin with that letter.

✔ Read a story and have your child call out the letter every time he or she hears a word beginning with that letter.

✔ Have your child make up sentences with words starting with the letter. Have the child bounce a ball for every word. Every time the word with that letter is said, the child has to lift his or her leg over the bounced ball. For example (did you ever learn this childhood game?), "A my name is Alice and my brother's name is Al. We live in Alabama and we sell apples." The child would lift his or her leg over the bouncing ball for *A*, *Alice*, *Al*, *Alabama*, *and*, and *apples*.

✔ Name the foods in your kitchen and have your child clap his or her hands when he or she hears a food that begins with that letter.

Tactile

Some children learn best by the sense of touch.

✔ Draw the letter with crayon and have the child trace over it with his or her finger.

✔ Have your child make the letter in finger-painting form.

✔ Have your child make a painting using the letter as a design.

✔ Take a paper plate and have your child write the letter with a squeeze tube filled with cake icing. Then take colored sprinkles (jimmies) and have your child place them on the icing until the letter is covered. Have your child trace over it (with clean fingers, of course) and then lick the tasty creation off his or her fingers!

✔ Another activity focusing on the child's sense of touch is screen writing. You can buy some wire mesh screening from a hardware store, cut it to the size of eight by eleven inches, and tape the edges with duct tape for safety. Place a sheet of paper on top of it. Using crayon, write the letter on the paper. The screen will cause the letter to feel bumpy. Remove the paper and have your child use his or her writing finger to trace over the letter. The child will remember the sensation of the raised crayon bumps on his or her fingertip. The sense of touch will help the child internalize the shape of the letter. If the child says the sound of the letter while tracing it, the additional sense of sound will help the child remember the letter more easily.

✔ You could also write the letter in glue and have the child stick unbaked macaroni, sand, or sparkles on it. These activities help the tactile child have a better feel for the letters.

Kinesthetic

Some children learn better through large-muscle movements and action.

✔ You can outline the letter with chalk on the sidewalk outside and have the child walk along or jump along the letter. Have your child say the sound of the letter while doing any of the above activities.

✔ Indoors, make the letter in large size by laying masking tape on the carpet to form the shape of the letter. Each letter should be about four, five, or six feet long. Have your child walk, run, skip, crawl, or march along the letter, in the direction which the letter would be written. Have the child say the letter as he or she marches or walks across it.

✔ Show food labels to your child and have your child jump up when he or she sees the letter you are studying.

For All Types of Learners

Almost all children enjoy this version of hide-and-seek.

✔ Have the child search the house for objects or pictures that have the selected letter in its name. For example, if you are teaching the short sound of *a*, as in *hat*, your child may look for objects or pictures with the *a* sound. They may find a mat, cat, bat, etc.

After finding the items, make a label for each object. Have your child write the word or trace over your writing of the word.

Letter Activities for Older Students

If you find that your preteen or teenager is having trouble with some of the letters here are some activities appropriate for older children of any learning type.

Getting to Know the Letters

1. Write the letter.
2. Tell your child the sound.
3. Have your child write it and say it.
4. Have your child draw his or her favorite things that start with that letter.
5. Have your child close his or her eyes and visualize the letter in his or her head. Tell him or her to say the sound. Then the child should trace the letter in the air with the writing finger while keeping his or her eyes closed. Have your child repeat this several times.

Book Search

After doing the above activities, have the child search through a book, looking for words that contain the letter on which you are working. For example, if you are working on *b*, have the child point to words with *b* in it. You may have the child copy the word on a list and draw a picture to go with it, if it is a word that can be drawn.

Read a Book

Select a book in which the chosen letters occur frequently. Before reading, point out all the words with that letter and have your child repeat the word after you. This helps the child get ready to look for those words and say them correctly. Then have the child read the book aloud. Help the child with the words having letters you have not yet worked on, but let him or her try reading by himself or herself the words you have practiced. You will find that after learning different combinations using that letter, your child will have less difficulty reading those words. With practice, those words will become part of your child's reading vocabulary.

The Reading-Writing Connection

Buy a special notebook with lined paper. You may want to buy one of those blank books with decorative covers for your child. If your child is reading picture books or easy reader books as he or she is learning the letter-sound relationships, have him or her write a sentence or two daily about a book he or she has read. Tell your child to write down all the sounds he or she hears in each word. For example, if your child plans to write *The clown from the circus was a hero*, but your child spells *circus* as *cs*, guide your child by asking, "What other sound do you hear after the *c*?" "What do you hear in the middle of the word?" In the early stages the child may only hear the initial sound and the final sound. Over time, and with your guided questions, your child will begin to recognize the vowel sounds and the sounds that come in the middle of the word. They will begin to make a connection between words and the letters and sounds that form them.

Noting Your Progress

Save a copy of the reading diagnosis that you did with the child and the list of sounds with which the child had trouble. As you work with the child on each sound, check off the sounds on the list as your child masters them. After working through all the trouble letters with the child, have him or her read the same passage to you that you used when you first did the diagnosis. On a fresh copy of the passage, circle the words and sounds that the child misses. You will most likely discover that the child no longer makes the same mistakes on the letters you worked on. What a feeling of accomplishment!

The above activities can be used to help your child through all the consonant letters and their various sounds. The above activities should be done with all the consonant letters. (Note: *y* can be pronounced as a consonant as in *yellow*, or as a vowel like *i* in *cry*, or *e* in *baby*. When teaching *y* as a consonant, use the sound of *y* as in *yellow*.

Learning the Vowels

The five vowels, *a*, *e*, *i*, *o*, and *u*, have a variety of pronunciations depending upon its placement in relation to other letters in the word, the way a syllable is divided, and the vowel's position at the beginning, middle, or end of a word. There are many rules for children to learn that deal with vowel pronunciation. Thus, vowels need to be taught in a way that children can learn each particular sound as well as the situation in which the vowel has that sound.

Teaching the Short Vowel Sounds

The following methods provide simple and effective ways to teach children the short vowel sounds. We begin with the short vowels first because they appear in the two- and three-letter words that children first learn. The rule is simple. Learning the rule will help children read multisyllable words with short vowel patterns later.

To begin with, these are the short vowel sounds:

a as in *hat,*

e as in *bed,*

i as in *pig,*

o as in *hot,* and

u as in *rug.*

When teaching the short vowel sounds, it is helpful to give children a picture to remember the sound. Tell the child that this picture or object will be their helper.

Teaching the Short A Sound

Tell them that for *a* the helper will be the word *apple.* Draw a large letter *a* on a chart and a picture of an apple next to it. For kinesthetic children, give them a plastic letter *a* and have them hold a real apple or a plastic apple. Then have the child make their own vowel chart. Have them copy the *a* onto their chart and draw an apple next to it. Tell them short *a* is like *a* in *apple.*

Next, show them a word that has a short *a* in it. Write the word *cat*, and draw a picture of a cat next to it. Tell them to repeat the sound of *a* as in *cat*, and read the word *cat* aloud. Trace the *a* in a different color. Point out to them that *a* comes between two consonants. Tell them: "This is a 'c-v-c' word—we have a consonant, a vowel in the middle, and a consonant at the end." Then explain, "Whenever we have a consonant-vowel-consonant, the vowel *a* in the middle will be said as *a* in *apple* or in *cat*.

Next, show them a list of words in which *a* is in the middle of two consonants and begin with a list of other words that have the *at* pattern that rhymes with *cat*.

bat	mat
cat	pat
fat	rat
hat	sat

Ask them to find what is the same about all these words. They may point out that they all have *a* in the middle and end with *t*. Point out to them that the words all have the *at* pattern in them.

Write the word *cat* on a large sheet of paper or a wallboard or chalkboard. Put an *at* under it. Ask them to turn *at* into *hat*. Guide them to add an *h* before the *at*. Then write *at* again and ask them to turn it into *mat*. They should write an *m* before the *at*. If they do not do it on their own, ask them what letter they hear at the beginning of *mat*. If they say *m*, then direct them to place it before "at." Have them say the word when they write it. Repeat for *fat*, *rat*, *sat*, and the other words on the list.

Write a sentence for them using the *at* words, and see if they can read it. Help them with the other words that do not have the *at* pattern if they do not know the words on their own.

Example: The fat cat with a hat sat on a mat. The cat saw a rat with a bat.

Have your child make up sentences using the words and write them on the paper for him or her. Have your child try writing his or her own sentences on paper and drawing a picture to go with it.

Other activities for short vowel patterns

Visual

✔ Write *at* on paper and have the child trace it in his or her favorite color. Have the child write words that rhyme with *at* using different colors.

✔ Show your child pictures of words that have *at* in their names and then match the pictures to the correct spelling.

✔ Have the child put glue on paper, spelling *at*. Sparkles can be placed on the glue to make an attractive "at" picture.

✔ Tell the child to look through a magazine or newspaper to circle *at* words.

✔ Have the child look for objects in the house with the *at* pattern and write a label for the object.

Auditory

✔ Have your child spell words aloud that rhyme with *at* and write them on a large sheet of paper.

✔ Spell the words with the *at* pattern aloud and have your child say the correct word.

✔ Have your child tell you a story with *at* rhyming words and write it on paper for him or her. Have the child read it back to you.

✔ If the child plays an instrument, have him or her make up a tune to go with the spelling of the *at* words. Put the words on musical note paper and have your child play a note on the instrument for each letter.

✔ Show your child how to trace *at* words in the air, and spell the words aloud. Have your child repeat with eyes closed, saying the letters aloud, and completing the spelling by saying the full word.

Tactile

✔ Have your child write *at* in finger paints.

✔ Have your child write *at* words in the sand.

✔ Have your child feel objects that have the *at* pattern and write the word for each: *bat, cat, mat, hat*.

✔ Have the child write *at* on a paper plate with a squeeze tube of colored frosting. Have the child say "at." Have the child spell other words that rhyme with *at* using the frosting. Then the child can add sprinkles to it and lick off the icing and sprinkles.

✔ Give your child some play dough to shape the letters *at*. Have him or her add other letters to make rhyming words with *at*.

Kinesthetic

✔ Have your child do jumping jacks, spelling *at* words and saying them as he or she jumps.

✔ Make a hopscotch board outdoors and place one *at* word in each box. Have your child throw a coin into the hopscotch box, jump in it, and read the word. Repeat until he or she jumps in every box and reads all the words in each box.

✔ Draw the *at* pattern on a large sheet of paper or with chalk on the sidewalk outdoors. Have your child move along it like a cat, saying the letters and the words as he or she moves. Then your child should move along it like a fat cat. Have your child jump or skip along the letters while saying them out loud.

✔ For every *at* word that the child reads correctly, he or she gets to toss a ball into a basketball hoop, or a ring onto a stick for ring toss.

✔ Have your child write the *at* words with his or her whole arm in the air, with eyes closed, visualizing the word, and saying each letter at the same time.

After establishing the *at* pattern, add other short *a* patterns. Teach your child the *am* pattern and the words that end with *am*. Use the same procedures described in the learning activities for *at*. After the child has mastered *am* words, go on to other patterns such as *ab*, *ad*, *ag*, *an*, and *ap*. Use the word lists in The Vowel and Consonant Guide for each pattern. (See The Vowel and Consonant Guide: Part C.)

Teaching the Other Short Vowel Sounds

The procedure used to teach the short vowel *a* can be used for the other four vowels. After introducing each vowel, try the same procedures used to teach the short *a*. Write each vowel followed by a key word. For *a* the key word is *apple*. Here are the key words to use for the other vowels:

e is *egg*

i is *in*, and draw a ball going *in* a basket

o is *octopus*

u is *umbrella*

If your child has some other favorite word starting with the short vowel sounds, use those instead. The key is that there be a picture that can go with the sound as a frame of reference for the child.

The Vowel Book

I have created a tool called *The Vowel Book* (Linksman 1993), which has successfully helped many students learn all the vowel sounds. It is reprinted here as Part I of the Vowel and Consonant Guide. It serves as a handy guide for each child to keep at his or her desk in school or carry as a helper when stuck on a word. Each child should make his or her own copy of the vowel book on drawing paper and use his or her own drawings to personalize it. The child looks up the vowel and uses the picture clue to help him or her pronounce the word. The first page of the vowel book contains the short vowels.

Two Ways of Presenting the Short Vowels

There are two ways of presenting the vowels. One way is to present all five in the same lesson, making a chart of the five short vowel sounds on the same day. This is good for children who are global learners that need to see the whole picture. In this way, in one lesson, you can teach him or her that there are five short vowel sounds. Explain that when the vowel comes in the middle of two consonants (a c-v-c word), the vowel will have a short sound.

For children who are sequential, or step-by-step learners, you may present one vowel at a time and go through all the different rhyming patterns for several days until presenting the next vowel.

Word Games With Vowels

As the child learns more vowel patterns, several games can be played to reinforce the skill.

Vowel Mix-Up

Use index cards cut in half or colored tagboard cut into small rectangles. On each card, write a word with one of the vowel patterns you taught. For example, on some cards write *cat*, *hat*, *fat*, *mat*, *rat*. On other cards, write *can*, *fan*, *man*,

Dan, etc. Have the cards mixed up face-up on a table. Have the child sort the cards trying to keep in one row words that rhyme. Then have the child read the words to you.

Vowel Card Game

Use the same flashcards you made in "Vowel Mix-Up." Make sure there are fifty-two cards. Mix up the cards face-down. Give each player four cards. Players take turns looking for rhyming patterns in their hand. Every time a player has two cards that rhyme, they call out "Rhyming words." They read the words aloud and then put them in their own pile. They get to replace the cards with two new cards from the deck. If they don't have two cards that rhyme, they get to pick a new card from the deck and throw one of their cards back into the bottom of the deck. If they pick a card that gives them a rhyming pattern, they call out "Rhyming words," read the cards, and get to pick two more cards to replace those they put on their own pile. The winner is the person with the most rhyming patterns.

Make a Board Game

You and your child can make your own board games using the rhyming pattern words. Get a big piece of tagboard. You can also use game pieces and dice from some of your child's other games. On the tagboard, draw a starting point, a finish point, and spaces in between on which the game piece can move. In those spaces, write various rhyming patterns, alternating *at* words, *an* words, *am* words, etc. Pick a theme for a game your child would enjoy. Some samples are:

Space Launch

Make the board like an outer space scene, with the spaces as stars from which the rocket must travel to the goal line. The goal line could be another sun or planet. Write a word on each star that the child must read correctly. If the child reads it correctly, he or she may throw the dice or get points. You can choose the rules you prefer for the game.

Football

Make the board like a football field, with the spaces as goal lines. Each new goal line has a word. The child moves from one goal to the next by throwing the dice and reads the word on the goal line.

Trip to the Zoo

You can make the spaces different animal cages with animal pictures and words which the child must read.

Flashcard Basketball

Make flashcards for each of the various rhyming words. If your child is playing alone, have him or her read a flashcard. If the word is read correctly, the child can toss the ball in a basketball net. If several children are playing, you can have teams in which they get points for their team when they read a word correctly and make a basket.

READING PRACTICE

Each day as you do these activities, you should also have your child read about fifteen minutes daily from a book at their level. It could be a storybook, picture book, fiction, or nonfiction book. Before reading, have your child look for words with the pattern they have been learning. If your child does not know many words, you may help them read aloud the words they do not know. When the child gets to a word with a short vowel pattern you have taught them, see if they can recognize it independently. If necessary, remind the child that it is one of the words they know. You may cover the first letter so that they can see the pattern. After the child reads the pattern (with or without your assistance), remove your finger to reveal the first letter. Have your child add the first letter to the pattern. Thus, if the word is *mat*, cover the *m* until they read *at*. Then ask, "What is *at* with an *m* in front of it?" If the child does not say it by himself or herself, guide the child to say "mmmm-at," "mat." Remember, you want to give the child a chance to try it, but you want them to feel successful, even if you have to assist them with the answer. After doing this over and over, the child will finally recognize the pattern on their own. Remember to smile and say something positive when your child gets the answer correctly, even if you assisted a bit. You can say, "Good! You saw the *at* pattern and added the beginning letter to it." Or, "You read that correctly."

You may select books that have many pattern words you have been working on to give your child practice reading. It is important that the child read books during this process. It is not enough just to teach the patterns, without reinforcing it by reading books.

One method that works well is to tell the reluctant reader that you will give them "freebies." A "freebie" is a word the child has not learned yet. You will read the "freebies," and the child will only have to read the words that you know they have already learned. This way you can take turns reading.

Another technique is reading the page to the child first, and then having the child read it back to you. Again, when it is the child's turn to read, guide them with words you know they have not learned, and let them figure out the words you know they have already worked on or studied.

REMIND THE CHILD OF THE C-V-C PATTERN

One remarkable thing about children is that they will learn whatever you teach them. It is important that each time you teach them a new short vowel rhyming pattern you remind them that this is a c-v-c word, with the vowel in the middle of two consonants. By repeating this frequently, they will learn it. Why is it important to learn this? This will help them distinguish when a vowel is read as a short sound as compared to the variety of long vowel sounds and irregular vowel sounds they will learn later. It will also be useful when the child learns multisyllable words further down the road.

To reinforce the c-v-c concept, draw three boxes. Have the child put plastic letters in the boxes to spell the c-v-c pattern words. (See illustration below.) Point out how the vowel in the middle will have the short sound, as in their key words *apple*, *egg*, *it*, *octopus*, and *umbrella*.

CONSONANT BLENDS

After the child has mastered the consonant sounds and the short vowel patterns, we can either go on to long vowel sounds or blends. I recommend blends because there are so many words that come up in the earlier grades that have blends, that it will be easy for the child to combine them with the short vowel rhyming patterns they have already mastered. In fact, as soon as the child gets the concept of short vowel words, you can even begin blends alongside the short vowel words. If they know that *at* is *at*, it is easy for them to learn that *fl* with the *at* is *flat*.

A blend is defined as two or more consonants that combine to be read together without any vowel between them. Here is a list of the blends:

bl, br, cl, cr, dr, fl, fr, gl, gr, pl, pr, sc, sk, sl, sm, sn, sp, st, sw, tr, tw, scr, spl, spr, str

Word Games With Blends

The activities used to teach consonants and short vowels can be used to teach blends. Find the activities from the ones listed earlier in this chapter that match your child's best learning styles.

Instead of rhyming patterns, we will use lists of words that begin with the same blend. (See The Vowel and Consonant Guide: Part D.)

Here are some blend activities you can do:

Read the Blends

Have the child figure out the words on a list containing the same beginning blends.

Blend Brainstorm

Have the child give you words that begin with that blend, and you write the words on a chart. The child copies them on his or her own list.

Blend Search

Have the child select a book at his or her grade level and search for as many words as he or she can find beginning with the blend pattern you are studying. Add them to the blend chart and have the child copy onto his or her own blend list.

Name Blend

Have the child think of people's names, or places that begin with the blend.

Car Blend Game

While driving, have the child find as many signs as possible with blend words.

Board Game Blend

Just as you made a board game for the short vowels, make a board game with a theme your child enjoys, using blend words in the spaces. As the child moves the game piece along the spaces, he or she has to read the blend word correctly.

Blend Sports

Make flash cards with the blend words. For every word the child reads correctly, the child gets to run to the goal line, toss a basket into a hoop, or have a turn at whatever sports game he or she enjoys.

Food Blends

Go through your kitchen and have the child find as many foods as possible that begin with blends. Make a blend drink out of those foods. How about strawberry-grape drink? Have your child write a label for the drink and make a poster of an ad selling the drink to others. How about "Scrumptious Strawberry?"

Clothes Blend Search

Have your child search through drawers and closets for clothing that begins with a blend and lay them out. Try *blouses*, *sweaters*, *sneakers*, *skirts*. Look for ending blends as well, such as *vest*, or *pants*.

Your child may draw a picture of himself or herself wearing those blend clothes, and label the words.

LONG VOWELS

There are some fun and easy rules to help make learning the long vowels simpler. Once the child has established the short vowels in memory, we can now add on long vowels. One of the simplest rules to learn is the "magic *e*" rule.

The Magic E Lesson

Write on a board or large sheet of paper the word *cap*. Tell the child: "If we add a magic *e* at the end of *cap*, it turns the cap into a cape. How? *E* will make the *a* say its name. Instead of *a* like *cap*, it will be *a* like the letter *a*—its own name." You can also explain to the child that when a vowel says its own name, it is called a long vowel.

Tell your child that this magic *e* works with all the vowels. Write the following list:

mat	mate	tap	tape
fat	fate	Sam	same
rat	rate	can	cane
fad	fade	man	mane
mad	made	van	vane

After reading *mat*, *mate*, and then *fat*, *fate*, and so on, point to different words, skipping around, and have the child read each one. Go from one column to the next, or go up one column and down the next, or go back and forth between columns. The idea is for the child to spot the *e* at the end and read the vowel with a long sound.

Another activity is saying the word and seeing if the child can write it correctly. Continue to remind the child that magic *e* at the end makes the vowel say its name. Its name is like the name of the letter.

Since the child has already learned all the short vowels, you can show him or her how magic *e* works for all the c-v-c short vowel words. Show the child how it works for each of the vowels by adding an *e* to the c-v-c words. Here are some samples:

pet	Pete	hop	hope
rip	ripe	hug	huge
rid	ride	tub	tube
not	note		

Repeat the activities described for the *a* patterns for words with *e*, *i*, *o*, and *u*.

Have your child look in the mirror and touch his or her mouth while he or she says the short *a* and long *a* sounds. The child will feel and see the difference between the two sounds. The long *a* makes the mouth smile when pronounced. Repeat the procedure for short and long *e*. Long *e* also causes the mouth to smile. Repeat the procedure for long and short *i*. Point out that for long *i* the mouth opens wide. Show your child the difference in pronouncing short and long *o*. Point out how long *o* makes the lips protrude into a small circle shape. Finally, have your child say a short and long *u*. Have the child feel how long *u* also makes the lips protrude into a small circle shape.

Have your child read through word lists with rhyming patterns. For example, when reading the *ide* pattern, have your child read words such as *hide*, *ride*, *side*, and *wide*. Use the word lists in The Vowel and Consonant Guide: Part E.

The games listed in the section for the short vowel patterns can be used for the long vowel words. Make flashcards to play sorting games and card games. Find objects with those patterns. Do sports activities with flashcards to reinforce the words. Any of the visual, auditory, tactile, and kinesthetic activities listed in the short vowel and consonant blend sections can be adapted to teach the long vowel pattern.

As you read books with your child, have your child search for words that are made of c-v-c words plus magic *e*. Point out the differences between c-v-c words like *mat* and c-v-c-with-magic-*e* words like *mate*. As your child reads, have him or her list the words they find that use a magic *e*.

Long Vowels With Other Patterns

The lesson on magic *e* is for some of the situations in which a vowel is pronounced as a long sound, or as its letter name. There are several other situations in which a vowel is pronounced with the long sound.

The Two-Vowel Rule

There is another rule you can teach your child to help him or her know when to say the vowel by its letter name. It is the two-vowel rule: "When two vowels are together, the first one does the talking and the second one does the walking."

Take the word *rain*. Point out that the first vowel, *a*, does the talking—and it will say its own name *a* as in *cape*. The second vowel, *i*, does the walking, which means it is silent, it disappears, it does not make any sound. Draw a line through the *i* to show the child to pretend it is not there. Thus, instead of reading *rain* as *ran*, we read it as *rain*, with a long *a* sound. After pointing this out, show the child a list of words with the *ai* pattern and help your child read it with a long *a* sound:

rain, pain, gain, main, lain, stain

Continue to show the *ai* pattern using *aid*:

maid, raid, paid.

Demonstrate the difference the second vowel makes in a word by showing these pairs:

ran	rain
pan	pain
man	main
mad	maid
pad	paid

You can continue to demonstrate how the two-vowel rule works for all the other vowels:

fed	feed
bed	bead
lid	lied
rod	road
	toe
	true
	suit

Again, giving the child word lists helps to fix the pattern in memory (see The Vowel and Consonant Guide: Part F). Couple this with activities and games, as well as reading books to see those words in context.

Long Vowels: One Vowel at the End of the Word

Show your child that when some single vowels come at the end of the word, they will have a long sound. (See The Vowel and Consonant Guide: Part G.) For example, *e* at the end of a word gives us the following words:

be, he, me, she, we

Long *i* at the end of a word will also sometimes sound like long *e*. For example:

ski, mi (as in the musical scale, do, re, mi)

For *o* at the end of the word, we get the long *o* sound:

go, Jo, lo, no, so

Tell your child that some words are rule breakers. They have their own sounds. For example: *to* and *do* are irregular and have the *oo* sound as in *boot*.

Consonant Digraphs

A consonant digraph is one sound formed by two letters. It is different from a consonant blend. In a blend, such as *tr*, you hear both the *t* and the *r*. In a consonant digraph, both letters combine to form a totally new sound. There are only five digraphs to learn: *ch* as in *chair*, *sh* as in *ship*, *th* as in *them*, *th* as in *think*, and *wh* as in *wheel*. Unless a child is taught how to say these digraphs, they may continue to read *ch* as "ca-ha," or *sh* as "sa-ha." The *wh* is different from the other digraphs in that it is like a single *w* and the *h* is silent. It is included because together *wh* makes one sound. Unless children learn this, they will tend to pronounce both the *w* and the *h* and may get confused.

The consonant digraphs appear frequently in many words in early readers, and this skill should be taught early. (See The Vowel and Consonant Guide: Part H.)

To introduce the digraphs, write the two letters and tell the child the sound it makes. Let us start with *ch*. Write it out for the child and say the *ch* sound as in the beginning of *chair*. Draw a picture of a chair. Then write other *ch* words and see

if your child can read them. Try to use vowel patterns the child
already knows:

chat	chick
chap	chime
chip	chin
chess	chop
chest	chum
check	

You can make flashcards to play any of the games used in
earlier lessons. You can do word searches in magazines, newspapers, and books or find objects in the house. While driving,
have your child look for signs with the pattern. Again, any of
the activities described in the short vowel and blend section
can be adapted for learning the digraphs. Remember to pick
activities that match your child's best learning style.

After teaching *ch*, you can introduce *sh*. Write *sh* on
paper or on a board, then say the *sh* sound as in the beginning of *shoe*. Then present a series of words beginning with
sh using vowel patterns your child has already learned. For
example:

shade	shine
shake	ship
shale	shone
shape	shop
share	shore
shave	shot
shed	shun
shell	shut
shin	

Show the child flashcards of both *ch* and *sh* words to give him or her practice in recognizing the difference between these two sounds.

When teaching *th*, you need to point out that *th* has two different sounds. It can be *th* as in *this* and *th* as in *think*. Have your child say *this* and feel how the tongue vibrates. Have your child say *think* to feel how the tongue does not vibrate.

Give the child a list of words with the vibrating *th*:

this, that, then, there, they, these, those

Then give your child a list of *th* words without the vibrating sound:

thank, think, thin, thick, thud, thug, thumb

Explain to your child there is no rule for when a *th* is vibrating or not. It is just a matter of remembering the words. Explain to your child that if he or she is not sure of which *th* sound to use, to try it both ways and see which way sounds like a word that he or she has heard, and to go with that choice.

The *wh* pattern is easy. Explain to your child that the *h* is silent. The child should just read *wh* as *w*. Show the child the different words that begin with *wh*:

what   white
when   while
where   whip
whine

This would be a good time to point out that there are some *wh* words with *o* that do not sound like *w*. These words sound like *h* words. This would be an appropriate time to remind your child that English is a difficult language and there are many "rule-breaker words." They will just have to remember that these *who* words sound like an *h* word instead:

who, whom, whole.

After the child has learned the five digraphs, you can do card games, board games, or sports activities to help your child to practice recognizing the different pronunciations of each. Use activities that match your child's learning style!

VOWEL COMBINATIONS

The next skill is probably the one that gives children the most difficulty. It is also the one that is the cause of many reading difficulties in children from grade four and up. If the child did not receive any systematic instruction in these vowel combinations, the child does not know what to do when he or she sees a new word with these patterns. The child will either skip over the word, mix up the letters to come up with a word that is familiar, or guess-read the word. Teaching the vowel combinations is a key element in unlocking a child's reading difficulties.

If you have done the diagnosis, you may have discovered your child is having trouble with many different vowel combinations. If your child knew half the words in that portion of the diagnostic test, do not assume they know those combinations. It could have been that they memorized those words from their sight word lists because they appear so frequently in their reading books. If the child missed many vowel combinations, it would be a good idea to teach all of them. Never assume they know these. If we make a wrong assumption, when these patterns come up in multisyllable words later in your child's school career, they will not know what to do with them unless they learn them now.

The best way to teach the vowel combinations is to teach all possible combinations for each vowel at once. This gives your child a total picture of how many different sounds the vowel can make and in how many ways they are combined with other vowels. For this, I have come up with *The Vowel Book*, and have used it successfully with students for several years (see The Vowel and Consonant Guide: Part I). I have found this tool to be highly effective with children of all ages. You can use it as a guide to help your child draw his or her own vowel book. The child can then take it to school and use it as a reference as he or she reads.

Your child's vowel book works as follows: The child will have a pictorial clue for each vowel combination. When the child reads a book and comes across one of the vowel combinations, he or she looks it up in the book. The child refers to the picture as a clue to the pattern's pronunciation, then figures out how to read the word. This helps the child read independently and empowers him or her to read far more words than he or she can learn using word lists. They now have a tool to help them read all possible vowel combinations in the English language. After this lesson they are well on the way to reading most of the one-syllable words and will have the tools to break up multisyllable words.

To teach each of the vowel sounds, show the child the pattern on a large chart or board. Say the sound. Then draw an illustration of a word containing that pattern and write the spelling of the word next to it.

There are two ways of teaching using the vowel book: by listing the different combinations and drawing the clue words, or by stopping after each vowel combination and giving your child some word lists to read with that pattern. Either method works. If a child is a global learner, I like to give him or her all the vowel combinations first and then go back and do the word lists for each one. If the child is a sequential learner, it may be better to do a pattern and then a word list. The second method may take longer to get through. I find that by teaching all the combinations at once all five vowels can be presented in five one-hour sessions. When the child has the total picture and can start using the book, we go back and work on word lists for each pattern.

Here are the different combinations for *a* and some picture clues you can use. Preferably, the clue should be a noun that can be drawn. In some patterns, there aren't any nouns, so pick a word for which some pictorial situation can be drawn. You will notice that among the combinations are some you have already taught your child—the short vowel pattern and the long vowel patterns. They will see the vowel with a consonant and a magic *e* at the end, and they will see the words that fit the two-vowel rule (*ai, ee, ea, oa, oe, ui, ue*).

Also explain that in some cases, *a* is combined with another vowel, and in other cases *a* is combined with a consonant which changes its pronunciation.

Word lists for each vowel pattern are provided in The Vowel and Consonant Guide: Part J, in the back of this book. Below are the different pronunciations of each vowel when combined with different letters.

A *Combinations*

a	cat
a-e	cake *(Explain to your child that the dash means that a consonant goes there.)*
ai	rain
au	faucet
ay	day *(Draw a sun. Explain that y is sometimes a vowel.)*
ar	car all ball

are	hare	ale	male
air	hair	alk	walk
aw	saw	alm	palm
al	pal	alf	half
alt	salt	alves	halves

E Combinations

e	bed
e-e	Pete (e-consonant-e)
e	he/she/we (when "e" is at the end of a two- or three-letter word)

ee	feet	er	her
ea	wheat	ere	here
ea	bread	ere	were
ea	break	ear	spear
ei	receive	ear	bear
ei	sleigh	ear	earth
ei	their	ear	heart
eau	beauty	eer	deer
eu	neutral	eir	their
ew	new	el	elf
ew	sew	ell	bell
ey	they	eal	seal
ey	key	eel	wheel

You need to point out that sometimes the same two letters together have different sounds, such as *ey* in *they* or *key*. When your child comes across a new word with *ey*, he or she should try pronouncing it both ways to see which one makes more sense or sounds like a word they know.

I *Combinations*

i	lid		
i-e	bike (*i-consonant-e*)		
ie	lie	ier	tier
ie	believe	il	milk
ieu	adieu	ild	wild
ir	bird	ill	pill
ire	fire	ile	smile
iar	friar	ial	dial
ier	flier	ind	kind

In later lessons on endings, the child will learn *io* as part of *tion*, *sion*, and *ion*.

The following are optional, since they are situations in which both vowels are pronounced separately. You may point them out, but do not include them in the main vowel book because they may confuse the child at this stage.

io	lion *(Explain that in some words both vowels are pronounced.)*
ia	Maria *(Explain that both vowels are pronounced.)*
ia	Miami *(another way to pronounce both vowels)*

O *Combinations*

o	pot		
o-e	rope (*o-consonant-e*)		
oe	toe	oth	brother
oa	boat	or	horse
oo	book	or	worm
oo	boot	ore	store

oo	flood	oor	door
oi	coin	oar	oar
oy	boy	our	hour
ou	soup	our	journey
ou	house	our	pour
ou	cough	oll	doll
ou	could	oll	troll
ou	touch	ole	hole
ow	cow	oal	goal
ow	snow		

U *Combinations*

u	sun		
u-e	flute *(u-consonant-e)*		
ue	blue	ul	bulb
ui	suit	ull	gull
ua	aqua	ull	bull
uo	duo	ule	mule
uy	guy	ual	equal
ur	purse	uel	fuel
ure	cure	uil	quilt
uire	squire		

Two Sounds of Y

y	baby
y	fly
ye	dye

As you can see, there are many combinations for children to learn. By having a chart or a vowel book, they can look up sounds, use the picture clues, and figure out many words.

By reading word lists with each pattern, the patterns will be established in your child's memory. This will help him or her not only to read short words, but to recognize these patterns in multisyllable words.

Vowel Followed by an *R*

We take it for granted that children will automatically read unusual patterns correctly. It is surprising how many children do not know how to read vowels followed by an *r*. Although vowels with *r* (also called *R*-controlled vowels) were given in the above vowel combination lesson, they should also be taught as a separate skill so that children can learn all possible *r* combinations. If the child does not learn them, and reads the vowel as a short or long vowel sound, they will not pronounce the word right or recognize it as a familiar one. Try it for yourself: *cat, car; fun, fur.*

Introduce each of the vowel-plus-r patterns (See The Vowel and Consonant Guide: Part J) and have the child make another page in the vowel book, or make a chart. This should also be kept by the child as a reference sheet or book while reading so that he or she can look up the correct pronunciation using a picture clue.

ar	car	iar	friar
are	hare	ier	flier
air	hair	ier	tier
er	her	or	horse
ere	here	or	worm
ere	were	ore	store
ear	bear	oor	door
ear	earth	oar	oar
ear	heart	our	hour

eer	deer	our	journey
eir	their	our	pour
ir	bird	ur	purse
ire	fire	ure	cure
		uire	squire

Contractions

you're	you are
we're	we are
they're	they are

You can refer to earlier sections and make a game or learning activity using the above patterns. Always couple these activities with reading from books so that the child can practice seeing these words in context. It is exciting for children to pick out words with the patterns they have just learned. It gives them a sense of pride that they can recognize more and more words each time.

VOWELS FOLLOWED BY *L*

Vowels followed by *l*, or *l*-controlled vowels, also give the vowel a slightly different pronunciation. For this reason, teach children the vowels followed by *l* as a separate lesson. These patterns appear in The Vowel and Consonant Guide: Part I (*The Vowel Book*), but they are isolated here so that you can focus on them in a separate lesson. You can use any of the activities appropriate for your child's learning style to introduce these patterns. Word lists for each of these patterns are in Part J of The Vowel and Consonant Guide.

al	pal	ill	pill
alt	salt	ile	smile

all	ball	ial	dial
ale	male	oll	doll
alk	walk	oll	troll
alm	palm	ole	hole
alf	half	oal	goal
alves	halves	ul	bulb
el	elf	ull	gull
ell	bell	ull	bull
eal	seal	ule	mule
eel	wheel	ual	equal
il	milk	uel	fuel
ild	wild	uil	quilt

Two Sounds of *C* and Two Sounds of *G*

This is a short lesson but must be taught. You will find that as your child masters the above vowel patterns, he or she may still be stumped on words with *c* and *g*. The letter *c* has two sounds: *c* as the hard *k* sound as in *cat*, or *c* with soft *s* sound as in *ice* or *city*. *G* also has two sounds: the soft *g* sound as in *cage* or *gem*, or the hard *g* sound as in *go*. (See The Vowel and Consonant Guide: Part K.)

Luckily, there is a rule to help children remember which is which. The rule works for many of the words, but there are exceptions.

The rule for hard *c*: When *c* is followed by *a*, *o*, or *u*, it has a hard sound as in *cat*.

Rule for soft *c*: When *c* is followed by *e*, *i*, or *y*, it has the soft sound as in *ice*.

Here are some word lists to use as examples of the above rules:

Hard C	Soft C
cat	cent
can	cell
cot	city
coat	cinch
cut	cycle
cute	cymbal

You can also show how the rule works when the *c* is in the middle of a word.

Hard C	Soft C
bacon	racing
chocolate	faces
acorn	receive
hiccup	lacy

The same rule applies to *g*:

The rule for hard *g*: When *g* is followed by *a*, *o*, or *u*, it is pronounced with a hard *g* sound as in *go*.

The rule for soft *g*: When *g* is followed by *e*, *i*, or *y*, most of the time it is pronounced with a soft *g* sound as in *germ*.

Here are some examples of hard and soft *g* words:

Hard G	Soft G
gas	gem
gave	gentle
got	gist
go	giant
gull	gym
gum	gyro

Point out the following words as rule breakers:

girl, get, give.

Show your child a list of words in which *g* comes in the middle of the word.

Hard *G*	**Soft *G***
again	age
ago	raging
August	huge

You may also at this time show them that *dge* is like the *g* with a *j* sound:

badge
wedge
ridge
lodge
budge

Also explain that by doubling the *g*, it will take on the hard sound of *g*.

nagging
legging
wiggly
foggy
buggy

SILENT LETTERS AND IRREGULAR CONSONANT PRONUNCIATIONS

Some letters are silent when combined with other letters. They are in the words but are not pronounced. Many students who are not taught the silent letter patterns are continually stumped when reading such words. They pronounce the silent letters and get confused because what they read does not sound like any word they have heard before. They may get so confused that they skip over those words without understanding the passage. Word lists for each of these silent letter patterns are found in The Vowel and Consonant Guide: Part L.

gn	gnome	*g* is silent
kn	knight	*k* is silent
wr	write	*w* is silent
ight	light	*gh* is silent
mb	lamb	*b* is silent
lf	half	*l* is silent
psy	psychology	*p* is silent

Ph *as* F *and* Sch *as* Sk

There are words in English with irregular consonant pronunciations. A common example is ph, which is pronounced as *f*. Unless this is pointed out to your child, he or she will read *ph* as "pa-ha" and will not understand the word. "Sch" is pronounced as "sk" in "school."

Examples:

phone	*(fone)*
telegraph	*(telegraf)*
physics	*(fisics)*
elephant	*(elefant)*
scholar	*(skolar)*
school	*(skool)*
scholarship	*(skolarship)*

IRREGULAR WORD PATTERNS

Just when you think you have found some rules to go by, your child will come across some words that just do not fit any rule. You are overjoyed that you taught them the magic *e* rule, the two-vowel rule, and all the different combinations. Then your child gets to a word like *been*. The child wants to read it as *bean*, but you have to explain that this is a rule breaker, in which *been* is pronounced more like *bin*.

Then you come to the word *were*, which does not fit the magic *e* rule. Instead of rhyming with *here*, it is more like the *er* in *her*.

You come across the word *was*, which does not have the short *a* as in *hat*. It is more like a short *u* sound as in *up*.

As your child reads aloud to you, you will spot many irregular words that do not fit the patterns your child has learned. What should you do with them? Point them out, say the correct pronunciation, and call it a rule breaker. Tell your child it is just one of those words that he or she has to remember.

Phew! So many patterns! Are you beginning to wonder how children even learn to read at all?

We have covered the general list of patterns used in schools, although there are variations from school to school. While there are other sound combinations, these are the main ones on which to concentrate. For the most part, the consonants and short vowels are mastered by the end of first grade. In some schools, students may even learn them in kindergarten. In other schools, students also master the long vowels by the end of first grade. In second grade, students continue to master the short and long vowels, the blends, and the digraphs. They also begin to learn how to read words with the different vowel combinations. By the end of third grade, or fourth grade at the latest, students should be able to decode all of the above sounds.

There are variations in instruction. In some schools, students systematically go through each sound as an isolated skill in a method of instruction called phonics. In other schools, the children learn these sounds grouped by similar patterns, in a method of instruction called linguistics. In many schools, a method called whole-language instruction is used, in which the students do not learn phonics or linguistics, but read from trade books. They learn the sounds as needed when they come up in the book. It is important that if the whole-language approach is used in your child's school, you are watching to see that your child is learning all the sounds. In some schools, teachers have totally replaced phonics instruction with the whole-language method, not recognizing that the students still need to be taught the letter-sound relationships even within their whole-language instruction. It is important that parents check up on their school's whole-language program to ensure that the child learns each of the sounds. The system used to teach the sounds may vary, but each of the sounds should be taught somewhere in the program.

PROBLEMS WITH LETTER-SOUND RELATIONSHIPS IN THE UPPER GRADES

Part of your older child's reading difficulties may be due to missed letter-sound relationships during the first three or four years of school. Once a child misses these skills at the earlier stages, they continue to have trouble until someone catches the problem. If a child does not know all the sounds and is asked to read materials in the higher grades, he or she ends up skipping those words or muddling through them incorrectly. As a result, the child does not know the word and misses the meaning of the sentence. If there are too many missed words, the child is not going to understand the passage or story. This is where reading comprehension problems enter the picture.

If you give a simple reading diagnosis test to your older child, asking him or her to read some passages or pages from one of their current textbooks, you will be able to identify what words and sounds your child is missing. Working with your child to teach him or her how to identify the sounds in a variety of words can help get him or her back on track. Teach your child the sound, and make lists of words with that sound. Have your child practice reading those lists back to you. Have your child find those words in books and practice reading those words in context to you. Have the child write sentences with those words.

Be aware that a missed letter-sound relationship could have caused the reading problems your child has had from grades three, four, five, and six up to grade twelve. At whatever grade your child is now, find out what sounds they cannot read correctly and work with him or her on those sounds.

The problem is not irreversible. By working with your child on the sounds, you can help bring up his or her reading level significantly. Steady work can bring your child back on track.

READING MULTISYLLABLE WORDS

Once a child has learned the main letter-sound relationships, they will need to learn how to break up words with two or more syllables to read the parts correctly. Many children in fourth grade and higher can read short words, but they do not know what to do with words with several syllables.

What is a syllable? A syllable is a sound unit containing one vowel sound. Every syllable needs a vowel sound. There are no syllables containing only consonants. The vowel sound may have a consonant before it, after it, or both; it is made up of one, two, or more vowel letters that make one sound. The vowel sound can precede or follow a consonant blend or digraph.

Here are some possible syllables found in words:

　　a from the word *a-gain*
　　mo from the word *motion*
　　cap from the word *cap-sule*
　　boat from the word *boat-ing*
　　stop from the word *stop-light*
　　trust from the word *trust-ing*

After a child has learned the letter-sound relationships, we need to show them how to break up a word into syllables. By doing so, the child will recognize the patterns they have already learned and will be able to read the parts. Then they can put the parts together into a recognizable word.

There are only two ways to break up a word into syllables: after the vowel sound or after the consonants following the vowel sound.

After the vowel sound would be: c-v- (consonant-vowel)

> Example: no-tion
>   bi-son

After the consonant following the vowel sound would be: c-v-c- (consonant-vowel-consonant)

> Example: fic-tion
>   man-tle

Here is another great rule to teach your child:

If the word is divided after the vowel, the vowel will be read as a long vowel. In *no-tion*, note how the first *o* is long. If the word is divided after the consonant following the vowel sound, the vowel will be read as a short vowel sound. Note that in *fic-tion*, the first *i* is short.

This rule works in most cases. Thus, we can tell the child to try dividing a word both ways: after the vowel, and after the consonant following the vowel. Read the first case with a long vowel, and the second example with a short vowel. After trying both ways, the child can see which word is a recognizable one.

Your child may wish to keep a small marker or card to help divide the words as he or she reads. Teach your child to break the words into syllables, and try to figure out which patterns he or she knows. (See The Vowel and Consonant Guide: Part M.)

Chapter 14

How to Diagnose Problems
With Vocabulary Skills

Your child has finally mastered all the letter-sound relationships. When he or she reads aloud, it sounds almost flawless. But ask your child to tell you what he or she read, and he or she hesitates. After a few moments of pressure from you, your child finally throws out a few points about the story, some accurate and some a bit off. You realize that your child does not fully understand what he or she has just read. What is the problem? It could be either a lack of comprehension skills or problems in understanding the vocabulary words.

As your child moves from grade to grade, the difficulty of vocabulary increases. Your child may know the meaning of many words when he or she begins to read, but material at higher grade levels uses new and more difficult words. Children do not automatically know the meaning of these words as they get older. They must continually be taught the meaning and usage of new vocabulary words.

How are vocabulary words taught in schools? Again, there are a variety of methods used in classrooms throughout the country. When reading textbooks (called "basal readers") are used, new words are introduced at the beginning of each new story. Teachers usually go over the new vocabulary words, and students do practice activities with the new words. Thus, when the child reads the story, they know the meaning, pronunciation, and usage of the new words in advance. Reading the new words in the story reinforces the meaning and usage in the child's mind. There may be periodic review activities in which the child can practice the new words.

In some schools, children use a vocabulary book to learn ten to twenty new words a week. The children study the words used in reading passages, answer questions about the words, and practice using the words in sentences. Sometimes, when there are no vocabulary books, teachers select words from word lists or the week's lesson, and the students look up the meanings in a dictionary.

In whole-language programs, students read from trade books or library books of their choice, locate new vocabulary words on their own, then look up the meanings in the dictionary. The teachers may offer them a variety of activities they can do with the new vocabulary words. In this approach, students do not learn a systematic list of words, but learn words as they come across them in their reading. If every child reads from different books, each child will have their own independent vocabulary list generated from their own books.

Although the above methods vary, all students should learn how to learn new vocabulary words. Whether the words are chosen from basal readers, vocabulary series, or from independent reading, all students should know how to find the meaning of unknown words. Some students may have reading problems if they do not know how to find the meaning of new words.

DOES YOUR CHILD HAVE PROBLEMS WITH VOCABULARY?

Here is a simple test you can give your child to find out if he or she has difficulty with vocabulary skills.

Step 1: Take a story or chapter from a reading book on your child's grade level. Select a chapter he or she has not yet read. Preread the chapter yourself and locate the most difficult vocabulary words in the chapter. Mark off a one-hundred-word passage that contains these difficult words. Write the words on paper. Look up the definitions of the words yourself and write them down next to the words, but do not show them to your child.

Step 2: Have your child read aloud the passage you selected. At the end of the reading, ask your child the meaning of the words you had selected. You may allow your child to look back in the passage to find the word and reread it in the sentence in which it is used. Note down your child's definition of these words.

Step 3: If you child says he or she does not know the meaning of the word, ask your child, "What can you do to find out the meaning?" Use the checklist below and observe which of the behaviors your child exhibits.

Step 4: If your child gives a wrong definition, tell your child that it is incorrect and then ask your child, "What can you do to find out the correct meaning?" Also use the checklist below and observe which of the behaviors your child exhibits.

Step 5: Note down how many words your child defined correctly and how many your child missed. Fill out the following checklist of behaviors your child showed in trying to get the word meaning:

a. Did your child know the meaning?   yes   no

b. Did your child guess the meaning
   correctly?   yes   no

c. Did your child guess the meaning
   incorrectly?   yes   no

d. Did your child look up the meaning
   in a dictionary or glossary?   yes   no

e. Did your child try to figure out the meaning
   from the context or clues in the sentence
   or paragraph?   yes   no

f . Did your child try to figure out what some
of the word parts mean, such as the root
of the word, the prefix, or the suffix?   yes   no

g. Did your child ask you to tell him or her
what the word means?   yes   no

h. Did your child sit there without responding,
drawing a blank?   yes   no

ANALYZING THE RESULTS OF THE DIAGNOSIS

If your child defined the words you selected correctly, you should repeat the activity with more difficult passages. Although it was a positive sign that he or she could understand the vocabulary words in the passage you selected, we also want to see what strategies he or she uses when faced with new words. It is important that your child knows what to do when he or she encounters new vocabulary words.

When you find that your child has missed some words, it is important to observe what behaviors or strategies he or she used to figure out the meaning. If your child demonstrated behaviors d, e, or f, your child knows the strategies for finding out vocabulary meaning. It indicates that your child is aware that he or she must look up the meaning in a dictionary or glossary, or figure out what meaning makes sense from the clues given in the context ("context clues"), or use knowledge of word parts such as roots, prefixes, and suffixes to figure out the word's meaning.

If your child guessed, asked you for the meaning, or sat there blankly staring at the word, it may indicate that your child does not know what to do to figure out word meanings. The number of vocabulary words missed in one passage can give you an idea of what is happening when your child reads in school or at home for pleasure. He or she may be skipping many words without trying to find the meaning. You can get some idea of the percentage of each passage your child may be missing due to lack of vocabulary skills. If your child misses ten words out of a passage of one hundred words, then your child may only understand 90 percent of what he or she is reading. If your child does not know the meaning of twenty words out of a hundred-word passage, then your child is only understanding 80 percent of what he or she reads.

Lack of vocabulary skills can be part of your child's problems with comprehension. It may be that your child's excellent comprehension skills are camouflaged by a lack of vocabulary skills. How can this happen? I have seen many students who understand what they read, but due to an inability to figure out the meaning of new vocabulary words, answer questions about the story incorrectly. Here is an example:

A child is reading a passage about a German shepherd. The child may understand everything else in the passage accurately, but thinks the German shepherd is a boy in Germany. See how the child may miss the comprehension questions.

> A man was skiing on a mountain. He fell down and hurt his ankle. It pained him so much that he could not move. None of the other skiers came down the same slope, so no one knew he was there. He cried for help. Night fell, but the man could not walk. He feared that he would freeze overnight. As his hands and feet began to stiffen, he heard a noise. He cried out for help. A German shepherd came down the slope. He pushed at the man, but the man could not move. The German shepherd ran up the mountain. Soon he returned with a woman who was able to get help for the fallen man.

> 1. Who is the hero of the story?

> 2. How was the man's life saved?

3. What senses did the German shepherd use to find the man?

The child reading the story does not know what a German shepherd is. The reader thinks a German shepherd is a boy who takes care of sheep. Thus, the child may incorrectly answer question 1 by saying that the hero is a boy. Someone reading the child's answer may think that the child has a comprehension problem, because the hero could be either the dog or, as a second choice, the woman. To question 2, the child, not knowing the German shepherd is a dog, would reply that a boy saved the man's life. And for question 3, the child may think the German shepherd only heard the man's cries, and not respond that the dog also used its sense of smell to find the man.

Missing the meaning of one or two key words in a story can make it appear that the child has poor comprehension, when in fact it is only a lack of vocabulary skills.

Chapter 15

Remedies for Problems With Vocabulary Skills

Your first approach to solving the child's vocabulary problem may be to teach the child hundreds of new words. That is a remedy, but not the cure. Only by teaching your child the strategy to learn *any* new vocabulary word can you teach him or her *how to learn* vocabulary words. Once children learn the basic strategies for attacking new words, they can repeat the technique with any new words they encounter.

There are three main techniques for getting the meaning of new words. The first is looking up the definition in a dictionary or glossary, a skill that every child needs to learn. The second approach is getting the meaning of the word from the context, which means using clues in the sentence or passage to figure out what the unknown word means. There are a variety of context-clue skills you can teach your child. The third is using knowledge of word parts—roots, prefixes, and suffixes—to figure out what the word means.

TEACHING YOUR CHILD HOW TO USE
A DICTIONARY OR GLOSSARY

If your child is in first through third grades, you will need a beginner's dictionary. If your child is in fourth through sixth grades, you will need an intermediate dictionary. If your child is in middle school or high school, you can use any standard dictionary.

Begin by pointing out how a dictionary is set up. Explain that the words are arranged alphabetically. If your child is in first, second, or third grade, he or she may not understand what alphabetical order is. You will have to explain that the words are listed in the order that letters appear in the alphabet.

Point out the guide words on the top of each page of the dictionary. Show your child that if you are looking up a word that starts with *h*, you have to flip through the book until you come to the *h* words.

Explain that the first guide word shows which word is at the beginning of the page. The second guide word shows which word is at the end of the page. All the words on the page will be in between the two guide words.

You must point out that there are many words that begin with *h*. After finding *h*, we must look at the second letter in the word. If the word is *hippopotamus*, we must then look up the guide words which have *hi*. After locating the *hi* words, we must look at the third letter, which is *p*. We must then look up guide words that have *hip*. If *hip* is not a guide word, we must look at the letter before *p*, such as *hio* and then *hin*, and after *p*, such as *hiq*, then *hir*, then *his*. When we find the guide words for *hip* words, we then know to look on that page. The entry words are written in darker black, or bold ink. We skim down the list of bold words looking for *hip*. When we get to *hip*, then we look at the fourth letter, which is *p*. We then begin looking for *hipp*. We continue to compare each letter of the word we want with the entry words until we find our word. For example:

hint	**history**
hint	his
hip	Hispanic
hipbone	hiss
hippopotamus	history

Next, you will need to teach your child what to do after finding the entry word. Explain that the definition of the word is written. There may be several definitions. The child will have to try each definition and see which fits the meaning of the rest of the sentence. To begin with, read the sentence, thinking of the word as meaning number 1. Ask your child, "Does this make sense?" If not, read the sentence, thinking of the word as meaning number 2. Again ask your child, "Does this meaning make sense?" If not, continue reading the word in the sentence, thinking about each of the meanings, until you find the one that makes sense.

Point out that the dictionary also gives the part of speech. This will be meaningful to children in grades four and up. They should be able to determine whether the word is a noun, verb, adjective, or adverb. In some dictionaries, the word is used in a sentence as an example. Point this out to the child. If the dictionary also gives synonyms or opposites, you can point that out as well.

WHAT TO DO WITH THE DEFINITIONS?

You will want your child to begin some kind of record-keeping for the new words he or she looks up in a dictionary. After looking up the word once, chances are that your child will forget the meaning. It is important for your child to write the word and its meaning and do some activities with the word that will help him or her remember its meaning. It is said that a person must use a word at least seven times to own it. Here are some ways your child can keep a record of new words, followed by activities to help your child remember the new word.

Record-Keeping of New Words

The style of record-keeping you choose will depend on your child's best learning style. Here are some record-keeping techniques that can be used with visual, auditory, kinesthetic, or tactile learners.

Visual Vocabulary Record-Keeping

Have your child make a booklet of new words. Your child can write the word and its meaning, then draw a picture to illustrate the meaning. Have your child use different colors for the pictures.

Have your child write sentences or make up a story using the new vocabulary words.

Have your child make a large chart for the wall. Divide the chart into nouns, verbs, adjectives, and adverbs. Have your child write the new word and its meaning on the chart, in the space matching its part of speech. Have your child make a small sketch next to the word, illustrating the meaning. On another sheet of paper, have your child write a story using the new words and then illustrate it.

Auditory Vocabulary Record-Keeping

Keep a small audiocassette recorder and a blank tape. As your child looks up new words, have him or her read the new word and its definition into the tape recorder. Have your child play back the list of new words over and over again.

Have your child tell a story using the new words.

Talk about the new words and have your child tell you examples of sentences or situations in which the word could be used.

Tactile Vocabulary Record-Keeping

Have your child type the new word and its definition on a computer or typewriter. Have your child type a sentence that goes with the word.

Have your child write each vocabulary word in a color, and its definition in another color. Have him or her use a third color to write a sentence for each word. Tell your child to make up a sentence telling how the word makes him or her feel. Or have the child write a sentence that relates to some emotion or feeling.

Kinesthetic Vocabulary Record-Keeping

After looking up the word, have your child act out a situation in which the word could be used. Have your child draw a cartoon action story in which the word is used, and have your child write the word in a bubble.

Make a semantic map in which the word goes in a middle bubble. Have bubbles shooting off the main word. In one bubble, have your child write the definition and draw a picture to show an action that goes with the word. In another bubble, write the part of speech, and in another write a synonym for the word. In another bubble write an antonym, or opposite. In a large bubble, have your child write a sentence using that word and draw an illustration that goes with it.

REMEMBERING NEW VOCABULARY WORDS

The key to keeping information in the long-term memory is attaching it to an emotion or some novel situation. You must take the word and think of it in an unusual way. The situation has to be as far-out and as outrageous as you can make it. Your child can either write down the situation, talk about it, act it out, or visualize it in the imagination. The more humorous, gross, or ridiculous your example, the more likely your child will be to remember the word and its meaning. Here are some examples:

taciturn: quiet

Have your child picture a dog named Taci taking a turn, and then sitting quietly. Have your child draw a cartoon of a dog or say aloud, "Taci, you dog, turn around and be quiet."

bifurcated: split into two

Explain to your child that *bi* means "two," as in *bicycle*, or "two wheels," or *bimonthly*, meaning "every two months." Then have your child picture a giant fork in the road that is split. One prong of the fork points to one road, and the other prong in the fork points to another road. Say, "*Bifurcated* is a 'fork' which is split into 'bi' or 'two.'" Have your child draw a giant fork, split into two parts, and say, "Bifurcated."

Try to find words your child knows that sound like the new word, and then create an image or picture. This will help bring back the word and meaning to your child's mind more easily. A list of words with possible associations is given in The Vowel and Consonant Guide: Part N. This will give you examples of associations for a variety of words to give you ideas to think of on your own.

Vocabulary Charades

Make a list of words and their definitions. Take turns with your child selecting a word and acting it out silently, so the other can guess which word is being dramatized. If you go first, select a word, act it out, and have your child guess which word you are acting out. Then have your child select a word and act it out, and you guess the meaning. Points can be awarded for each correct guess.

Vocabulary Search

Award your child a point each time your child uses a new vocabulary word correctly throughout the day. Have your child search for opportunities to use the new word. Each time you catch your child using the new vocabulary word correctly, give him or her a point. Determine the number of points needed to win a prize.

Dictionary Cross-Country

Give your child practice in looking up words in a dictionary. Provide your child with a list of ten new words selected from a current book your child is reading. Use a stopwatch to see how quickly your child looks up each word. Chart the results. Each day, give your child ten new words and see if your child can beat his or her own record.

Alphabetical Card Sort

Write a list of words on flashcards. Mix them up. Have your child arrange the cards in alphabetical order. This will provide practice for looking up words in alphabetical order in a dictionary or glossary.

TEACHING YOUR CHILD ABOUT CONTEXT CLUES

Using context clues to derive word meaning is one of the skills taught in schools. It is like detective work. One must figure out the meaning of the new word by using clues provided in the rest of the sentence. Here is an example:

John was elated when he won the race.

Suppose your child did not know the meaning of the word *elated*. To figure out its meaning from the context, you would ask, "How do you think John felt when he won the race?" Your child may say, "Happy." Then you would say, "That's correct. So *elated* must mean something like 'feeling happy.'" To confirm the meaning, look it up in the dictionary.

Why would one want to use context clues in place of using a dictionary? Often, when reading for pleasure, or when time is short, one does not have the time to look up the word. Thus, one could figure out what the word might mean by using the context without breaking the reading to find a dictionary. Ideally, students should keep a list of new words and the page they find them on, and look them up at some point in order to expand their vocabulary. But if this is not possible due to a time constraint, students can use context clues.

There are various types of context clues one can use. In one case, the new word is given and its meaning is also provided in the sentence:

On a nature walk, Jill saw a heron, a type of bird.

In this case, the new word, *heron*, is defined as "a type of bird." In many textbooks the new word is often defined in the same sentence.

Another type of context clue gives the opposite meaning:

Unlike easygoing, agreeable Sally, Pat was obstinate.

From this sentence, one gets a clue that *obstinate* must be the opposite of easygoing and agreeable.

A third type of context clue gives the meaning through information provided in the entire passage.

Bill had worked hard to try out for the baseball team. His older brother, Tom, kept telling him he would not make it. Tom's friends even made fun of Bill. Bill

wanted to try out anyway. On the day of the tryouts,
Tom and his friends were there to watch. Bill tried his
best, but missed the ball every time. Tom and his
friends would laugh. Every time Bill missed the ball,
Bill felt so chagrined he wanted to hide.

To determine the meaning of *chagrined*, the reader would
have to figure out how they would feel in Bill's place. Some
would say they felt embarrassed or humiliated, which is the
correct meaning. Using context clues is not as accurate as
looking the word up in a dictionary, but one can come fairly
close. In the above example, some students may say that Bill
felt frustrated or angry, which is not the correct meaning.
There is room for error in the context-clue method. But one
would have the clue that Bill was not happy about the situation and was not feeling good.

HOW TO USE CONTEXT CLUES

Go over the three types of context clues given in the examples above with your child. Then take one of your child's
books and locate some words that your child does not know.
Science and social studies textbooks are filled with examples
in which new vocabulary can be figured out using context
clues. Guide your child to find the words' meanings by using
the context clues. See which type of context clues are given.
Is the meaning given in the sentence? Is the opposite meaning given? Or does one have to figure out the meaning from
the situation in the sentence or paragraph? Have your child
identify which type of context clue is used.

Context Clue Search

Make a chart with three headings:

Definition Given in the Sentence or Passage	Opposite Meaning Given in the Sentence or Passage	Clues Given in the Situation Described in the Passage

Search in books for new words, and have your child identify which of the three types of context clues is used. List the words under the appropriate heading on the chart. Have your child find out which type of clue they find more of in their books.

Context-Clue Olympics

As you read with your child, have your child identify new words he or she does not know. Have your child figure out the meaning using the context clues. Then look up the word in the dictionary. See if your child's definition matches the dictionary's. For every time the definition your child figured out from the context clues was the correct one according to the dictionary, award him or her a point. Determine the number of points your child needs for a reward. The reward could be going out to your child's favorite restaurant, buying your child a new book, or going to a place of amusement your child enjoys. Sometimes when the task is difficult, like spending time on vocabulary building, including a reward makes it more like a game for the child.

USING WORD PARTS TO DERIVE WORD MEANING

A third method of figuring out the meaning of a new word is using word parts. Some words are made up of two parts: a root word and a prefix, or a root word and a suffix. There are some words that have a root, a prefix, and a suffix. In the following subsections, you will learn what these words mean.

How Knowledge of Prefixes Helps to Derive Word Meaning

A prefix is a group of letters added to the beginning of a word. The prefix gives the word a new meaning. Some prefixes are *re-*, *de-*, *pre-*, *un-*, *dis-*, *con-*, etc.

For example, *re* means "to do over" or "do again."

When *re* is added to the word *write*, we get *rewrite*, which means "to write again." When *re* is added to the word *do*, we get *redo*, which means "to do again." By knowing the meaning of the prefix *re*, the child can figure out many words:

> redraw
>
> revisit
>
> regain
>
> retry
>
> remake

Here is another example. *Pre* means "before." When *pre* is added to the word *test*, we get *pretest*, or "to test beforehand." We know that a pretest is a test the child receives before the actual test. When *pre* is added to the word *view*, we get *preview*, or "to view or see before." In a preview of a movie, we see the movie before it comes out to the general public. If the child knows that *pre* means "before," the child can figure out the meaning of many words that start with *pre*:

> preassign
>
> predate
>
> prepay

Other prefix definitions are:

dis:	not	quin:	five
un:	not	sex:	six
con:	against	sept:	seven
ir:	not	oct:	eight

be:	to be	nov:	nine
non:	not	deca:	ten
uni:	one	cent:	hundred
bi:	two	milli:	thousand
tri:	three	semi:	half
quad:	four	hemi:	half

(See The Vowel and Consonant Guide: Part O, for lists of words with prefixes.

Prefix Word Search

Make a chart listing the prefixes given above. Have your child find as many words as possible that begin with those prefixes and write them in the columns. This can be done two ways. The child can search for words starting with those prefixes in his or her books or look up those prefixes in the dictionary and list the words they find. Next to each word, have your child write the definition of the word using the prefix meaning. For example:

> bimonthly: two times a month
> hemisphere: half a sphere
> dissatisfied: not satisfied

Prefix Clues

While reading with your child, point out some of the words that begin with a prefix. Have your child look up the meaning of the prefix and figure out what the word means using the prefix meaning. For example:

Lilly had to rewrite her lesson.

Your child will look up *re* and find that it means "to do again." Your child should figure out that *rewrite* means "to write again."

How Knowledge of Suffixes Helps to Derive Word Meaning

A suffix is a group of letters attached to the end of a word. The suffix gives the word a new meaning. Some suffix endings are *-able*, *-ful*, *-ily*, *-ness*, *-less*.

For example: the suffix *ful* means "full of." If *ful* is added to the word *beauty*, we get *beautiful*, or "full of beauty." If *ful* is added to the word *sorrow*, we get *sorrowful*, or "full of sorrow."

The suffix *less* means "not having" or "having less." Thus, *penniless* means "not having a penny."

The suffix *able* means "able to." Thus, *lovable* means "able to be loved." *Livable* means "able to be lived in." (See The Vowel and Consonant Guide: Part P for lists of suffixes.)

Suffix Search

List a variety of suffixes on a chart. Have your child search for words in his or her books that end in those suffixes and list them on the chart. Next to each word, have your child write the definition, using the suffix meaning. For example:

excusable: able to be excused

Suffix Race

Using the suffix chart created above, have your child see how many of each suffix he or she can find. Then have your child make a graph to show which suffix appeared most frequently in his or her books.

Suffix Board Game

Make a game board in which a word with a suffix is written in each space on the game board. The theme of the game can be a car race, space race, boat race, motorcycle race, or anything in which your child is interested. The game can be played by throwing the dice and moving a game piece around the board. The player must correctly read the word on the space in order to stay on the spot. Otherwise, the player must return to his or her previous position. The first player to cross the finish line wins.

How Knowledge of Roots Helps Derive Word Meaning

A root word is the base word upon which prefixes and suffixes are added. Many of the words in the English language are derived from other languages, such as Latin or Greek. Knowledge of the original Latin or Greek can give clues to word meaning. For example, if one knows that the Greek word part *ology* means "study of" and *bio* means "life," we will know that *biology* means "the study of life." If we know that *geo* refers to the earth, we will know that *geology* is the study of the earth. If we know that *zoo* means "animals," then *zoology* is the study of animals.

If we know that *optic* refers to the eye, then we can have a good idea of the meaning of *optometrist*, *ophthalmologist*, and *optician*, as those who work with the eye. (See Vowel and Consonant Guide: Part Q for lists of roots and word parts.)

Root Word Search

Give your child the following root words and see how many words they can find in their books or in a dictionary which use that root:

ped:	foot	scope:	to see
cardio:	heart	graph:	to write
cycle:	wheel	astro:	space
mobile:	moving	aqua:	water
tele:	far	geo:	earth
phone:	sound	marine:	water
vision:	to see		

Examples: telephone, television, telecommunications, telegraph

Next to each word, ask your child to write the definitions. For example:

> telephone: sound from far away
> television: to see from far away

Invent a Word

Have your child combine roots, prefixes, and suffixes to invent new words and write the meanings of each. For example:

> aquascope: a machine to see water
> astrocycle: a bicycle to ride in space.

Ask your child to draw a picture of their newly invented word as well.

Magazine Search

Have your child search through a magazine to look for root words he or she knows and circle them with a colored magic marker or pen. Help your child figure out the meaning of the words using the knowledge of the root's meaning.

PULLING IT ALL TOGETHER

After going through the different methods one can use to figure out the meaning of new words, review them with your child. Ask your child to tell you what he or she can do to figure out the meaning of a new word. Your child should be able to tell you the following techniques:

✔ look it up in a dictionary or glossary

✔ use the context clues

✔ use knowledge of prefixes, suffixes, or roots

As you read with your child and he or she gets stumped by a new word, instead of telling your child what to do, ask, "What technique can you use to figure out the word?" It is important that your child remember the strategies, because you will not always be with your child when he or she reads, such as when he or she is in school. Your child needs to know the strategies in order to read and learn independently. If your child still cannot repeat to you any of the three strategies listed above, repeat the lessons given in this chapter for those techniques they forgot. The time you spend on these vocabulary activities will be time well spent, for your child will need these skills for his or her entire school career and later in life.

Keep a Personal Dictionary

As your child looks up new words, help him or her start a personal dictionary. You can buy one of the decorative blank books sold in bookstores or make your own book. Your child may wish to list new words alphabetically or by category. He or she may wish to list words by part of speech, such as nouns, verbs, adverbs, or adjectives, or your child may wish to list them according to categories such as sports, medicine, foods, animals, etc. Periodically review with your child the words in the dictionary to reinforce them. Remember, words must be used about seven times in order for them to become part of one's memory.

FOR HIGH SCHOOL STUDENTS: PREPARING
FOR COLLEGE ENTRANCE TESTS

If your child is in high school, he or she may want to prepare for college entrance tests, one portion of which involves vocabulary. There are books to help your child study for these tests. These preparatory books contain lists of words frequently used in these tests. You can use some of the techniques described above to help your child memorize the words. Teach your child to create novel, absurd, and outrageous pictures in his or her mind or to connect the word with an emotion in order to memorize the meanings. Many of the words in the lists are built from roots, suffixes, and prefixes your child can learn. The techniques in this chapter can help your child study these lists in preparation for the college exams.

Vocabulary-Building Audiotapes

There are a variety of audiotapes on the market which help build vocabulary. If your child is an auditory learner, he or she may learn quickly from these audiotapes. Some of the audiotapes not only give the word and its meaning, but give you stories and passages in which the word is used in context. You may wish to supplement the audiotape with the other techniques in the chapter to reinforce the words.

Use Your Child's Words in Your Own Speech

Once you know the new words that your child is trying to learn, look for opportunities to use them in your speech when your child is around. See if your child recognizes the word and what you mean in your usage of the word. Have bonus words for the day. Tell your child that you are going to use some of the new vocabulary words and to keep his or her ears open for them. Whether or not you give your child a tangible reward for noticing that you used the new word, your child will appreciate the interest you are taking in his or her vocabulary work. At heart, children love the attention they receive from parents as you take the time to help them improve in the various skills.

Chapter 16

How to Diagnose Comprehension Problems

As your child reads, he or she may pronounce the words correctly, but still not understand what he or she is reading. This could indicate a problem in understanding vocabulary or in comprehension of the passage. You can tell whether the problem is due to poor vocabulary skills or comprehension difficulties if you give your child a passage to read with simple vocabulary. If your child still has difficulty understanding what he or she has read, then he or she probably has comprehension problems.

Comprehension is the ability to understand what was read. It is the ability to convert symbols on the page into pictures in the mind's eye. Many children can say the words aloud, but do not know what they read. Reading is not just saying the words on the page; it is getting mental pictures, thoughts, ideas, or feelings from those symbols. It may be hard to believe, but I have taught high school students who drew a blank when I asked them what they see in their mind as they read. When I told them that they should be getting pictures in their heads as if there were a movie going on inside them, they were amazed. After working with them intensively to help them "picture" what they read, they told me, "This is fun. I never knew that this was what reading is." For years, they thought that if they sounded out the symbols on the page, they were reading. They were surprised and delighted to learn, even though it was a little late, that reading was seeing movies inside their heads!

We do not need to wait until children are in high school to teach them how to comprehend. We need to teach them from the very outset. I emphasize the word *teach*, because I have found after years of teaching reading that comprehension is not picked up by osmosis. We have to teach children to comprehend what they read. We cannot take it for granted that they will comprehend what they read automatically.

TESTING FOR PROBLEMS IN COMPREHENSION

Select two passages from your child's textbooks to read. For this activity, you may wish to select two different fiction stories that contain action. Your child should read one of the passages aloud, the other silently.

Oral Reading Passage

Have your child read aloud a passage from one of the stories. You will ask the child aloud the following sample questions and record the answers on paper. *Note*: These are general questions which may fit a wide variety of stories, but if they do not apply to the story you selected, alter the questions to fit.

Questions About Details

1. Who is this story about?
2. What is the character doing?
3. Where does the story take place?

4. When does the story take place?

5. What color is _____ ?

6. What did _____ say to _____ ?

Note: You can make up questions that can be answered by a sentence in the story. If a child cannot answer these simple questions, it may indicate that the child is not comprehending the details of the story.

Questions About the Main Idea

Ask your child what the main idea of the story is. If the story is about a boy who lost his dog, the child should be able to tell you that. If the child says he or she doesn't know, or gives you something that is way off base, he or she may have a problem understanding the main idea.

Questions About Time Order

Ask your child to list the events of the story in order. You may also wish to list the events of the story in a mixed-up order on paper and have the child number which event came first, which came second, which came third, and which came fourth. If the child gets this wrong, you know he or she could have a problem with time order.

Questions About Inference

Sometimes there are feelings or ideas expressed in the story that are not stated, but a reader can infer or assume what they are from other clues in the story. For example, if a character named John in the story is angry, the story may not say, "John was angry." Instead, the story will portray John as shouting and slamming doors. From those clues, the reader will get the idea that John was angry. Ask your child some of the following inference questions:

1. What do you think this character was feeling and why?

2. Why do you think the character did what he or she did?

3. What mood is this character in?

If the child cannot answer these questions correctly, he or she may be having difficulty with inference questions.

Questions About Predictions

Readers often anticipate what will occur next in the story. During a good break point in the story, have the child stop reading, and ask him or her:

1. What do you think will happen next?

2. Why do you think that?

If the child cannot answer these questions, it could mean problems with prediction.

Judgment Questions

Ask your child:

1. Do you think the character did the right thing?

2. What do you think the character should have done instead?

If your child's answer is not logical or he or she cannot answer these questions, he or she may be having trouble with judgment questions.

Silent Reading Passage

For the second reading the child will read silently. You will then ask your child the same questions listed for the oral reading passage. You can ask the questions orally, and your child will respond orally. Again, write down the child's responses.

Chart the Responses

Complete the chart (see The Vowel and Consonant Guide: Part S) by checking off which types of questions your child answered correctly for both the oral and the silent reading passages. Note which questions your child missed. Comprehension involves a variety of skills. It involves understanding details, main idea, time order, judgment, inference, and the ability to make predictions. Your child may be able to answer certain types of questions but not others. By charting the responses, you will know the areas in which your child needs more assistance.

ANALYZING THE RESULTS

You may find that your child missed all the questions. If this is the case, there could be several reasons. The reading level may be too high for your child, and the material may be far too difficult for your child to understand. If this is the case, you may repeat the diagnosis using materials from an earlier grade level. For example, if you had your third-grade child read to you from a third-grade book, your child may need second-grade material. Ask your child's principal or teacher to loan you a second-grade or even a first-grade book so that you can repeat the diagnosis. You may find that your child comprehends accurately at a lower grade level. This will tell you that the child is reading below grade level.

A second possibility is that your child does not yet know that he or she must picture in the mind's eye what the words say. Some children just sound out the words without thinking about their meaning, not because they cannot do it, but because no one has yet taught them that is what they are supposed to be doing! You may discover that your child is not comprehending his or her third-grade material because they do not know what comprehension is. You may have dropped back to a second- or first-grade book and discovered that your child could not comprehend those either. If this is the case, then you will need to do some activities listed below to teach your child how to comprehend. (Make sure the diagnosis is done using stories without pictures, or your child may be guessing the stories from the pictures!)

You may discover that your child missed the comprehension questions due to problems understanding the vocabulary. The child may have responded incorrectly to the questions because he or she did not know the meaning of some of the key words in the story. If this is the case, you should refer back to the previous chapter related to vocabulary skills. Lack of an adequate vocabulary can masquerade as comprehension problems: In reality the child may have good comprehension, but does not know the meaning of many difficult words.

A third cause for comprehension errors is problems with memory. Your child understood the passage while reading it, but forgot what happened by the time you asked the questions. He or she may retain the events of the story in his or her short-term memory, but forgets it quickly. It is not staying in his or her long-term memory. Your child may need training in remembering what is read. Again, these are skills that must be taught. We cannot assume every child is going to know how to do these things by himself or herself.

You may find that your child does better on the oral reading passage than the silent reading passage, or vice versa. This can be due to differences in learning style. An auditory learner may do better reading the material aloud, while a visual or kinesthetic learner may have to read silently and take the time to internalize and picture the material. Your child's performance on the oral and silent reading passages can give you and your child an indication of which type of reading helps the child comprehend better.

If your child missed some questions and responded correctly to others, you can analyze which types of questions your child had trouble with and which types your child understood. This will help you pinpoint the areas that need work. You may find that your child missed the same areas in both the oral and silent reading passages. This will help confirm the type of comprehension questions on which you need to focus.

You may be surprised to find that your child stumbled over many words yet scored high on the comprehension questions. You may wonder how your child comprehended so well yet missed reading so many words. The child has learned to compensate for word-reading problems by using his or her intelligence. Your child has a good sense of the language. He or she may have stumbled over words, but used his or her intelligence and logic to make sense out of the story. This is a good sign. It means your child is using context clues to make sense out of words he or she does not know. It means that your child has a good grasp of the language and can figure out what is happening. Of course, you want to go back to the chapter on letter-sound relationships to help your child read all types of words and letter combinations, but at least you do not have to worry about comprehension. If your child is stumbling, you should correct the problem, because as the work gets harder, there will be too many difficult words for your child to rely on context clues and logic. When the number of words your child misses becomes too great, even their intelligence and logic may not be able to help them compensate. Generally, a child can compensate for poor letter-sound relationship skills or poor vocabulary skills up to fourth grade. But at fourth grade they will find it harder and harder to compensate, and many reading problems start to show up.

Chapter 17

Remedies for Comprehension Problems

Once you ascertain that your child has difficulty with comprehension skills, you need to start teaching them how to comprehend. This is probably the one area in which many schools are weak. They may do a good job in teaching letter-sound relationships or vocabulary, but they do not teach comprehension. They may assess comprehension by having the child answer questions about the readings. But they often just score the responses from here till kingdom come and never teach the child how to remedy their incorrect responses. One of the biggest revelations that teachers have when I do teacher-training seminars is that children need to be *taught* how to comprehend. Teachers may spend time going over the correct answers, but generally do not teach the child *how* to comprehend. This is where a parent's support is invaluable. The following section will teach you how to teach comprehension skills to your child.

The very first lesson in teaching comprehension skills is to help children understand that when we say the words on the page, we should get pictures or movies in our heads. We should see what is happening inside our minds. We should hear the sounds and the words being spoken. We should smell the smells, taste the flavors, and feel the emotions of the characters. Reading is the process of making the words come alive so that we can see the movie and live the story inside of us.

The act of picturing can be taught to children. The first step is to begin with picturing words.

PICTURING WORDS

Select a storybook, preferably one with a good amount of imagery. An action story, adventure, or fairy tale is a good choice with which to begin. Have your child begin reading aloud the first sentence. Stop the child on a noun. Tell your child to close his or her eyes and tell you what he or she sees. Suppose the word is *frog*. Have your child describe to you the frog. Ask, "What color is it? How large is it? What is it doing?" When the image is fixed in your child's mind, say to your child, "Just as the word *frog* gave you a picture in your head, so should all the words create pictures." Have your child continue to read. At the next noun, stop your child and again repeat the process of having him or her picture the word in his or her head, while explaining what he or she is seeing.

PICTURING PHRASES

The next step is for your child to picture each phrase that he or she reads. The phrase will not only involve a noun, but may include adjectives to describe the noun, verbs to explain the action, and other connecting words and articles. After each phrase that lends itself to an image, stop your child and have him or her see the image (with either open or closed eyes), and tell you what is seen. As the child reads, explain, "As you read, imagine that you are seeing it like a movie, video, or television show in your mind. Tell me what scene you see in your mind." Remind the child to pretend he or she is watching this as a movie. The child should be able to describe back to you the sentence he or she read. For example:

The brown dog jumped over the fence and ran home.

Say to your child, "What do you see?" The child should say, "A dog." Ask, "What color is the dog?" The child should say, "Brown." Ask, "What do you see it doing?" The child should respond, "I see it jumping." Ask, "What do you see it jumping over?" The child should say, "A fence." This dialogue will alert your child to the fact that what was read aloud should be pictured in his or her head. Continue with the next phrase, "and ran home." After your child reads this phrase, ask the child, "What do you see the dog doing now?" The child should say, "The dog is running home."

If the sentence is, "John jumped on a red bike and rode to the park," ask detailed questions, such as: "Who is the boy in the sentence?" (John.) "What did he do?" (He jumped on a bike.) "What color is the bike?" (Red.) "Where did he ride to?" (The park.) If the child misses any of these, have him or her reread the sentence until he or she answers correctly. Then go to the next sentence. Have the child read the sentence and picture the scene in his or her mind. Then ask several detailed questions about it. Continue reading the whole story in this manner. At times, you may want to ask questions about how the character felt or why the character did what he or she did in the story.

Continue reading the story in this manner, phrase by phrase. Tell your child, "Now I am asking you questions as you read. But you should ask yourself these questions as you read by yourself. You should make sure you are picturing everything. If you are not picturing the words and sentences in your head, then you are not reading. Whenever you find you have stopped picturing, you must go back to the last place you pictured, and start reading from there. When you stop picturing, it means you have blanked out and are just saying the words. Unless you know what you read, you are not reading." In this way, you are training your child to monitor his or her reading to see whether he or she comprehends or not. By repeatedly performing this activity of picturing the words, phrases, and sentences, your child will eventually get the message and begin modeling what you are doing. By hearing you ask these questions over and over, the child will start asking the questions to himself or herself automatically. When this occurs, your child will have internalized the skill of comprehending and will be on the road to successful reading.

PICTURING SENTENCES

After a week or two of picturing phrases, move on to having your child picture a whole sentence. This is a bit more complex, as there may be several images and events described in one sentence. Continue the same line of questioning: "Who or what do you see?" "What is he [or she or it] doing?" "What is happening?" At this point you may add the following question: "If you were making a movie of this sentence, what would you see or hear or feel happening on the screen?" Tell your child that he or she is the movie director and must explain to the actors or actresses what they are doing on the screen. Go through each sentence of the story in the same manner.

It may seem slow going at first, and with this method it may take you a long time to get through each page. But remember, the key here is not speed-reading. The key is to teach your child to picture everything in the mind. The slow pace here is essential for them to get used to picturing everything. After it becomes automatic, their speed will pick up and eventually even accelerate, for they will not have to reread the same page over and over due to lack of comprehension. They will be able to continue reading at a good pace, because they will start to automatically picture whatever they read.

PICTURING PARAGRAPHS

After a week or two of picturing each sentence, you can start to move on to having your child picture a paragraph. You will then stop your child to ask questions only at the end of each paragraph. In some cases, where the paragraphs are only one or two sentences long, you may stop them after several paragraphs. Continue questioning them: "What do you see or hear or feel happening in your head?" "Tell me what you see." "What color is this?" "What is so-and-so doing?" "Where are they?" "How does so-and-so feel?" etc.

PICTURE PAGES

You will eventually stop your child only after an entire page to ask questions about what he or she is picturing. At this point your child is beginning to get the idea of comprehension. If you find that your child cannot relate back to you what happened on the page, then go back to picturing paragraphs. Remind the child that if they missed some of the events, that means they have stopped reading at some places and have blanked out. Teach your child to go back and reread the portions they missed.

Continue this process every day. After a while the child will realize, "Oh, while reading, I should be picturing everything!" This great revelation will be the key to understanding that reading means making a connection in his or her mind with the words on the page.

TEST YOUR CHILD'S COMPREHENSION

After working with this procedure of picturing for several weeks or a month, have your child read a passage and ask the same type of comprehension questions again as you did in diagnosing the silent and oral reading passage. You should find that your child's comprehension abilities have increased. Your child's memory of the story should also have improved, because he or she will have a picture in mind to recall. When he or she did not picture anything, there was nothing to remember. But as he or she develops the ability to picture what is being read, the likelihood that he or she will remember the material increases.

STRATEGIES FOR CHECKING ANSWERS

When you ask your child a comprehension question, you can teach your child how to skim through the story to check the answer. Ideally, your child should remember the story. But oftentimes people remember the main idea or the big picture, but forget the details. In school, students are often graded on the comprehension questions at the end of a story. They will need to learn the skill of checking back in the story to verify their responses. Many students guess the answers and continue to score poorly on comprehension. By teaching your child to check back in the story before responding, you will be helping to eliminate guessing and will help your child to be more accurate in his or her responses.

Prove Your Answer

This activity can help your child develop the habit of checking his or her answers. Have your child read a passage. Prepare beforehand written or oral questions about the passage. Ask the questions, but before allowing the child to respond, have him or her go through the passage and point to the sentence that gives the answer. Do not allow the child to write the answer until he or she finds it in the passage. You may wish to have the child mark the page number, paragraph number, and sentence number next to each answer. If you can get your child into the habit of looking for the answers in the passage, you will help him or her cut down on guessing. Teach your child that when answering detail or time-order questions in school, he or she should prove the answers by finding them in the story. Explain that for inference questions, the answers are not stated in the story. Instead, your child will need to find the clues in the passage that lead him or her to make a particular inference.

Skimming for Key Words

In going through the story to look for answers, teach your child that he or she does not need to reread every word. This could take too long a time to find the answer. Instead, teach your child to skim for key words. If the question asks the reader to find out what Susan wore to the party, have the child skim for the words *Susan* and *party*. When those words are found, your child should then read the sentence before that sentence, that same sentence, and the sentence after it. Tell your child that chances are likely that that is the place the answer can be found. If the answer is not in that first place the key word appears, have the child continue to scan the page for each time the key word appears until he or she finds the answer to the question.

Give your child practice in skimming quickly for certain key words. For example, if the question is, "Where did Sally lose her key?" the key words to locate are *Sally*, *lose*, and *key*. If one remembers where that portion is, one can go right to that section and find the answer. If one does not remember where that portion is, one has to skim the entire story look-ing for the key words in order to locate the answer.

It is important to teach your child to verify the answer by checking back in the text. This will help ensure the accuracy of your child's responses. It can make the difference in your child's reading grades and in scores on standardized tests. More importantly, it will help your child be a more accurate reader, especially when each bit of data forms the base for fur-ther learnings. If the child can comprehend accurately at each stage, it will make for more solid understanding and provide a stronger foundation for further readings.

TEACHING SPECIFIC COMPREHENSION QUESTIONS

As described earlier in the chapter, there are a variety of com-prehension questions. From the comprehension diagnosis, you should have identified the types of questions with which your child is having problems. Sometimes children may have diffi-culty with a particular category of questions. They may be good at details but poor at questions about inference. They may be good at details and inference, but have trouble with time-order and sequence questions. The diagnosis gives you a baseline to determine the areas in which your child needs more work. You now have the information you need to discuss the problem with your child's teacher and come up with a plan for remediating the situation. There are also activities given below that you can do at home to solve your child's comprehension problems.

Factual Questions

Factual questions are those which have answers stated in the passage. One can actually locate a sentence in which the ques-tion is answered. They usually deal with details that answer the questions who, what, where, when, how, and why. Detail questions are usually the easiest comprehension questions to answer because one can check back in the passage to locate the answers.

If a child has trouble with factual detail questions, he or she may be a learner who concentrates on the big picture or main idea. They are reading to grasp the total idea of the passage and do not focus on details. This is a matter of learning style. These types of readers will need to learn to find the answers to detail questions in order to survive in school situations where the teacher or the test requires answers about details. Readers who grasp the whole picture are comprehending what is important to them, but they need to learn strategies to remember detailed information. They need to learn the technique of checking the passage for the answers and skimming for key words, as described earlier in the chapter. They need to understand that there is nothing wrong with reading for main ideas, but that they need to learn the strategies for checking over the passage for the smaller details as well.

Another reason why children may have trouble with details is that they forget them when they are finished reading. Again, some of the comprehension techniques for picturing what you read can help these students form clearer images in their minds. They need to practice asking themselves to picture the characters, their description, their actions, and what they see, hear, smell, taste, and feel. The more vivid the images they create in their minds, the better chance they have of recalling what they read.

Younger children may need to be taught the meaning of some of the question words. We should not take it for granted that a child knows what the question "Who?" or "Where?" means. Children need assistance in understanding these words and the type of reply they require. Here are some explanations you can use to teach your child the meaning of the various types of question words:

"Who?" is asking to tell the name of the person or animal in the story. For example:

Marge had a pet cat. The cat's name was Ginger. Every day, Marge fed the cat milk. After drinking the milk, Ginger would climb into Marge's lap and fall asleep.

Ask your child, "Who is the story about?" and point out that the word *who* is asking you to name the person in the story. Your child should tell you that the story is about Marge. Then ask, "Who is Marge's pet?" Again, explain to your child, "The word *who* is asking you to name the animal." Your child should say, "The cat named Ginger," or "The cat," or "Ginger."

Have your child read some passages aloud. Ask your child "who" questions and have your child point to words that answer the question correctly.

Repeat the same activity with "when" questions. Explain that *when* refers to the time that an event happened. Teach them that *when* can refer to a time of day, a clock time, a day, a week, a month, a season, a year, or a period of history. Give your child practice in locating answers to "when" questions.

The same activity should be used to teach your child how to answer "where" questions. Explain that *where* refers to the place at which the story happens or the place at which an event happens. The answer to a "where" question can be a city, state, country, or planet, or it can be "on a spot," "in a hole," "at a home," "on top of a horse," or any location. Find a storybook and have your child locate the "where" responses on each page.

"What" refers to a variety of questions like "What is he wearing? What is she doing? What is happening? What is he playing with?" It can refer to an activity, an event, a happening, or an object. Read a story aloud and ask your child a variety of "what" questions, guiding him or her to locate the correct answer.

Teach your child that "why" questions ask for reasons. It is like asking, "What is the reason that such and such happened?" Sometimes the answers to "why" questions are stated in the story and sometimes they are not. When dealing with factual questions, look for answers that your child can pick out in the story. The story may tell you *why* the clown was sad. It may state that the clown was sad because the elephant ran away from the circus. Point out that "why" questions are sometimes answered with statements that start with *because*. Practice asking "why" questions, and have your child find the answer. In the beginning, you may have to help your child find the correct response, but after modeling several times, he or she will get the idea and will be able to answer by himself or herself.

Teach your child that "how" questions explain the steps needed to get something done or the method used to do something. Find stories in which some steps or procedures are explained. Guide your child to locate *how* something is done. Have your child tell you *how* the turtle won the race, or *how* the bird escaped from the cat, or *how* cookies are made.

If you find your child has some trouble with any of these question words, you can well imagine what is happening to the child in school when these questions are asked. It gives you a sense of how much we take for granted that children know, and how much instruction is really needed in order for them to be successful.

Twenty Questions

After reading two pages from a story, prepare twenty detail questions for your child. Give your child points for each one correctly answered. Then you read aloud the next two pages of the story, and your child must ask you twenty questions. Have your child award you points for each question correctly answered. At the end, total the scores and see who wins, you or your child.

Question Balloons

Draw six large balloons on large construction or butcher block paper. Label the top of the balloons as "Who?" "What?" "Where?" "When?" "Why?" and "How?" After reading a story, have your child draw a picture in each balloon to answer the questions. For "Who?" have your child draw who the story is about. For "Where?" have your child draw the place where the story takes place. For "When?" have your child draw the time on a clock or calendar as to when the story takes place. For "What?" have your child draw a scene to tell what happened. For "Why?" have your child draw the cause of one of the events of the story. For "How" have your child draw the steps explaining something that took place in the story.

Prove It

Take turns with your child asking detail questions and finding the sentence that contains the answer. You can ask a question and your child has to locate the sentence that contains the answer. Then your child can ask you a question and you have to locate the sentence that contains the answer. Points are given for each correct answer. Total the points and see which of you wins.

Factual Main Idea

Main-idea questions can be of two types. The factual main idea is stated in the story. You can actually locate a sentence that states the main idea. Inferential main ideas are not stated in the story. You have to figure them out from clues given in the story. Factual main ideas are easier to locate than inferential main ideas. But for many children, the concept of a main idea is still a difficult one.

Tell your child that the main idea is "what the story is about." It is the point of the story or a statement summarizing the story in a few words. Details tell you more information about the main idea.

After reading a story, ask your child to tell you in a nutshell what the story is about. Stop them before they go into the details. They should say something like "This story is about a girl who makes it to the top of the highest mountain," or "This story is about a baby lion who runs away from its mother." The main-idea statement will usually contain the main character and what happened to the character.

The hardest part of teaching a main idea is showing the child how to discriminate between a main idea and a detail. The key rule to tell the two apart is, "The detail tells more about the main idea."

One way to teach a main idea is to give your child a group of four words, three of which are details and one of which is the main heading. For example:

>red
>blue
>color
>yellow

Tell your child to decide which of the four words are details and which is the main heading for the rest. They should tell you that the heading is *color*, and that *red*, *blue*, and *yellow* are the details that tell more about the word *color*.

Here is another example:

>lion
>elephant
>giraffe
>animal

See whether your child can pick out the word *animal* as the main idea.

When helping your child select the main idea that is stated in a paragraph, ask your child to locate the sentence that tells what all the rest of the sentences are about. To help your child visualize what you are trying to explain, draw a diagram or map in which each sentence appears in a box. Point to each sentence and ask, "Is this the sentence all the other sentences are describing?" Continue until the child locates the correct main idea.

Explain to your child that the main-idea sentence of a paragraph can appear anywhere. It can be the first sentence, the last sentence, or the middle sentence. Wherever it is, it will tell what the paragraph is about, and all other details will give more information about it.

Find the Main Idea

Use a child's magazine or newsletter, or make copies of pages from one of your child's science or social studies books. Have your child use a marker and find the main idea of each paragraph. Go over your child's responses and explain why your child answered correctly if he or she did so. If your child did not identify the correct main idea, talk about which sentence is the main idea and explain why.

Main-Idea Topics

Give your child a list of words and have him or her find the main-idea topics:

List 1	List 2	List 3
bananas	sports	rain
fruit	baseball	snow
cherries	football	sleet
grapes	basketball	weather

Have your child make up his or her own list of words with a topic for you to figure out.

Time Order

Time-order questions are also called sequencing questions. Usually, in practice exercises in school, events in a story are provided in a mixed-up order, and the student has to put them in correct chronological order. Sometimes an event is named, and the student has to tell what event came before or after it in the story.

Time-order questions are difficult for younger children or for those who are not sequential learners. Young children who do not work in a step-by-step or sequential manner may need to see a concrete representation of the story to succeed with time-order questions. They may have to make a drawing or cartoon of the events of the story in order to put them back together in sequential order.

One technique that works well is locating each sentence listed in the time-order question. They need to go back to the story and underline or mark the sentence where each choice appears. Only after doing this can they number the events that they underlined in the story: 1, 2, 3, and 4. Then they must correlate the first event with the event from the mixed-up list and number the event as 1. Next, they go to the second event underlined, and correlate it with the same event from the mixed-up list, labeling it as 2. Continue in that way until the four events are numbered. This matching activity can help the younger child or those who are not sequential thinkers.

Draw a Time Line

Another approach to teaching time order is telling the child to draw a time line as he or she reads. Each event should be listed on the time line. When the mixed-up events are read, the student can match them to their location on the time line and then put them in the right order.

Time-Order Puzzles

Draw four or five cartoon pictures to illustrate events in the story. Mix them up and have your child try to put the pictures in the correct time order.

Watch Out for Trick Questions

Children need to watch out for one trick question that appears in school exercises: the question that asks the student to put events into *the order in which they appear in the story*. This may or may not be in time order. The events can be written in flashback form in which the story jumps from present to past and back again. The more usual time-order question will ask the student to put the events into chronological order or time order. This would mean that they must be listed from past to present, beginning with the earliest time and proceeding to the latest time. Children must be taught the difference between these two types of questions.

Prediction Questions

Sometimes children are asked to predict what they think will happen next in the story. A prediction question is a way of getting readers involved in a story. It asks them to apply their thinking to figure out what the next event in the story will be. Prediction questions require a higher level of thinking than factual questions. In order to make a prediction, readers must use their knowledge of what has already happened and make an educated guess about what the characters will do next. Readers are asked to step into the story and tell what they would do if they were the character. There is usually no right or wrong answer to a prediction question, but the answer must be logical.

You can give your child practice in making predictions as you read aloud together. After each crisis point in a story, or at the end of each chapter, pause and ask your child to predict what will happen next, and ask your child to explain the reason for his or her prediction. This not only stimulates higher levels of thinking, but also gives your child a reason for wanting to read on in the story—to see if his or her prediction was correct.

Inferential Questions

Inferential questions are usually the hardest ones for students to answer. These are questions that require children to figure out the answers from clues given in the passage and from their own experience. The response is not stated in the passage.

For an inferential question, you have to figure out how a character feels, what motives a character has, why a character did what he or she did, and what the underlying causes for an event were. Here is a sample passage followed by an inferential question:

> Laila's face looked pale. She leaned back in her chair with her eyes closed. She kept rubbing her forehead. While the teacher lectured, Laila put her head down on her desk. Finally, she raised her hand. Her teacher thought she was answering a question, but instead Laila asked, "May I please go to the nurse?"

The question is, "How does Laila feel?"

Nowhere in the passage does it tell you how Laila feels. We only have clues such as that Laila looked pale, Laila kept rubbing her forehead, Laila had her eyes closed at her desk while the teacher was lecturing, and Laila wanted to go to the nurse. We can infer, or take an educated guess, that Laila felt sick. It is not stated in the passage that "Laila felt sick," but we can figure out from the rest of the description that Laila was ill.

Inferring is a skill that takes a higher level of thinking. To become proficient at drawing inferences, children need to have knowledge of nonverbal communication. They need to know that certain facial expressions, tones of voice, and nonverbal gestures indicate a person's state of mind or emotional condition. In my twenty years of teaching, I have noticed that there has been an overall decrease in students' ability to draw inferences in the last few years. Students may be able to locate answers stated in their text, but they have a difficult time figuring out how characters feel or think or what their motives are if it is not stated. In giving this some thought, I came to the conclusion that much of their ability to infer has been lost due to the increased influence that watching television, videos, and movies has had in their lives. If you have ever read a book and then watched the same story portrayed in the movie, one of the key differences you may have noticed is that a book allows you to get inside the thoughts and feelings of a character. The movie version only shows you the action, the dialogue, and the outer facial expressions, gestures, and tones of voice without telling you what they mean. As children watch more and more movies and read fewer and fewer books, they lose the exposure to the underlying thoughts and feelings of the characters in the story. Unless there are adults to engage them in dialogue about the underlying motives, thoughts, and feelings that are expressed by certain nonverbal gestures or tones of voice, they will not be able to figure them out for themselves.

One method that parents can use to provide children with the background knowledge to make inferences is talking to them about the books they are reading and even the movies they watch. Children need to be taught what the various human emotions are and how they are expressed through actions, facial expressions, gestures, and tones of voice. There needs to be discussion about cause-and-effect relationships. When an event happens, discuss what previous actions or events might have caused it, and what the possible results are. Children need to begin to think beyond the face-value action. They need to think of causes and effects. They need to think of the thoughts and feelings of the characters and how they cause certain events to happen.

What is valuable about the skill of drawing inferences? Students often ask this question. I tell them, "We are not learning the skill just to pass a standardized test or a reading checkup at the end of a chapter in the literature book. This skill is used by people in daily life. We use the skill in communicating with and relating to people around us. For example, your brother comes home and slams the door. He throws down his baseball hat and storms upstairs. What can you infer from his behavior? You know that he is upset about something, whether it was due to losing a game or getting into a fight with someone on the team. Your inference that he is upset will guide your behavior toward your brother. You may infer that it is not a good time to ask to borrow his car. Or you may infer that it is a good time to be a friend, talk to him, and help him through his crisis. You may infer that it is a bad time to break the news to him that you have lost his favorite CD that you borrowed. This is one example on how we make inferences in our relationships with others.

"If we become a medical doctor, we may have given our patient a particular treatment. By watching the patient's reaction to the treatment, we will be able to infer whether the medicine is working or not. We will have to make a decision on what to do next based on the data we receive and the inferences we draw from that data. If our inference is correct, the patient will continue to improve. If our inference is not correct, we may be pursuing a treatment that is not helping the patient."

Here are some sample questions you can use to engage your child in conversations that strengthen his or her inferential skills. The conversations can be based on events in your day-to-day life, on a television program or movie you watch together, or on a book that you read together. These experiences are important in helping build your child's abilities to make inferences.

✔ How does the character feel? What makes you think that?

✔ Why did the character do what he or she did?

✔ What caused the character to act this way?

✔ What emotion is the character feeling? Why?

✔ Why do you think this event happened?

✔ What do you think the character will do about this situation?

If you spend time discussing questions like these with your child about events in your daily lives, the child will understand more when he or she reads a book. The experience of reading will be enriched by the background of a character's feelings and emotions that he or she brings to the action. It is the difference in richness of depth and quality that we receive from reading the book as opposed to seeing the movie. Why do people often say the book is better than the movie version? It is the depth of a character's personality, thoughts, and feelings that we read in a book that makes us relate to the character and feel a part of the character's life. Drawing inferences is the ability to get inside people's heads and hearts to understand them better and to relate to them.

Inferring Emotions

To help younger children become familiar with the wide range of human emotions and how they are expressed through the face, cut out pictures from magazines to reflect people's faces when they are experiencing happiness, sadness, anger, joy, depression, guilt, fear, ecstasy, worry, anxiety, tension, etc. Have your child tell you what feelings the person is showing. If you find the child's vocabulary is limited to a few words such as *happy* or *sad*, teach them the variety of words to show the emotions illustrated in the pictures. Discuss what it means to feel that way. Take turns giving examples of times you and the child felt that way. By enriching the child's vocabulary of human emotions, you are opening up a whole new depth of meaning for the child as he or she reads.

Match the Action to the Emotion

Either use pictures of people engaged in action that you cut out from magazines, or show a video movie that portrays people expressing a wide variety of emotions. Have the child match the action to a feeling the person may be having. For example, if the picture shows a runner crossing the finish line first, ask your child, "What do you think this person is feeling?" The child may say, "Happy." After telling the child that he or she has made a correct inference, also guide the child to other choices of words as well, such as thrilled, overjoyed, elated. Even if your child may seem too young for certain vocabulary words, such as *elated*, expose him or her to the words anyway. It may be the only time and place in which the child will learn the word! You will be pleased to hear the child start to use the bigger vocabulary words in his or her speech as well. Here is a list of some actions and some possible responses, although your child may think of other responses that will be just as correct:

Action	Possible Responses
a child falling down	pained, embarrassed, upset
a couple getting married	excited, happy, joyous
a baby's first step	happy, excited, proud
a dog seeing the owner come home	excited, comforted, happy
a boy at a funeral	sad, depressed, fearful
a child snuggled in parents' arms	safe, secure, content

Reverse the activity by having the child cut out the pictures of different actions and write down on the back of each picture the emotion it expresses. Then let the child have you infer the emotions. Let your child tell you if you inferred correctly.

Why Did This Happen?

List a series of events from your daily life, and have your child infer what caused them to happen. Practice inferring by using events in your daily life or by selecting events from a video movie and discussing what caused the selected events to happen.

Here are some examples you may wish to start with in your daily life:

✔ A dish breaks.

✔ Someone falls down outdoors.

✔ A cat is meowing loudly in the middle of the night.

✔ A sibling is crying.

✔ Someone comes home in a happy mood.

✔ The television has static.

✔ The cake in the oven burns.

✔ Neighbors are arguing next door.

For each of the above events, or for each event taken from your own life, have your child give you an explanation as to why he or she thinks it happened. Have your child give you evidence to support his or her reasons. Explain that inferring requires more than guessing; it requires analyzing clues that lead us to think the way we do about a particular happening.

Although you may not know the exact cause of some of these incidents, the exercise will give your child practice in trying to infer possible causes based on his or her background knowledge about the situation.

Inferring Incidents in a Book

From incidents in daily life and movies, move on to practicing drawing inferences from books. Have your child read aloud to you from a fiction story. Periodically stop the reading to ask the child to infer what has caused certain incidents in the book. You may also stop and ask how he or she thinks the character feels. If a character acts in a certain way, ask your child to infer what thoughts or feelings caused that action.

Cause-and-Effect Questions

Often in school, children are asked to identify the relationship between cause and effect. In some cases the cause-and-effect relationship is stated and in some cases it must be inferred. Your child will be presented with an incident and may be asked to find what caused the incident. In other cases, your child will be presented with an incident and will be asked to find what effect that incident will have. This is another difficult skill, as it requires a higher level of thinking. Unless we give our children practice in the thinking skills needed to see cause and effect, they will have difficulty figuring out these kinds of comprehension questions when they read.

"Cause" Questions and "Effect" Questions

In these types of questions, if the cause is stated, the reader has to figure out the effect it has. If the effect is stated, the reader must find the cause. Here are some examples to illustrate what these types of questions are like:

Fluffy was an active cat. She liked to climb the shelves in her owner's house. One day, while climbing, she tipped over a shoebox filled with yarn. Fluffy became frightened and jumped off the shelf, landing in the yarn. Her paw got stuck in the ball of red yarn. The more she tried to pull her paw out, the more stuck she became. She struggled for hours. When the owner came home, he found a big ball of red yarn with whiskers sticking out of it. He did not know what it was until he got closer. Fluffy meowed loudly, and the owner jumped back. He then realized what had happened.

The following is a "cause" question:

> The effect is: Fluffy was covered with yarn.
> What was the cause?

When your child rereads the passage, he or she will find that the cause is stated in this sentence: "The more she tried to pull her paw out, the more stuck she became."
The following is an "effect" question:

> The cause is: Fluffy knocked over a box of yarn.
> What was the effect?

When your child rereads the story, he or she will find that the effect of Fluffy knocking over the box of yarn is Fluffy getting stuck and being covered up with the red yarn.

You can give your child practice with cause-and-effect relationships by citing examples from everyday life. Practice giving your child causes and ask him or her to name the effect it may have. Here are some examples you may start out with:

- ✔ The cake was left too long in the hot oven.
- ✔ The water ran too long in the stopped-up bathtub.
- ✔ No one shoveled the snow from the driveway in front of the garage where the family car is parked.
- ✔ The child forgot to take a packed lunch to school.
- ✔ The car window was left open on a rainy night.

Your child will then name the effect of each of these events.

Conversely, you can give your child a series of effects from everyday life and your child will have to find the cause. Here are some examples:

✔ You are late for work.

✔ The baby came down with a cold.

✔ The car has a flat tire.

✔ The child won an award.

✔ Money was found on the sidewalk in front of your house.

Your child will then need to come up with possible causes for each of the above events.

By practicing these cause-and-effect questions from everyday life, your child will be better able to understand cause-and-effect relationships in stories that he or she reads.

Find the Cause and Effect in Books

After practicing examples from your own life, help your child see the cause-and-effect relationships in books. As you read aloud with your child, stop the child when you find an event that looks like a cause of another event. Have your child name the effect. Also, stop your child when there is an event that looks like an effect and have your child name the cause. In some cases, the cause may be stated in the story. In other cases, it may not be stated, and your child will have to infer or use clues to figure out what the cause was.

The Importance of Recognizing Cause and Effect

Understanding cause and effect helps people use their common sense in day-to-day life. When we know that a certain action will produce a particular effect, we will be more cautious about taking that action. Being aware of cause and effect makes us more thoughtful in our actions and decisions in life. How frustrated parents can become when a child does something without thinking of the results or consequences! Thinking about cause and effect helps us to raise children who are more aware of the effects they have on others. They also become aware of the effect people's actions have on each other and on society. Unless someone guides children to understand these relationships, they will not necessarily come to understand them on their own. They may have to learn cause and effect the hard way, by trial and error in their own lives, if they learn it at all. We can help our children learn responsibility and gain awareness of the effects that actions and events have on life by giving them practice in cause-and-effect relationships.

THE BENEFITS OF TEACHING OUR CHILDREN COMPREHENSION SKILLS

Although comprehension is a skill area on which our children are tested, graded, and measured in school, the purpose of mastering this skill is not only for a grade. Comprehension is an essential component of the reading process. Without comprehension, reading is a mechanical act of sounding out letters and words. Comprehension is the communication between the writer and the reader, in which the reader makes meaning out of the symbols on a page to understand the author's message. Comprehension is thinking about and interacting with the thoughts of the writer and developing one's own ideas and thoughts about a subject.

Comprehension is the ability to think. Besides being essential to reading, comprehension skills help us analyze, assess, interpret, and interact with the events in our lives. They help us develop a higher level of thinking ability. We no longer become passive viewers of life, but come up with our own opinions, thoughts, and ideas that we can express to others. We are able to make sense out of the world around us.

By taking the time to help our children develop comprehension skills, we can help them develop their thinking abilities so that they can reach their highest potential. We are creating human beings who can think deeply and clearly about the world around them, about life, and about themselves.

Chapter 18

How to Diagnose Problems With Independent Reading Strategies

Our knowledge of independent reading strategies has grown out of analyzing what good readers do. Studies have isolated certain strategies used by people who read well. From this analysis, educators can try to teach all students those strategies in the hope that they too will develop into good readers.

In some schools, students are taught the strategies to be independent readers at an early age. In other schools, the strategies are not taught at all. To better understand what independent reading strategies are, let us use the example of sports. If you are learning to play tennis, you will study the moves that professional tennis players make. You may watch a certain series of steps or movements that make up the serve. You repeat the movements in your head and hope these thoughts will guide your body to follow through with the correct action. In reading also there are a series of steps one can follow in order to read better. These steps are not actions, though. The steps are thoughts or questions that one asks oneself as one reads. These steps are designed to help readers when they become stuck on a word that they do not know.

The basic questions a good reader asks when stuck on a word are as follows:

1. What sounds do I know in this word?

2. Are there any picture clues that can help me figure out the word?

3. What word would make sense here?

4. If I reread the sentence or read ahead, are there any other clues that would help me figure out the word?

You may wonder, why would anyone go to all the trouble of asking these questions when the reader can just "sound out" the word? That is a valid question. These strategies come in handy in the following situations:

✔ The student has not yet learned all the sounds, but wants to keep reading to figure out the story.

✔ The reader does not want to stop reading to spend time on figuring out the word, because it stops the flow of the reading.

✔ The reader has sounded out a new word, but does not know the correct pronunciation or on which syllable to place the stress. As a result, the child cannot recognize the mispronounced word as familiar.

By combining knowledge of letter-sound relationships and independent reading strategies, the child can read a wider variety of materials without the assistance of parents and teachers.

DIAGNOSING INDEPENDENT READING STRATEGIES

Find a reading selection from material that your child has not yet read. You may pick a reading textbook from school and use a passage from the end of the book. You want material that will be slightly more difficult than your child's reading level. You may have to use something in the next grade level up. For this you may have to borrow a book from the school or from an older student. The key to the selection lies in picking text in which there will be some unfamiliar words.

Have your child read a story aloud. For this exercise, you want to see what your child does when he or she comes across a new or difficult word. You also want to observe what the child does when he or she makes an error in reading.

Watch for the following:

1. What does your child do when he or she comes across new words in the text?
   ✔ Does the child skip the new word?
   ✔ Does the child say the first letter and make up another word that begins with the letter even though it does not make sense?
   ✔ Does the child say the first letter and make up another word that begins with the letter that does make sense in that sentence?
   ✔ Does the child ask you to tell him or her the word?
   ✔ Does the child look it up in the glossary or dictionary?
   ✔ Does the child become frustrated and stop reading?
   ✔ Does the child make up another word that does not begin with the same letter?
   ✔ Does the child read the rest of the sentence and come back to the word to try to figure it out?
   ✔ Does the child reread the sentence a few times until he or she finds the word that makes sense?

2. What does your child do when he or she misreads a word or makes an error in reading?
   ✔ Does the child misread a word and go on as if it were correct?
   ✔ Does the child misread a word, stop, and realize that it was the wrong word but does nothing about it?
   ✔ Does the child misread the word, stop, and ask you to help him or her with the word?

✔ Does the child misread the word, stop, and try to figure it out by looking at the letters in the word?

✔ Does the child misread the word, stop, and try to figure it out by rereading the sentence to see what word would make sense?

✔ Does the child misread the word, stop, and use a picture clue to figure out the right word?

✔ Does the child misread the word, stop, and use a combination of looking at letter clues and rereading to see what makes sense?

ANALYZING THE RESULTS

If your child tries to figure out the new word by using picture clues, the letters in the word, rereading or reading the rest of the sentence to see which word would make sense, then your child has good independent reading strategies. If your child recognizes that he or she has made a mistake because what was read does not make sense, then that is another sign that your child has good strategies for independent reading. But if your child does not know what to do with a new word, does not recognize that he or she has made a mistake and is not making sense, then he or she needs some instruction on what good reading strategies are. If your child asks you to assist with the missed word, or becomes frustrated and wants to stop reading, that is also a signal that it is time to teach your child these good strategies for reading independently.

Chapter 19

Remedy for Problems With Independent Reading Strategies

The first step in teaching your child independent reading strategies is to explain to your child, "There are certain habits that good readers have that you can also learn. These are steps they follow to read without the help of their parents and teachers. If you learn these steps, you can read on your own without any help. That means you can read whatever you want to read and you will be able to figure out new words for yourself."

TEACHING YOUR CHILD HOW TO FIGURE OUT NEW WORDS

In the chapters on letter-sound relationships and vocabulary, you learned how to help your child sound out words and figure out their meanings from context. This independent reading skill of figuring out new words is slightly different. It will come in handy when your child encounters words that are beyond the letter-sound relationship skills they have learned, words that have an irregular pronunciation, or words that the child cannot figure out from his or her knowledge of word parts, prefixes, and suffixes.

Explain to your child that there are words that do not fit the letter-sound relationships he or she has learned. There are words that are irregular, or words that have meanings not covered in their earlier lessons. Tell your child that these are the steps they can take to try to figure out what he or she is reading:

Step 1: Figure out as much of the word as you can from the letter-sound relationships you already know.

Step 2: Look at any picture clues for help with the unknown word.

Step 3: Read the rest of the sentence and possibly the next sentence for context clues as to what word with those letters would make sense.

Step 4: Reread the entire sentence several times, making the sounds of the letters of the unknown word as well as you can, until a word that sounds familiar and logical pops into your head.

For example, the child comes across this sentence:

The little boy held on to his father's hand.

If the child does not know how to read the word *little*, have him or her reread the sentence as follows:

The l＿＿＿ boy held on to his father's hand.

Tell your child to ask himself or herself, "What word do I know that starts with the *l* sound that would make sense here?" Your child may come up with *large* or *little*.

Next, ask your child to name the letter after *l*. Your child will say *i*. Ask your child whether *large* or *little* has an *i* after the *l*. Your child may be able to tell you that *little* has an *i* sound. Have your child see whether there are other letters in the word *little* that match the word in the sentence.

This question-and-answer technique may seem a bit tedious, and you may be tempted to just tell your child the answer, but please have patience and restrain yourself! By going through this dialogue with your child, you are training him or her to ask these questions of himself or herself. After repeatedly going through this back-and-forth dialogue, your child will mimic you and begin to ask these questions of himself or herself. You are training your child how to analyze the situation alone and figure out the word. Remember, you will not always be with your child in school when he or she encounters new words. By training him or her to ask these questions, you are developing an independent reader.

HOW TO TEACH YOUR CHILD TO SPOT MISCUES

Spotting errors in one's own reading is also called self-monitoring. A child needs to be aware of when they make an error in reading so that they can take steps to correct the mistake. There are two ways for a child to spot errors in reading. One is to recognize that what they just read did not make any sense. The second is to check the word that they read with the spelling of the word on the printed page.

To detect whether the word made sense, the child needs to comprehend what is being read. If you have successfully taught your child the comprehension skills described in the earlier chapter, they will be picturing what they read as their eyes travel across the printed words on the page. If the picture in their mind does not make sense, or there is an error in the sentence structure or syntax, the child needs to be taught to stop reading, look more closely at the word, and figure it out.

Miscues of unimportant words do not matter that much in terms of understanding the meaning of the sentence. For example, often while reading along, readers will substitute *a* for *the*, *the* for *these*, or *on* for *upon*. These are considered minor miscues and will not interfere with your child's comprehension of the passage. But if your child misses significant words that affect the meaning of the passage, tell them to stop and try to figure out a word that makes more sense and matches the spelling of the word on the page.

For example, if the sentence says, "The boy fell on the ground," and your child reads, "The boy fell on the garden," ask them, "Can someone fall *on* a garden, or do they fall *in* the garden?" From their knowledge of the spoken language, they will hear the mistake. Then instruct your child to think of another word that starts with *g* that makes sense and to look at the other letters in the word *g-r-o-u-n-d*. If your child knows the *gr* pattern and the sound of *ou*, they should come up with *grou* and say, "The boy fell on the grou——." Tell them to search their memories for other words that would make sense there. If your child does not know the *gr* pattern or the *ou* pattern, ask your child to think of other places that start with *g* on which someone can fall. Guide your child to the answer, but try not to say it except as a last resort. You can ask leading questions such as "What do we walk on?" They may say, "Grass." Then say, "Okay, let us check it against the word *g-r-o-u-n-d*. What does *grass* end with?" They should be able to tell you that it ends with *s*. Tell them to check whether *g-r-o-u-n-d* ends with *s*. They will say that it does not. Then ask, "What other names do we have for what we walk on or fall on?" Continue this line of discussion until they come up with the word *ground*. When they suggest the word *ground*, again ask them to check what sound *ground* ends with. They should be able to say that it ends with *d* or *nd*. Have them check it against the spelling of *g-r-o-u-n-d*. They will discover it ends the same way.

Tell your child that these questions you are asking are questions that they should learn how to ask themselves in order to be a good independent reader. Continue this process over a period of weeks and even months. This process of questioning will become a part of your child's thinking.

As parents and teachers, we can monitor the child's errors when they read aloud, but as the child grows, they will be reading silently in school and at home more and more and will need to monitor themselves for errors. Listening for whether their reading makes sense will provide the child continual and immediate feedback on whether their reading is correct. In sports, a child knows when they have dropped a ball. In music, they know when a wrong note has been hit on the flute or guitar or piano. Similarly, in reading, a child needs to learn when a wrong word has been hit and what to do to correct it.

Chapter 20

Reading as a Pleasurable Activity

Throughout the entire process of helping your child with letter-sound relationships, vocabulary, comprehension, and independent reading strategies, there is one underlying principle that must run like a thread through beads: Reading should be a pleasurable activity. While all these skills are being taught, the act of reading and the material read should be enjoyable for the child if we want him or her to develop into a lifelong reader. You may wonder how you can combine the teaching of skills and fun. It is definitely possible. First we must understand what constitutes "fun" and "enjoyment."

Those who study human motivation have found certain ingredients need to be present in order for a person to experience an act as pleasurable, enjoyable, or fun. These ingredients are:

- ✔ interest
- ✔ recognition and approval
- ✔ a challenge that can be met
- ✔ emotional satisfaction
- ✔ comfort and security
- ✔ a sense of belonging
- ✔ a sense of gaining power over one's life

✔ a sense of accomplishment

✔ the satisfaction of curiosity

✔ having novel or unique experiences

Let us look at each of these areas and see how reading can meet these criteria.

INTEREST

Each person has particular interests in life. For some these may include sports, an art, a hobby, a famous person, history, animals, or a branch of science. When we have an interest, we want to know more about that subject. It is important that parents be aware of their children's interests in order to provide them with books in those fields. We ourselves know how we would rather read a book of our own choice than one that is assigned to us or given to us by someone else. At times we may take the recommendation of others about a good book or magazine article. But we like to be the ones who have the freedom to decide whether to take their suggestions. Children are no different. They like to choose their own books according to their interests. Our role is to guide them to the places where they can find the books that interest them.

No matter what your child's interest, there will be reading matter on that subject. Any interest can be a springboard for a reading experience. For example, I have worked with students who were referred to me by other teachers. They would tell me that these children had never read a book in their lives and they had no interests. Of course, when a teacher is the "last resort" or "last hope" for a child's progress, they cannot throw up their hands in defeat. Taking a positive attitude and believing that every child has some talent, interest, or hobby that can be used as a base for a reading list, I get to know my students. I talk to them about what they do after school or during their vacation time. I give them questionnaires to find out everything under the sun in which they have some knowledge or interest. Even the most obstinate of students will tell me that they enjoy "listening to music" or "playing video games." That is all I need to know. I will dig further to find out what kind of music or what kind of video games. They are now like flies caught in a spider's web—there is no escape for them. We go to the library to find books and magazines about these favorite subjects. The music lovers return with books and magazines on their favorite musicians, music reviews about their favorite records, or books on how to play electric guitar or how to be a disc jockey. The video game players return with books and articles on video games, or instruction manuals on how to play a video game they never played before. There is always something for everyone. Before they read the material, we discuss some questions they hope to have answered by reading the book. This gives them a designated purpose for reading. I have yet to see a student refuse to read a book or magazine on a topic in which he or she is interested.

Following the same principles, you can list your child's skills, interests, and hobbies. You know your child better than anyone else. Then guide your child toward books and magazines or even newspaper articles along those lines. Let those materials be the ones with which you do the practice activities suggested in this book. In this way they are not only practicing their new skills, but enjoying the topic. Your child will become so involved in the article, he or she will want to continue reading even by himself or herself in order to learn more about his or her favorite subject.

Here are some interests young people may have and books that would match those interests:

Interest	Book Subjects
drawing	how-to art books
	lives of famous artists
football	how to play better football
	biographies of football players
	books about teams
	history of football
clothing	fashion design how-to books
	how clothing is made
	how to make clothing
	books about fashion designers
	fiction books about fashion designers
computers	computer instruction books
	history of computers
	computer careers
airplanes	history of airplanes
	how to make paper airplanes
	famous aviators
	types of aircraft
	how planes fly
	fiction books involving flying
gymnastics	books about the Olympics
	biographies of gymnasts
	how to be a gymnast
science	how to do experiments
	nonfiction on different topics
	biographies of scientists
	science fiction

These are but a few examples to get you started. You can also go to your local library or bookstore and ask for suggested books on the topics that interest your child. Then have your child pick out the ones he or she wants to read. You may wish to buy a subscription to a magazine that contains articles on your child's hobby. Keep your eye open for newspaper articles on the subject. If your child resists, explain, "You will need to put in time reading for practice anyway, so why not read something you like?" They will see your point!

RECOGNITION AND APPROVAL

One need that human beings have is to receive recognition, whether it be quiet appreciation or public fame. Some people enjoy the public limelight for their accomplishments, while others wish simple appreciation and approval from the significant people in their lives for their accomplishments. Reading should be an opportunity to give your child appreciation and approval for his or her success. At all costs, you want to prevent reading time from becoming a time for discouragement and a sense of failure. You do not want it to be a time in which the child leaves the session feeling as though he or she has failed or has earned your disapproval. You can add to your child's sense of pleasure from reading by making sure they receive your appreciation and approval. How can you do this? You must celebrate your child's every success. No matter how small it is, you should appreciate whatever your child has done successfully. Every time your child reads with you, you should find at least one positive thing he or she has done. You should state the positive in a specific term so that your child knows what act he or she has done well. In this way, he or she will know what behavior to repeat the next time.

As stated earlier in the discussion of self-esteem (Chapter 4), you should accompany your positive statement with positive body language. There should be a smile on your face, soft and approving tones in your voice, and caring body language. The child will derive pleasure from your approval statements and gestures and will wish to return another time for a reading session to experience that pleasure again. Whenever I have given approval, appreciation, and recognition to my students for their reading success, I have found they wanted to read with me again and again. They would often show up at my room at unscheduled times of day in order to have more of my time and the approval I gave them. They would find ways to get a pass from their teacher on some flimsy excuse just to come to my room to work with me, even though it was not their scheduled time to do so. When I analyzed this frequently occurring phenomenon, I realized it was because they enjoyed having someone appreciate, respect, and approve of them.

You will be amazed at the wonders you will bring about by giving your child approval during the reading practice sessions or the shared reading sessions. You will be building a strong foundation of love for reading out of your child's need for recognition and approval.

A CHALLENGE THAT CAN BE MET

Another factor that contributes to the pleasure of an experience is that it presents a challenge that engages a person yet is not so difficult that it cannot be successfully met. If a task is too simple, a person loses interest and walks away saying, "That's boring," or "That's too easy." If a task is slightly more difficult, a person wants to attempt it, as if it were a game or a chance to see if one's abilities can rise to the occasion.

There is a sense of accomplishment when one has undertaken a difficult task and accomplished it successfully. But if a task is so difficult that it is impossible to achieve, then frustration sets in and a person either gives up in midstream or decides never to attempt such a task again.

When it comes to reading, we want to avoid presenting a challenge that is so Herculean and so impossible that the child gives up and decides that he or she hates reading, and never wants to try it again. Thus, we do not want to present the child with reading material or tasks that are so far beyond their ability level that they become frustrated. We also do not want to provide reading materials that are so easy that the child says, "This is baby stuff." It is a delicate balancing act in which we provide—or rather help the child select—materials that are going to be within his or her range of capabilities, but with a slightly higher level of difficulty to present a challenge. When we assist the child and teach him or her the necessary skills, the child will feel a sense of accomplishment and mastery that he or she was able to meet the challenge.

Earlier it was mentioned that there are three levels at which people can work: independent level, instructional level, and the frustration level. Independent level is the level at which the child can read independently without difficulty. Independent level is good when the child is reading for enjoyment. He or she can breeze through the material with ease. We want some of the books to be at this level so that the child can gain the practice needed to become a quick, fluent reader. But we do not want all the materials to be at independent level. If all the books the child reads are at this level, then the child is not being challenged with harder vocabulary, or more difficult and complex word patterns, such as those that are found in multisyllable words. The child needs to see more difficult words repeatedly in order for them to become easily recognizable. The more a child reads a word, the more a child will recognize it. In this way, we move a child up to higher and higher levels.

Thus, we want to offer the child materials at instructional level. This means that the basic material is at the child's level, but harder vocabulary words, more complex word patterns, and higher levels of ideas are being presented. While a child reading at independent level will make zero or one mistake per hundred words of reading, at instructional level they should make from two to four or so mistakes. That means there are two to four challenges per hundred words that the child can undertake, and after successfully figuring out those challenges, the child will have had exposure to some new items that will then become part of his or her normal reading vocabulary. If you look at school textbooks in reading, you will find that about ten new words are introduced in each new chapter. It should be the same for reading material you use with your child at home. Thus, help your child select materials that will have about a dozen new words so that your child will grow from the reading. Your child will feel good when he or she is able to read material that is slightly harder than the previous books. This sense of accomplishment adds to the enjoyment the child will get from reading.

How do you select a book from the library or bookstore? I have always taught my students to do two things: one is to read the blurb on the back cover or the inside flaps to see if the book is about a subject that will interest them; and the second is to read a paragraph or page from the beginning of the book and see whether it looks too easy, too difficult, or just right. I explain that "just right" means that they know most of the words, yet there are a few new words for them to figure out. If they find themselves struggling with every word, then the book is too hard. If they read through it and find the words too simple, then it may be for those reading at an easier level. If they read through most of the words with ease and occasionally find a word that they have to figure out, then that could be the book for them.

EMOTIONAL SATISFACTION

To add to the pleasurable experience of reading, the child should have emotional satisfaction. This can be provided in several ways. There is emotional satisfaction from the loving experience that comes with shared reading. When a parent reads with a child, the child should feel a sense of love, warmth, and caring. The child will begin to associate reading with a loving experience. Parents who take their children in their laps and read books to them from their infancy are building a foundation of positive, emotional bonding during the reading act. Whether or not the child has learned to speak yet, they will subconsciously remember reading as an experience in which they felt warm and loved. Many children who were read to in this warm, caring way grew up to be people who loved to read.

Therefore, as parents, we want to make sure that children associate reading time with positive emotions. It needs to be a time when we leave our stresses and strains at the door. We need to be in a calm, cool, and upbeat mood. If we are angry, impatient, distracted, or distraught, it is not a good time to read with our child. We want to build a feeling that reading time is a time when they feel loved and cared for.

In schools, many teachers from elementary school to high school have instituted a time in which they read to their class. It has been found to be a positive experience even for high school students. Besides being an opportunity to hear good writing read to them, it is also a time when they experience a closeness, a sharing, and a warmth between them and their teacher, as well as between them and their classmates. It is important for a parent to create this same kind of environment during reading time at home. Whether it is a shared reading time or a time for you to help the child with skills, your attitude should be loving, warm, and supportive. This will help your child to associate reading with positive emotions.

Another way students can derive emotional satisfaction is by reading books that address their emotional needs. Books in which the main characters deal with emotional issues can help children work through their own feelings and problems. Once children gain the skill of comprehension, they will find a whole new world opening up for them. They will meet characters just like them. They will realize that other people go through the same problems and crises they are going through. By relating to a character with difficulties who ultimately finds a solution, they can discover ways to solve their own problems. There is one area of reading, called "bibliotherapy," in which children work through their own problems by reading about the problems of characters in books. Reading can put your child in the company of many people from the past and the present, from many countries around the world, and from many backgrounds who have lived through the same problems.

Even if a child does not have major problems, they will experience the emotions and feelings of the characters, including the satisfaction, relief, and joy the character feels when his or her problem is resolved. They will be transported into another world through reading and will learn the happiness and satisfaction they can experience through books.

COMFORT AND SECURITY

Along with providing children with an opportunity to feel loved and cared for during reading time, we can also provide them with a sense of comfort and security. Feeling safe adds to the experience of pleasure. Each of us does not have to think hard to recall the sensation of feeling threatened, fearful, or uncomfortable. Can we enjoy anything in that state? On the other hand, when we feel safe, secure, and comfortable, we are in a better frame of mind to experience pleasure and joy.

Children will have better associations with reading if they feel comfortable, secure, and unthreatened. Parents can provide this type of environment for their child in several ways. Comfort can be physical or emotional. For physical comfort, we can make sure the temperature of the room is not too hot or too cold. We can make sure the spot selected for reading is physically comfortable. A soft, stuffed easy chair may be more comfortable than a hard dining room chair. Some children prefer to stretch out on the floor with pillows.

While physical comfort can add to the enjoyment the child has while reading, parents can make their child comfortable emotionally by eliminating fear and threats. We have to make reading time a time in which the child feels free from being harmed by abusive words or negative nonverbal signals. If a child experiences any of these negative reactions, they may start to resist reading.

There are many ways that parents unknowingly make a child feel fearful and threatened. If a child makes a mistake and the parent reacts by making fun of the child, putting the child down, or criticizing the child, it is a form of verbal abuse that the child will associate with reading time. If the child's feelings are hurt or the child fears being reprimanded or punished for mistakes, the child will begin to associate those feelings with reading. The tendency then will be to resist reading time. They will feel, "Whenever I read with my parents, they get angry with me and criticize or scold me. I would rather not read with them so as to avoid those bad feelings I get."

Parents need to be on continuous guard against making their children feel threatened or fearful. Children need to be taught that it is okay to make mistakes, that errors are a part of learning, and that mistakes are a way for us to learn what actions not to repeat the next time. They need to know that they are still worthy and valuable even if they make a mistake. If you find yourself becoming frustrated with your child, you need to hide it. Take a deep breath, change activities, take a walk, but under no circumstances should you make your child feel uncomfortable or threatened. Needless to say, we definitely do not want to hit or strike our child out of anger or frustration, because that may be the death knell for the child's feelings about reading. We want to keep the reading experience positive, safe, and comforting.

Sometimes a child who is a perfectionist is hard on himself or herself for making a mistake. The parent needs to counteract this by letting the child know that it is all right to make mistakes, that we all make mistakes, and that we do not have to put ourselves down for it.

Our tone of voice can go a long way in making the child feel safe. If we speak with soft tones, with gentleness, and with patience, the child will relax and be more comfortable. If our voice is harsh, angry, impatient, and critical, the child will feel uncomfortable and will start to feel threatened, and those emotions will become a hindrance that may interfere with the child's ability to concentrate on reading. Over time the child may develop a dislike for reading, not because of the reading process itself, but because of the bad experiences associated with it due to feeling threatened or fearful of criticism or verbal attack.

A SENSE OF BELONGING

In the field of education, attention is being given to making children feel that they belong to a group. A sense of belonging adds to one's self-esteem and self-worth. It is feared that if children do not gain a sense of belonging to positive class-room experiences, they will look for other peer groups per-haps, or some even turn to gangs or groups that engage in behaviors that are harmful to themselves and others. The responsibility of parents and teachers lies in helping children feel that they belong. How do we do this? The child has to feel respected, valued, and appreciated. If these elements exist in a relationship, the child will return to that group again and again because of the good feelings they receive.

Parents can give their child a sense of belonging by appre-ciating, valuing, and respecting them. During reading time, the child can be made to feel respected and valued. If we talk to them with respect for their ideas and feelings, if we make pos-itive comments about what they say and think, and show that we like who they are, they will enjoy that time. They will wish to return again and again to that shared reading time. We must always be on guard to avoid making any comments that will make them feel that they are not respected and valued. It is sad that although one positive comment does not build a long-term relationship, one negative comment can destroy it. A long-term relationship requires many positive comments over a long period of time. Once that relationship is solidly established, it can endure a negative comment here and there, because both parties know the deep feelings they have for each other. But until the long-term positive relationship is established, there is little toleration for even a single negative comment. Without the solid positive relationship, we can turn off a child from reading by speaking in a way that shows the child we do not respect or value them.

What are some ways to show that we value our children? When they talk to us, we can listen attentively and with inter-est. We should affirm them by letting them know we have heard what they said and that we understand how they feel. We may or may not agree with them, but by affirming them with comments that show that we listened, that we understand how they feel, and that we care, they will know that they are valued. Even when disagreeing, we can let them know that we understand how they feel, even though we may not feel that way ourselves. In our dialogue with them about the books or the skills on which we are working, we can listen to them with respect and consideration. They will get the message that they are important to their parents and will respond by returning again and again to the reading sessions.

A sense of belonging to the family through reading is a powerful tool. Reading time has to compete with television and video games. Television and video games may be initially more entertaining, but if we provide children with the pleasure of belonging and the positive feelings of being valued and respected, we will be giving them much more than they can get from a dead video game or television set. The television and computer cannot provide those kinds of feelings. I have seen children who chose reading or working with me over seeing movies or playing games in their classroom. Why? Because feeling valued and respected is more pleasurable and fulfilling than watching a screen that does not respond to you as a person. If television has attracted the attention of millions of children for six or seven hours a day, could it be because no one is offering them anything better to meet their needs? Look at the rare child who would rather work on a project, read a book, develop a talent, or spend time with his or her family than watch television. They are deriving pleasure from the activity, and that pleasure is a result of a sense of self-worth, achievement, and emotional satisfaction. If we are to counteract the effects of television, we must provide something more that the child cannot get from the box. By providing time in which the child feels valued and respected and cared for, we are offering them a powerful alternative to television. If we make sure they feel good during reading time, they will develop a love of reading because of the positive feelings they derive from that activity.

A Sense of Gaining Power Over One's Life

Having power and control over one's life and destiny is a human motivator. Power in this sense does not mean over people but over one's own life. The opposite is feeling powerless. We feel powerless when we cannot do a task, when we feel we have no control over a situation, or when we feel others can do things we cannot do.

Children also want to have some power and control over their lives. We can teach them that knowledge is also a form of power, and we can help our children understand the following ways in which knowledge can empower us:

- ✔ When we become good readers and learn to study well, we become more proficient and our classwork becomes easier. We will not have to spend extra time doing schoolwork or making up work and tests in which we did poorly; this leaves more free time to do other activities that we enjoy.

- ✔ When we are at the top of our class, sometimes we are selected for special opportunities, and more choices are available to us.

- ✔ Those who do well can win scholarships to help pay college tuition costs and have a better chance of being accepted to the school of their choice.

- ✔ To stay on a sports team in school, we may have to keep our grades up to a certain standard or we cannot play on that team.

- ✔ Knowledge opens up more doors for us and gives us more choices.

✔ Reading helps us learn more about a variety of different subjects and helps us find different fields that interest us.

✔ Those who do well in school have a better chance of doing well in college or vocational school and a better chance of getting a good job, which in turn may pay better money and give us a better standard of living.

✔ Those who do well have more choice in the type of career they pursue and have more opportunity to work at something they really enjoy.

While knowledge and learning bring their own intrinsic rewards, there are other benefits, many of which can give a person more control and power over one's own life. The feeling of being master of one's destiny is a positive one and can add to the enjoyment one experiences at a task. If children can master reading, they will have a sense of power and control over a difficult task. For some, this is a satisfying experience that adds to the pleasure of reading.

Merely talking about the power and control children can gain from reading may give them an awareness, but will not give them that experience. The experience will come when they are successful at reading. Parents can provide the environment and the assistance to help them be successful. The satisfaction from being in control by reading successfully will come as a by-product.

A Sense of Accomplishment

We all know how we feel when we accomplish a difficult task. Whether it is building a piece of furniture, playing tennis, knitting, taking a course in school after many years, doing well in the stock market, or succeeding at a new career, we experience the thrill of doing well at something we never dreamed we could do. Children experience the same joy from doing well and accomplishing a task that was difficult.

We can provide continual opportunities for our children to derive a sense of accomplishment. Each time we present a challenge and give our children the skills to meet it, we have set the stage for them to experience satisfaction. Remember, we do not want to overwhelm them with something that is impossible for them to achieve at their level. We want to offer them a slight challenge and then teach them what they must do to succeed. Every time our children experience success, we have added to their enjoyment of the reading process. They will look forward to the next challenge eagerly and will continue to do their best to achieve it. They want to repeat the enjoyable experience, just as they like to return to their video games day after day. It is not the game that is exciting—it is the thrill of the challenge and trying to win against odds. When they do win, it is satisfying because they beat the odds with their own skill. Reading can provide a challenge as well; and the same enjoyment they receive from winning at a game, they can have from mastering challenging skills. That challenge can be reading a more difficult book. Young children are excited when they move from picture books to "chapter books." It gives them a sense of accomplishment to move up a level in reading. Older children may find satisfaction in getting higher grades because they have improved their reading and study skills.

Even though some children may appear too "cool" to admit to receiving satisfaction from doing well in reading, do not let their outer bravado fool you. Inside they are as human as the rest of us. They love to do well and to feel the sense of accomplishment. We can provide opportunities for them to experience this by presenting them with challenges and helping them to succeed at them.

THE SATISFACTION OF CURIOSITY

Watch infants or young children. See how they explore the world around them. They want to touch everything in sight. They want to break away from the parent's hold to check out everything around them. They seem to enjoy playing with objects that hold absolutely no interest for us. They have an innate curiosity that drives them to investigate the world around them.

That curiosity does not die at a certain age. We know that each of us is curious about the unknown. We may want to find out whether there really is life on Mars, or whether our next-door neighbor is expecting another baby. See how our curiosity is peaked by coming attractions in a movie theater, or by the teasers for the upcoming news magazine programs on television, or by the blurb of a best-selling novel.

School-age children are also curious, and we can harness that trait to engage them in reading. We need to find out what they are curious about and provide them with the right materials to satisfy that curiosity.

In education, there is a practice called anticipatory reading that has become part of most classrooms. Using anticipatory reading, the stage is set to motivate the children to read. This is accomplished by stimulating the children's curiosity to read a certain selection. They may look at the illustrations or the chapter headings and come up with their own questions on what they hope to learn from the chapter. Even during the reading process, they are asked to predict what they think will happen next. Naturally, they become curious to see whether their prediction was accurate. This spurs them to read on.

We can generate interest by using our child's natural curiosity. We can discuss topics of interest to the child and find out what questions the child would like answered about the subject. Then we can guide the child to reading materials that would provide some answers. We can present books that arouse their interest and have them think of questions they hope the book will answer. As we read with them, we can ask them to make predictions about what they think will happen next in the book, and then read on with them to see if they were correct.

Keep an ear open for topics in which your child shows interest, and have him or her list a series of questions or mysteries related to the subject. Then look for books in which he or she may find answers to those questions. Children's innate curiosity can work as a catalyst to lead them to explore books.

NOVEL OR UNIQUE EXPERIENCES

What do you remember best—those things that were presented in a unique or novel way, or those routine things that were repeated or presented in the same way over and over again? We perk up when we hear or see something presented in a unique and novel manner. Advertising companies thrive on finding new ways to sell us the same product over and over again. Our interest is engaged when we see something different.

We can use that same principle to stimulate our child's interest in reading. We can find novel or unique ways to activate their interest in reading. For example, throughout this book you learned a variety of ways to present skills. We used color, sound, games, movement, the sense of taste, imagination, visualization, the sense of touch, kinesthetic activities, and emotion. To a child who is used to learning only through lecture methods or seeing the printed work and copying from a board, these are unique and novel approaches. By varying the way we present materials or skills, we can pique their interest. Also, we need to make sure we *continue* to vary the activities. Even if something is new one day, if we keep repeating the same activity, that too will become old. As soon as we see our child tiring of something or complaining that it is boring, we need to alter the approach to reignite their interest.

We can help ensure that our child remembers what they learn by doing our best to present it in a new and interesting way.

Chapter 21

Hope for Your Child's Progress

Although there are a large variety of reading difficulties, the categories in this book—letter-sound relationships, vocabulary, comprehension, and independent reading strategies—cover a large portion of them. Having taught reading for over twenty years and having worked with elementary, middle, and high school students as well as adults with reading problems, I know that a majority of reading problems can be resolved by using these simple methods of diagnosis and remediation. I have seen students accelerate one, two, and even three years in their reading levels by using these methods for even one year.

When a child has an undiagnosed reading problem, several main things happen: the child feels like a failure, their self-esteem drops, they resist reading, and their reading level drops progressively from year to year.

We know how we ourselves resist doing what we cannot do well. Similarly, children who are not given the instruction they need in reading and begin to fail will resist reading. They will feel like a failure, and they will begin the cycle of continual failure. They will not want to try because they feel there is no hope. By working with them to reteach skills they missed, they will begin to feel successful again. They will see that they can do it. It is important to make them feel that they do not have a reading problem because they are "stupid," but because there are some steps they missed along the way. By backtracking and reteaching those steps, the students will begin to see they are not "dumb," and that they are in control again. They will feel great about themselves when they can retrace their steps and begin their climb up the stairs.

Studies have shown that reading progress also depends upon time spent in reading. Good readers spend at least ten minutes every day reading for pleasure. Reading is a skill that needs to be practiced, just as one must exercise daily to be physically fit. Every time someone reads, they increase their speed and their ability to comprehend. But every time students "struggle read," or have trouble reading the words or understanding the meaning, they are not increasing their reading ability. That means that those ten minutes of reading are not moving them ahead, for they are not understanding the words or the meaning of the passage.

To increase reading speed and comprehension, they should be reading ten minutes per day at independent level, or at best, instructional level. Each day that children read at frustration level, they are not reading at a point that will increase their speed and progress.

To ensure that our child reads daily at independent level, we need to let them read materials for pleasure that are not too difficult. While the materials they use during instructional time should be at their instructional level, the child should be allowed to read for a minimum of ten minutes daily from materials of their choice that they can read independently. Let them choose books of interest to them. In the beginning, to develop their interest, let them even read books that look a bit easier for them. Initially, they need that feeling of success. It is only when reading becomes enjoyable that they will wish to continue to pursue it as a lifetime reader. By making the reading task easy, we increase the likelihood that they will keep reading. This continual exposure to reading will automatically improve their reading ability.

As they progress, develop confidence, and start to enjoy reading, then we can start to challenge them with materials that have more difficult words and more complex ideas. We must walk a continual tightrope, avoiding material that is too easy and material that is so difficult that they become frustrated and give up. We need to always watch the balance so that they are presented with materials that can be read with ease, yet with just enough new words, new patterns, or new ideas to challenge them and give them more exposure to higher levels of skills.

No reader is hopeless. Every child, with proper instruction and guidance, can become a successful reader. As parents, you can help diagnose and pinpoint your child's problem and remedy the situation. We owe it to ourselves to give the gift of reading to our children. It is in every parent's power to bestow this gift on their children.

The Vowel
and Consonant Guide

Part A

Skills Checklist for Letter-Sound Relationships

Consonants

___ Initial consonants (knows the consonant sounds when they appear as the first letter of a word):

___b ___c ___d ___f ___g ___h ___j ___k ___l ___m

___n ___p ___q ___r ___s ___t ___v ___w ___x ___y

___z

___ Final consonants (knows the consonant sounds when they appear at the end of a word):

___b ___c ___d ___f ___g ___h ___j ___k ___l ___m

___n ___p ___q ___r ___s ___t ___v ___w ___x ___y

___z

___ Medial consonants (knows the consonant sounds when they appear in the middle of a word):

___b ___c ___d ___f ___g ___h ___j ___k ___l ___m

___n ___p ___q ___r ___s ___t ___v ___w ___x ___y

___z

Vowels

___ Short vowels:

___a ___e ___i ___o ___u ___y (as short *i*—gym)

___ Short vowel patterns:

   ___ab ___ack ___ad ___ag ___al ___am___an ___ap

   ___as ___at ___ax ___eb ___eck ___ed ___ef ___eg

   ___ell ___em ___en ___ep ___es ___ess ___et.___ib

   ___ick ___id ___ig ___il ___ill ___im ___in ___ip ___is

   ___it ___ix ___ob ___ock ___od ___og ___oll ___om

   ___on ___op ___oss ___ot ___ox ___ub ___uck ___ud

   ___uff ___ug ___ull ___um ___un ___up ___us ___uss

   ___ut

___ Long vowels:

   ___a ___e ___i ___ o ___u ___ y (baby) ___ y (cry)

___ Long vowel patterns:

   ___a-e (cake) ___ai (rain) ___ay (day) ___e-e (Pete)

   ___e (he) ___ee (feet) ___ea (eat) ___ei (receive)

   ___ey (key) ___i-e (ride) ___ie (tie) ___i (I) ___ight (light)

   ___ild (wild) ___ind (kind) ___o-e (rope) ___o (go)

   ___oa (boat) ___oe (toe) ___ough (dough) ___ow (snow)

   ___u-e (tune) ___ue (blue) ___ui (suit)

___ R-controlled vowels:

   ___ar (car) ___are (hare) ___are (are) ___air (hair)

   ___er (her) ___ere (here) ___ear (bear) ___ear (earth)

   ___ear (heart) ___eer (deer) ___eir (their) ___ear (spear)

   ___ir (bird) ___ire (fire) ___iar (friar) ___ier (flier)

   ___ier (tier) ___or (horse) ___or (work) ___ore (store)

___oor (door) ___oar (oar) ___our (hour) ___our (pour)

___our (journey) ___ur (purse) ___ure (cure)

___uire (squire)

___ *L*-controlled vowels:

___al (pal) ___al (salt) ___all (ball) ___ale (male)

___alf (half) ___alves (halves) ___el (elf) ___ell (bell)

___ eal (seal) ___eel (wheel) ___il (milk) ___ill (pill)

___ile (smile) ___ial (dial) ___oll (doll) ___oll (troll)

___ole (hole) ___oal (goal) ___ul (bulb) ___ull (gull)

___ull (bull) ___ule (mule) ___ual (equal) ___uel (fuel)

___uil (build)

___ Other vowel patterns:

___au (auto) ___aw (saw) ___ave (have) ___ea (bread)

___ei (weigh) ___eu (neutral) ___eau (beauty) ___ew (few)

___ey (they) ___ie (retrieve) ___ieu (lieu) ___oo (book)

___oo (boot) ___oo (flood) ___oi (oil) ___oy (boy)

___ou (route) ___ou (out) ___ou (touch) ___ou (should)

___ow (now) ___ua (aqua) ___uo (duo) ___uy (guy)

Consonant Combinations

___ Consonant digraphs (two consonants that make one sound):

___ Initial consonant digraphs (digraphs at the beginning of a word):

___ch (chair) ___sh (ship) ___th (think) ___th (then)
___wh (wheel)

___ Final consonant digraphs (digraphs at the end of a word):

___ch (lunch) ___tch (catch) ___sh (fish) ___th (bath)
___th (with) ___the (bathe)

___ Medial consonant digraphs (digraphs in the middle of a word):

___ch (richer) ___tch (watching) ___sh (wishing)
___th (ether) ___th (bathing) ___ wh (awhile)

___ Consonant blends:

___ Initial consonant blends (blends at the beginning of a word):

___bl ___br ___cl ___cr ___dr ___fl ___fr ___gl ___gr
___pl ___pr ___sc ___sk ___sl ___sm ___sn ___sp ___st
___sw ___sch ___scr ___spl ___spr ___squ ___str ___tr
___tw

___ Medial consonant blends (blends in the middle of the word):

___bl ___br ___cl ___cr ___dr ___fl ___fr ___gl ___gr
___pl ___pr ___sc ___sk ___sl ___sm ___sn ___sp ___st
___sw ___sch ___scr ___spl ___spr ___squ ___str ___tr
___tw

Two Sounds of C

___ Initial *c* (*c* at the beginning of a word):

___hard *c* (cake) ___soft *c* (city)

___ Medial *c* (*c* in the middle of a word):

___hard *c* (vacuum) ___soft *c* (racing)

Two Sounds of G

___ Initial *g* (*g* at the beginning of a word):

___hard *g* (gum) ___soft *g* (gem)

___ Medial *g* (*g* in the middle of a word):

___hard *g* (wagon) ___soft *g* (caged)

___*dg* like soft g (lodging)

Word Endings

___ Ending markers:

___ed (walked) ___s (boys) ___es (boxes)

___ing (tracking) ___'s (girl's) ___ies (babies)

___er (faster) ___est (fastest)

___ Doubling rule:

When adding *ed*, *er*, *est*, or *ing* to a c-v-c word, double the final consonant to keep the vowel short:

___running ___tanning ___hotter ___batted

___fatter ___hopped

If the final consonant is not doubled, the vowel will be pronounced as a long vowel sound:

___fuming ___cuter ___finest ___tuned ___baking

___hoping

Word Parts
___ Prefixes:

___re- ___de- ___pre- ___bi- ___be- ___a- ___un- ___dis-

___en- ___tri- ___quad- ___quin-

___ Suffixes:

___-able ___-ible ___-ly ___-ily ___-ness ___-ful ___-age

___-iage ___-tion ___-ion ___-sion ___-le ___-ble ___-dle

___-gle ___-al ___-ance ___-ence ___-ar ___-iar

___ Root words and other word parts:

___ped ___cycle ___aqua ___tele ___micro ___vision

___phone ___graph ___ology ___onomy ___bio ___astro

___ogist ___ist ___geo ___sphere

Compound Words and Multisyllable Words
___ Compound words (can read compound words):

___firehouse ___baseball ___football ___treetop

___popcorn ___sidewalk

___ Multisyllable words (can read multisyllable words):

  ___ 2-syllable words:

    ___letter ___spider ___candle ___runner

  ___ 3-syllable words:

    ___microscope ___finally ___happiness

  ___ 4-syllable words:

    ___terrifying ___disappointed ___wonderfully

Silent Letters and Irregular Consonant Pronunciations

___gn (gnat) ___kn (know) ___wr (write) ___ight (night)

___mb (lamb) ___lf (half) ___lve (halves) ___ps (psychic)

___ph (phone) ___sch (school)

Part B

Skills Checklist for Letter-Sound Relationships: Diagnosing Errors

Directions: After your child reads from oral reading passages and word lists, put an X on the line next to the skills with which your child had difficulty. Optional: If you have the time, you can also write the number of errors made for each skill and record it next to the "X."

Consonants

___ Initial consonants (knows the consonant sounds when they appear as the first letter of a word):

___b ___c ___d ___f ___g ___h ___j ___k ___l ___m

___n ___p ___q ___r ___s ___t ___v ___w ___x ___y

___z

___ Final consonants (knows the consonant sounds when they appear at the end of a word):

___b ___c ___d ___f ___g ___h ___j ___k ___l ___m

___n ___p ___q ___r ___s ___t ___v ___w ___x ___y

___z

___ Medial consonants (knows the consonant sounds when they appear in the middle of a word):

___b ___c ___d ___f ___g ___h ___j ___k ___l ___m

___n ___p ___q ___r ___s ___t ___v ___w ___x ___y

___z

Vowels

___ Short vowels:

   ___a ___e ___i ___o ___u ___y (as short *i*—gym)

___ Short vowel patterns:

   ___ab ___ack ___ad ___ag ___al ___am___an ___ap

   ___as ___at ___ax___eb ___eck ___ed ___ef ___eg ___ell

   ___em ___en ___ep ___es ___ess ___et___ib ___ick

   ___id ___ig ___il ___ill___im ___in ___ip ___is ___it

   ___ix___ob ___ock ___od ___og ___oll ___om ___on

   ___op ___oss ___ot ___ox___ub ___uck ___ud ___uff

   ___ug___ull ___um ___un ___up ___us___uss ___ut

___ Long vowels:

   ___a ___e ___i ___ o ___u ___ y (baby) ___ y (cry)

___ Long vowel patterns:

   ___a-e (cake) ___ai (rain) ___ay (day) ___e-e (Pete)

   ___e (he) ___ee (feet) ___ea (eat) ___ei (receive)

   ___ey (key) ___i-e (ride) ___ie (tie) ___i (I) ___ight (light)

   ___ild (wild) ___ind (kind) ___o-e (rope) ___o (go)

   ___oa (boat) ___oe (toe) ___ough (dough) ___ow (snow)

   ___u-e (tune) ___ue (blue) ___ui (suit)

___ *R*-controlled vowels:

   ___ar (car) ___are (hare) ___are (are) ___air (hair)

   ___er (her) ___ere (here) ___ear (bear) ___ear (earth)

___ear (heart) ___eer (deer) ___eir (their) ___ear (spear)

___ir (bird) ___ire (fire) ___iar (friar) ___ier (flier)

___ier (tier) ___or (horse) ___or (work) ___ore (store)

___oor (door) ___oar (oar) ___our (hour) ___our (pour)

___our (journey) ___ur (purse) ___ure (cure)

___uire (squire)

___ *L*-controlled vowels:

___al (pal) ___al (salt) ___all (ball) ___ale (male)

___alf (half) ___alves (halves) ___el (elf) ___ell (bell)

___ eal (seal) ___eel (wheel) ___il (milk) ___ill (pill)

___ile (smile) ___ial (dial) ___oll (doll) ___oll (troll)

___ole (hole) ___oal (goal) ___ul (bulb) ___ull (gull)

___ull (bull) ___ule (mule) ___ual (equal) ___uel (fuel)

___uil (build)

___ Other vowel patterns:

___au (auto) ___aw (saw) ___ave (have) ___ea (bread)

___ei (weigh) ___eu (neutral) ___eau (beauty) ___ew (few)

___ey (they) ___ie (retrieve) ___ieu (lieu) ___oo (book)

___oo (boot) ___oo (flood) ___oi (oil) ___oy (boy)

___ou (route) ___ou (out) ___ou (touch) ___ou (should)

___ou (cough) ___ow (now) ___ua (aqua) ___uo (duo)

___uy (guy)

Consonant Combinations

___ Consonant digraphs (two consonants that make one sound):

   ___ Initial consonant digraphs (digraphs at the beginning of a word):

   ___ch (chair) ___sh (ship) ___th (think) ___th (then)

   ___wh (wheel)

   ___ Final consonant digraphs (digraphs at the end of a word):

   ___ch (lunch) ___tch (catch) ___sh (fish) ___th (bath)

   ___th (with) ___the (bathe)

   ___ Medial consonant digraphs (digraphs in the middle of a word):

   ___ch (richer) ___tch (watching) ___sh (wishing)

   ___th (ether) ___th (bathing) ___ wh (awhile)

___ Consonant blends:

   ___ Initial consonant blends (blends at the beginning of a word):

   ___bl ___br ___cl ___cr ___dr ___fl ___fr ___gl

   ___gr ___pl ___pr ___sc ___sk ___sl ___sm ___sn

   ___sp ___st ___sw ___sch ___scr ___spl ___spr ___squ

   ___str ___tr ___tw

   ___ Medial consonant blends (blends in the middle of the word):

   ___bl ___br ___cl ___cr ___dr ___fl ___fr ___gl

   ___gr ___pl ___pr ___sc ___sk ___sl ___sm ___sn

___sp ___st___sw ___sch ___scr ___spl ___spr ___squ ___str ___tr ___tw

Two Sounds of C

___ Initial c (c at the beginning of a word):

___hard c (cake) ___soft c (city)

___ Medial c (c in the middle of a word):

___hard c (vacuum) ___soft c (racing)

Two Sounds of G

___ Initial g (g at the beginning of a word):

___hard g (gum) ___soft g (gem)

___ Medial g (g in the middle of a word):

___hard g (wagon) ___soft g (caged)

___dg like soft g (lodging)

Word Endings

___ Ending markers:

___ed (walked) ___s (boys) ___es (boxes)

___ing (tracking) ___'s (girl's) ___ies (babies)

___er (faster) ___est (fastest)

___ Doubling rule:

When adding ed, er, est, or ing to a c-v-c word, double the final consonant to keep the vowel short:

___running ___tanning ___hotter ___batted ___fatter ___hopped

If the final consonant is not doubled, the vowel will be
pronounced as a long vowel sound:

___fuming ___cuter ___finest ___tuned ___baking

___hoping

Word Parts

___ Prefixes:

___re- ___de- ___pre- ___bi- ___be- ___a- ___un- ___dis-

___en- ___tri- ___quad- ___quin-

___ Suffixes:

___-able ___-ible ___-ly ___-ily ___-ness ___-ful

___-age ___-iage ___-tion ___-ion ___-sion ___-le

___-ble ___-dle ___-gle ___-al ___-ance ___-ence

___-ar ___-iar

___ Root words and other word parts:

___ped ___cycle ___aqua ___tele ___micro ___vision

___phone ___graph ___ology ___onomy ___bio ___astro

___ogist ___ist ___geo ___sphere

Compound Words and Multisyllable Words

___ Compound words (can read compound words):

___firehouse ___baseball ___football ___treetop

___popcorn ___sidewalk

___ Multisyllable words (can read multisyllable words):

___ 2-syllable words:

___letter ___spider ___candle ___runner

___ 3-syllable words:

___microscope ___finally ___happiness

___ 4-syllable words:

___terrifying ___disappointed ___wonderfully

Silent Letters and Irregular Consonant Pronunciations

___gn (gnat) ___kn (know) ___wr (write) ___ight (night)

___mb (lamb) ___lf (half) ___lve (halves) ___ps (psychic)

___ph (phone) ___sch (school)

Short Vowel Pattern Words

ab	ack	ad	ag	al	am
cab	back	bad	bag	gal	ham
dab	hack	Dad	gag	pal	jam
gab	Jack	fad	hag	Sal	Pam
jab	lack	had	lag		ram
lab	pack	lad	nag		Sam
nab	quack	mad	rag		yam
tab	rack	pad	sag		
	sack	sad	tag		
	tack	tad	wag		
			zag		
blab	black	Brad	brag		clam
crab	clack	Chad	drag		cram
drab	crack	clad	flag		gram
flab	flack	glad	shag		scram
grab	shack		snag		slam
slab	slack		stag		tram
stab	smack				
	snack				
	stack				

an	ap	as	at	ax	-ass
ban	cap	gas	bat	ax	bass
can	gap	has	cat	fax	pass
Dan	lap		fat	Max	mass
fan	map		hat	tax	
Jan	nap		mat	wax	
man	rap		pat		
Nan	sap		rat		
pan	tap		sat		
ran	zap		Tat		
tan			vat		
van					

bran	clap		brat	flax
clan	flap		chat	
Fran	snap		flat	
plan	strap		scat	
scan	trap		slat	
Stan			that	
than				

eb	eck	ed	ef or eff	eg	ell
Deb	deck	bed	Jeff	beg	bell
web	neck	fed		leg	dell
	peck	led		Meg	fell
		Ned		peg	sell

eb	eck	ed	ef or eff	eg	ell
		red			tell
		Ted			well
		wed			yell
	check	bled	clef		shell
	fleck	bred			smell
	wreck	fled			spell
		shed			swell
		sled			
		sped			

em	en	ep	es	ess	et
gem	Ben	pep	yes	Bess	bet
	den			less	get
	men			mess	jet
	pen			Tess	let
	ten				met
	hen				net
					pet
					set
					vet
					wet
					yet
stem	glen	prep		bless	Chet
	then	step		chess	fret
	wren			dress	stet

ib	ick	id	ig	il	ill
bib	Dick	bid	big	nil	Bill
fib	kick	did	dig		dill
nib	lick	hid	fig		fill
rib	Mick	kid	jig		gill
	Nick	lid	pig		hill
	pick	rid	rig		ill
	quick	Sid	wig		Jill
	Rick		zig		kill
	sick				mill
	tick				pill
	wick				quill
					sill
					till
					will
crib	brick	grid	twig		chill
glib	chick	skid			frill
	click	slid			grill
	flick				krill
	slick				skill
	stick				spill
	trick				still

im	in	ip	it	ix
dim	bin	hip	bit	fix
him	din	lip	fit	mix

im	in	ip	it	ix
Jim	fin	quip	hit	six
Kim	kin	rip	kit	
rim	pin	sip	lit	
Tim	sin	tip	pit	
	tin	zip	quit	
	win		sit	
			wit	

im	in	ip	it
brim	chin	chip	flit
grim	grin	clip	grit
prim	shin	drip	knit
skim	skin	flip	skit
slim	spin	grip	slit
swim	thin	ship	spit
trim	twin	skip	split
		slip	
		snip	
		strip	
		trip	
		whip	

ob	ock	od	og	oll	op
Bob	dock	cod	bog	doll	bop
cob	lock	god	cog		cop
job	mock	nod	dog		hop
mob	rock	pod	fog		lop

ob	ock	od	og	oll	op
rob	sock	rod	hog		mop
sob		sod	jog		pop
			log		top
blob	block	plod	clog		chop
knob	clock	prod	flog		clop
snob	frock		frog		crop
throb	shock		smog		drop
	smock				flop
	stock				plop
					prop
					shop
					stop

oss	ot	ox
boss	cot	box
loss	dot	fox
moss	got	lox
Ross	hot	pox
toss	jot	
	lot	
	not	
	pot	
	rot	
	tot	
cross	blot	
dross	knob	

oss	**ot**	**ox**
floss	Scot	
gloss	shot	
	slot	
	spot	
	trot	

ub	**uck**	**ud**	**uff**	**ug**	**ull**
cub	buck	bud	Buff	bug	gull
dub	duck	cud	cuff	dug	hull
hub	luck	dud	huff	hug	lull
rub	puck	mud	puff	jug	
tub	suck			lug	
	tuck			mug	
				pug	
				rug	
				tug	

club	Chuck	spud	bluff	chug	skull
flub	cluck	thud	fluff	drug	
grub	pluck		gruff	shrug	
snub	snuck		stuff	slug	
stub	stuck			snug	
	struck				
	truck				

um	un	up	us	uss	ut
gum	bun	cup	bus	fuss	but
hum	fun	pup	Gus	Russ	cut
sum	gun		pus		gut
	pun				hut
	run				jut
	sun				nut
					rut
chum	shun		plus		glut
drum	spun				shut
glum	stun				strut
plum					
slum					
strum					
swum					

Consonant Blends

bl (as in *blouse*)	**br** (as in *braid*)	**cl** (as in *clock*)	**cr** (as in *crown*)	**dr** (as in *dress*)	**fl** (as in *fly*)	**fr** (as in *frog*)
black	Brad	clam	crab	drab	flab	frame
bland	brag	clap	crack	drain	flack	free
blast	braid	class	cram	drag	flair	freed
bled	brain	claw	crank	drape	flan	freeze
bleed	bran	clean	crash	dread	flap	fresh
blend	brand	clear	crate	dream	flat	fret
bless	brass	cleat	crave	dress	flaw	fridge
blimp	brat	click	cray	drink	flax	fried
blind	brave	cliff	craze	drip	fled	friend
bliss	bread	clip	cream	drive	flee	frisk
blob	bred	clock	crest	droll	fleece	frock
blond	bride	clone	crib	drop	flesh	frog
blot	broach	clop	cried	dross	flew	from
blouse	brown	close	crime	drove	flex	frond
blue	brute	clot	crimp	drug	fly	front
blunt		cloud	croon	drum		frost
blur		clown	crow			frown
		club	crown			fry
		clue				

gl (as in *glove*)	**gr** (as in *grapes*)	**pl** (as in *plate*)	**pr** (as in *prize*)	**sc** (as in *scarf*)	**sk** (as in *ski*)	**sl** (as in *sled*)
glad	grab	place	pray	scab	skate	slab
glass	grapes	plaid	prep	scan	ski	sled
glaze	grate	plan	press	scarf	skill	slip
glean	graze	plate	price	scarves	skip	slot
gleem	great	play	pride	scat		slump
glib	green	pleat	prime	Scott		
glob	grid	plod	prize			
glove	grill	plop	probe			
glum	grim	plot	prod			
	grime	ploy	prom			
	grin	plug	prone			
	grip	plum	prop			
	grit	plume	prose			
	groan	plus	prove			
	grope		prowl			
	gross					
	grove					
	grow					
	grown					

sm (as in *smile*)	**sn** (as in *snow*)	**sp** (as in *spot*)	**st** (as in *star*)	**sw** (as in *swing*)	**scr** (as in *screen*)	**spl** (as in *splash*)
smack	snack	space	stack	swab	scram	splash
smart	snip	speck	star	sweat	screen	splat

sm	sn	sp	st	sw	scr	spl
smell	snow	spell	steep	sweet	scribe	spleen
smile	snug	spill	stem	swing	scroll	split
smog		spot	step	swum	scrub	
smug		spun	still			
			stove			
			stub			

str	tr	tw	thr
(as in *street*)	(as in *train*)	(as in *twins*)	(as in *thread*)
strait	train	twins	thrash
strap	trek	twirl	thread
street	tribe	twist	thrice
stripe	troll		throw
stroll	trump		thrush
strut			

Part E

Word Lists for Magic *E* Words

a-e
(as in *cake*)

Abe	dane	Jake	pane	vase
ace	dare	Jane	quake	wade
ade	date	kale	race	wage
age	Dave	Kate	rage	wake
ale	daze	lace	rake	wave
ape	face	lake	rare	Yale
ate	fade	lame	rate	
bake	fake	lane	rave	
bale	fame	late	safe	
bane	fare	mace	sage	
bare	fate	made	sake	
base	gale	make	sale	
cage	game	male	same	
cake	gate	mane	sane	
came	gave	mare	save	
cane	gaze	mate	take	
cape	hale	maze	tale	
care	hare	name	tame	
case	hate	pace	tape	
cave	haze	page	vale	
dale	jade	pale	vane	

287

e-e
(as in *Pete*)
eke
Pete
Steve

i-e
(as in *bike*)

bike	like	ripe
bile	lime	rise
bite	line	side
cite	live	sire
dice	mice	site
dime	Mike	size
dine	mile	tide
dive	mime	tile
file	mine	time
fine	mire	tire
fire	nice	vibe
five	nine	vine
hide	pile	wide
hike	pine	wife
hire	pipe	wine
hive	quite	wipe
jive	rice	wire
kite	ride	wise
life		

o-e
(as in *rope*)

bone	joke	rode
code	Jove	role
coke	lone	rope
cone	lore	rose
cope	mode	rove
core	mole	sole
cove	mope	tome
dole	mopre	tone
dome	nose	tore
dote	note	tote
dove	poke	vote
doze	pole	woke
fore	Pope	wore
gore	pore	wove
hole	pose	yoke
home	quote	yore
hone	robe	zone
hope		

u-e
(as in *tune*)

cube	jute
cure	lute
cute	mule
duke	muse
dune	mute
dupe	pure
fume	rude
fuse	tube
huge	tune
juke	yule
June	

Part F

Word Lists for the Two-Vowel Rule

Rule: When two vowels are together, the first one does the talking (says its name) and the second one does the walking (is silent).

ai (as in *rain*)	**ay** (as in *day*) (y serves as vowel)	**ea** (as in *wheat*)		**ee** (as in *feet*)	
aid	bay	beach	read	bee	seek
aim	cay	bead	ream	beep	seem
air	day	beak	reap	beet	seen
bail	Fay	beam	rear	deed	seep
bait	gay	bean	sea	deep	seer
fail	Jay	bear	seal	deer	sees
fair	Kay	beat	seam	feed	tee
gain	lay	deal	sear	feel	teen
gait	may	dean	seas	feet	tees
hail	nay	dear	seat	heed	veer
hair	pay	fear	tea	heel	wee
jail	ray	feat	teak	jeep	weed
lain	say	gear	teal	jeer	week

290

ai	ay	ea		ee	
lair	way	heal	team	keel	weep
maid		heap	tear	keen	
mail		hear	teas	keep	
maim		heat	veal	leek	
main		lead	weak	leer	
nail		leak	weal	meek	
paid		lean	wear	meet	
pail		leap	wheat	need	
pain		meal	year	peek	
pair		mean	zeal	peel	
quail		meat		peep	
raid		near		peer	
rail		neat		queen	
rain		pea		reed	
sail		peak		reek	
tail		peal		reel	
vain		pear		see	
waif		peas		seed	
wail		peat			
wait					

ei (as in *receive*)	ey (as in *key*)	ie (as in *tie*)	oa (as in *coat*)	oe (as in *toe*)	ou (as in *dough*)
deceive	donkey	die	boar	doe	although
receive	honey	hie	boat	foe	dough
	key	lie	coal	hoe	though

ei	ey	ie	oa	oe	ou
	lacey	pie	coat	Joe	
	money	tie	foal	Moe	
	monkey	vie	foam	toe	
			goad	woe	
			goal		
			goat		
			hoax		
			load		
			loaf		
			loan		
			moan		
			moat		
			oat		
			road		
			roar		
			soak		
			soar		
			toad		

ue
(as in *blue*)

blue	hue
clue	rue
cue	true
due	
glue	

ui
(as in *suit*)

juice
fruit
suit

Part G

Vowels at the End of a Word

Long Vowel Sounds

Rule: When the vowels *e*, *o*, and *u* come alone at the end of a word, most of the time they have the long vowel sound.

e (as in *me*)	**o** (as in *go*)	**u** (as in *Peru*)
be	go	gnu
he	Jo	Lu
me	lo	Peru
she	no	menu
we	so	snafu
ye	*Exception:* do, to	

Other Vowel Sounds at the End of Words: A

When *a* comes at the end of a word, it is generally pronounced as "uh" as in *America*. It is mostly used in names of people and places:

Africa	Ghana
Alaska	Gina
Alberta	Guyana
America	India
Antarctica	Indiana
Argentina	Maria
Arizona	Nebraska

Australia	Nevada
Bolivia	Nigeria
British Columbia	North Carolina
California	Oklahoma
Canada	Pennsylvania
Colombia	South Carolina
Czechoslovakia	Tina
District of Columbia	Virginia
Florida	West Virginia

I

When *i* comes at the end of the word, it is generally pronounced as long *e* as in *ski*. It is also found in many names. Sometimes it is pronounced as long *i* as in *pi*, the mathematical term.

I as long *i*:	*I* as long *e*:	
hi	Billi	ski
I	Bobbi	spaghetti
pi	Cindi	Vicki
	Hawaii	Walli
	macaroni	ziti
	Mardi	
	Nicki	
	Nikki	
	Ricki	
	rigatoni	
	Sandi	

Part H

Word List of Digraphs

Initial **ch** (as in *cheese*):	Final **ch** (as in *torch*):	Final **tch** (as in *watch*):	Initial **sh** (as in *ship*):	Final **sh** (as in *fish*):	Initial **th** (as in *thumb*):
chart	church	batch	shade	bash	thank
chat	brunch	botch	shame	bush	thesis
check	lunch	catch	shape	cash	theta
cheer	lurch	ditch	share	dash	thick
cheese	much	hatch	shave	dish	thin
chess	rich	hutch	shear	fish	think
chest	torch	latch	shed	gash	thought
chick	touch	march	shell	lash	thud
child	such *march*	~~match~~	sheet	lush	thug
chime		patch	shin	mash	thumb
chin		pitch	shine	mush	thump
chip		stitch	ship	nosh	three
chive		watch	shrink	posh	thrill
choke			shock	push	thrive
choose			shone	rash	throb
chop			shop	rush	throne
chore			shot	sash	
chose			shrug	wash	
chum			shut	wish	

Final **th** (as in *bath*)	Initial **th** (as in *them*)	Final **th** (as in *with*)	Final **the** (as in *bathe*)	Initial **wh** (as in *wheel*)	Exceptions: Sometimes *wh* sounds like *h* and *the w* is silent.
bath	than	with	bathe	whack	who (hoo)
Beth	that		lathe	wham	whom (hoom)
both	the		loathe	what	whole (hole)
faith	their		writhe	wheel	whose (hooz)
forth	them			wheeze	
fourth	then			when	
hearth	there			where	
path	these			whet	
teeth	they			which	
tooth	they're			whiff	
	this			while	
	those			whim	
	thus			whine	
				whip	
				white	

Medial Digraphs

ch (as in *lunches*)	**sh** (as in *lashes*)	**th** (as in *bathtub*)	**th** (as in *father*)	**wh** (as in *every-where*)	**tch** (as in *catcher*)
lunches	bushel	bathtub	bother	awhile	catcher
lurching	lashes	pathway	brother	everywhere	latched

ch	sh	th	th	wh	tch
richer	mashed	toothache	father	somewhere	stitching
richest	mushy		mother	somewhat	watching
touching	washing		other		
	wishing		weather		

Part I

The Vowel Book

In the following exercise, your child should draw his or her own picture flashcards for these words and vowel sounds.

Example:

A

Short a:

a   apple

        cat

Long a:

a-e   cake

ai   rain

ay   day

Other *a* patterns:

au	faucet
aw	saw
ave	have

R-controlled *a*:

ar	car
are	care
air	hair

L-controlled *a*:

al	pal
al	salt
all	ball
ale	male
alk	walk
alm	palm
alf	half
alves	halves

E

Short *e*:

e	elephant	bed

Long *e*:

e-e	Pete
e	he
ee	feet
ea	eat
ei	receive
ey	key

Other *e* patterns:

ea	bread
ea	break

ei	weigh
eau	beauty
eu	neutral
ew	flew
ew	sew
ey	they

R-controlled *e*:

er	her
ere	here
ere	were
ear	bear
ear	spear
ear	earth
ear	heart
eer	deer
eir	their

L-controlled *e*:

el	elf
ell	bell
eal	seal
eel	wheel

I

Short *i*:

| i | in, lid |

Long *i*:

i-e	bike
ie	tie
i	I
ight	light
ild	wild
ind	kind

Other *i* patterns:

i	ski
ie	retrieve
ieu	adieu

R-controlled *i*:

ir	bird
ire	fire
iar	friar
ier	flier
ier	tier

L-controlled *i*:

il	milk
ill	pill
ile	smile
ial	dial

O

Short *o*:

o	octopus, pot

Long *o*:

o-e	rope
o	go
oa	boat
oe	toe
ou	dough
ow	snow

Other *o* patterns:

oo	book
oo	boot
oo	flood
oi	coin

oy	boy
ou	soup
ou	house
ou	cough
ou	could
ou	touch
ow	cow
oth	brother

R-controlled *o*:

or	horse
or	work
ore	store
oor	door
oar	oar
our	hour
our	pour
our	journey

L-controlled *o*:

oll	doll
oll	troll
ole	hole
oal	goal

U

Short *u*:

| u | up, sun |

Long *u*:

u-e	tune
ue	blue
ui	suit

Other *u* patterns:

ua	aqua
uo	duo
uy	guy

R-controlled *u*:

ur	purse
ure	cure
uire	squire

L-controlled *u*:

ul	bulb
ull	gull
ull	bull
ule	mule
ual	equal
uel	fuel
uil	build

Y

y as long *e*	baby
y as long *i*	cry
ye	bye
eye	eye

Part J

Word Lists for Other Vowel Patterns

A Patterns

au (faucet)

		aw (saw)	**ave** (have)
August	pause	brawl	have
auk	sauce	claw	
aura	Saul	crawl	
caught	taught	draw	
cause	taupe	drawl	
daughter	vault	flaw	
faucet	*Exception:*	jaw	
fault	laugh	law	
gaudy		paw	
haul		raw	
haughty		saw	
laud		shawl	
launch		slaw	
mauve		straw	
naught		thaw	
naughty			
Paul			
pauper			

R-controlled *a:*

ar (car)	**are** (hare)	**air** (hair)
bar	bare	fair
car	care	flair
far	dare	hair
jar	fare	lair
mar	flare	pair
par	glare	stair
star	hare	
tar	mare	
Exception:	pare	
war	rare	
	spare	
	stare	

L-controlled *a:*

al (pal)	**al** (salt)	**all** (ball)	**ale** (male)
Al	halt	ball	bale
gal	malt	call	dale
Hal	salt	fall	gale
pal		gall	hale
Sal		hall	kale
Val		mall	male
		stall	pale
		tall	sale
		wall	tale
			vale

alk (walk)	**alm** (palm)	**alf** (half)	**alves** (halves)
talk	balm	calf	salve
walk	calm	half	halves
	palm		

E Patterns

ea (bread)	**ea** (break)	**ei** (sleigh)	**eau** (beauty)	**eu** (neutral)
bread	break	freight	beautiful	Eugene
breakfast		neighbor	beauty	feud
breath		sleigh		neutral
dead		weigh		teutonic
dread				
feather				
head				
heather				
lead				
leather				
read				
tread				
weather				

ew (new)		**ew** (sew)	**ey** (they)
chew	grew	sew	grey
dew	new		hey
drew	pew		they
few	stew		whey
flew	threw		

R-controlled *e*:

er (her)		**ere** (here)	**ere** (were)
berth	perch	here	were
fern	perk	mere	
gerbil	perm	there	
germ	pert	where	
her	serf		
herb	serve		
herd	term		
jerk	terse		
kernel	verb		
merge	verge		
nerf	verse		
nerve	were		
per			

R-controlled *e*:

ear (bear)	**ear** (spear)	**ear** (earth)	**ear** (heart)	**eer** (deer)	**eir** (their)
bear	clear	dearth	heart	cheer	heir
pear	dear	early	hearth	deer	their
tear	dreary	earth		jeer	
wear	gear	heard		leer	
	hear	learn		seer	
	near	pearl		sheer	
	rear				
	shear				
	smear				
	spear				
	year				

L-controlled *e*:

el (elf)	**ell** (bell)	**eal** (seal)	**eel** (wheel)
el	bell	deal	eel
elf	dell	heal	feel
elm	fell	meal	heel
elves	quell	peal	kneel
gel	sell	real	peel
melt	smell	seal	reel
	spell	steal	steel
	swell	teal	wheel
	tell	veal	
	well	zeal	
	yell		

I Patterns

ie (retrieve)	**ieu** (adieu)
believe	adieu
retrieve	lieu
allieve	

R-controlled *i*:

ir (bird)	**ire** (fire)	**iar** (friar)	**ier** (flier)	**ier** (tier)
birch	dire	briar	crier	tier
bird	fire	friar	drier	
birth	hire	liar	flier	
chirp	sire		plier	
dirge	tire			
dirt	wire			

ir (bird)

fir	mirth
firm	stir
first	swirl
girl	twirl
girth	

L-controlled *i*:

il (milk)		**ild** (wild)	**ill** (pill)		**ile** (smile)
film	nil	mild	bill	pill	bile
filter	quilt	wild	dill	quill	file
hilt	silk		fill	sill	pile
jilt	silt		gill	spill	smile
kiln	silver		hill	still	tile
kilt	tilt		Jill	till	while
lilt	wilt		kill	will	
milk	zilch		mill		

L-controlled *i* (continued):

ial (dial)

dial
vial

Other long *i* patterns:

ind (kind)

bind
find
kind
mind
rind
wind

O Patterns

oo (book)	oo (boot)		oo (flood)	oi (coin)	oy (boy)
book	boo	pool	blood	boil	boy
brook	boom	proof	flood	broil	coy
cook	boon	room		coil	joy
crook	boost	root		coin	loyal
foot	boot	scoop		foil	ploy
good	bloom	soon		hoist	Roy
gook	broom	sloop		join	royal
hood	cool	spoon		joist	soy
hook	coop	stool		moist	toy
look	doom	stoop		noise	
nook	food	swoon		oil	
rookie	fool	too		point	
shook	goo	tool		poise	
took	goose	toot		soil	
wood	groom	troop		spoil	
woof	hoop			toil	
wool	hoot			voice	
	loom			void	
	loop				
	loose				
	loot				
	moo				
	mood				
	moon				
	moose				
	noon				

ou (soup)	**ou** (house)		**ou** (cough)	**ou** (could)	**ou** (touch)
coup	bough	mound	bought	could	couple
rouge	bout	mouse	cough	should	double
route	doubt	mouth	fought	would	enough
soup	foul	noun	sought		rough
troupe	found	pouch	thought		touch
	gout	pound	wrought		tough
	ground	pout			
	grout	sound			
	hound	south			
	house	trout			
	loud	wound			

ow (cow)			**oth** (brother)
bow	drown	now	brother
brow	frown	scowl	mother
brown	gown	town	other
clown	how	vow	
cow	howl	vowel	
crown	jowl	wow	

Other long *o* *R*-controlled *o*: patterns:

ow (snow)	**or** (horse)		**or** (worm)	**ore** (store)
bow	born	torch	word	bore
flow	cord	torn	work	core
flown	cork	worn	worm	fore

ow	**or**	**or**		**ore**
glow	corn	morse	worth	gore
grow	dorm	nor		lore
know	for	norm		more
low	ford	or		pore
row	forge	porch		sore
sow	fork	pork		shore
show	form	port		store
slow	fort	sort		snore
snow	horn	short		spore
stow	horse	stork		tore
tow	morn	storm		wore

| **oor** | **oar** | **our** | **our** | **our** |
(door)	(oar)	(hour)	(journey)	(pour)
boor	boar	flour	journey	pour
door	board	hour		tour
floor	hoard	sour		your
moor	oar			
poor	roar			
	soar			

L-controlled o:

oll (doll)	**oll** (troll)	**ole** (hole)	**oal** (goal)
doll	droll	dole	coal
	poll	hole	foal
	roll	mole	goal
	toll	pole	shoal
	troll	role	
		stole	

U Patterns

ua (aqua) **uo** (duo) **uy** (guy)

| aqua | duo | buy |
| suave | | guy |

R-controlled *u*:

ur (purse) **ure** (cure) **uire** (squire)

blur	hurl	cure	acquire
burn	nurse	lure	esquire
burst	purr	pure	require
curb	purse	sure	squire
curd	surf		
curl	surge		
curt	turf		
curve	turn		
fur			

L-controlled *u*:

ul (bulb) **ull** (gull) **ull** (bull) **ule** (mule) **ual** (equal)

bulb	gull	bull	mule	dual
bulge	hull	full	rule	equal
bulk	mull	pull		
gulf	null			
gulp				
mulch				
pulp				
pulse				
sulk				

L-controlled u (continued):

uel (fuel)   **uil** (quilt)

cruel	build
duel	built
fuel	guild
	guilt
	quill
	quilt

Y as a Vowel

y (baby)	**y** (cry)	**ye** (dye)
(y as long e)	(y as long i)	
baby	by	bye
cloudy	cry	dye
crazy	dry	eye
funny	fly	lye
handy	fry	rye
jumpy	my	
lady	pry	
ninety	shy	
penny	sly	
rainy	sty	
stormy	try	
tiny	why	
windy		

The Two Sounds of *C* and the Two Sounds of *G*

The Two Sounds of C

When *c* sounds like *s*:

Rule: When c is followed by *e*, *i*, or *y*, most of the time it will sound like *s*:

cellar

cement

cent

cider

city

civil

cycle

cyclone

deceive

face

race

racing

receive

When *c* sounds like *k*:

Rule: When *c* is followed by *a*, *o*, or *u*, most of the time it is like a *k* sound.

call	come
can	cow
cap	custard
cat	cut
coin	cute
color	

The Two Sounds of G

When *g* sounds like *go*:

Rule: When *g* is followed by *a*, *o*, or *u*, most of the time it has the hard sound of *g* as in *go*.

game	gone
gas	good
gate	gull
go	gum
goal	guts

When *g* has the sound of *j*:

Rule: When *g* is followed by *e*, *i*, or *y*, most of the time the *g* sounds soft like *j*.

gem	gym
gentle	gyro
gesture	Rule breakers: give, girl
gist	

Part L

Silent Letters and Irregular Consonant Pronunciations

gn
(*g* is silent)

gnat
gnome
gnu

kn
(*k* is silent)

knight
knit
know
known

wr
(*w* is silent)

wrestle
write
wrong

ight
(*gh* is silent)

height
light
night

mb
(*b* is silent)

climb
lamb
limb

l/or lv
(*l* is silent)

half
halve
salve

dge
(*d* is silent)

edge
fudge
ledge

ps
(*p* is silent)

psychiatrist
psychic
psychologist
psychology

ph
(*ph* as *f* in phone)

elephant
phone
phonics
phony

sch
(*sch* as *sk* in school)

scholar
scholarship
school

Dividing Syllables

C-V-C

If a word is divided after a consonant-vowel-consonant (c-v-c), the vowel will be pronounced as short:

bat/ter	hun/ter
bet/ting	med/al
bat/tle	mus/tard
din/ner	tod/dler
fan/tas/tic	win/dow

Note: The c may be made up of a single consonant, a blend, or a digraph. For this rule, the vowel will be a single vowel.

Other examples of c-v-c, when c can be a blend or a digraph:

blast/ing	grand/ma
blis/ter	shop/ping
blot/ter	shut/ter
branch/es	trust/ed
ched/dar	wheth/er
chim/ney	

C-V

If a word is divided after the consonant-vowel, the vowel will be pronounced as long:

bu/gle	fi/nal	lo/cal
de/cide	la/cy	

Note: The consonant can be a single consonant, a digraph, or a blend.

Other examples of c-v when the consonant is a digraph or blend: cra/dle

bri/dal   stru/del

bro/ken   the/sis

Part N

Associations to Remember Vocabulary Words

To help remember new vocabulary words, it helps to make an association that is far-out, wild, and ridiculous. Also, making up funny and strange sentences that have similar sounds to the syllables of the words can help one remember the meaning.

Word	Definition	Associations to Help Remember the Meaning
arcane	secret, known only to a few	Picture an arcade and that you are playing video games and only you know how to win. Someone else comes along and is frustrated because they do not know the secret of winning, and they start hitting the game with a cane.
culpable	guilty, deserving blame	Picture a culprit making mischief and tearing up the neighbor's flower garden. The culprit is caught and is declared guilty.
jocund	merry	Picture someone telling jokes and making others merry.
tenuous	slender, weak	Picture how "thin-you-was" (ten-u-ous) when you were weak.

tress	long lock of hair	Picture a girl's hair looking like a long *t* down the back of a girl's dress.
turbid	cloudy	Picture being in an airplane, and the clouds surrounding the plane are "turbulent."
yegg	robber	Picture a robber trying to steel jewels, who ends up finding eggs and then asks, "*Y* did this happen?"

Part O

Prefixes

Prefix	Meaning	Example Words	Meaning of Example Words
a-	on, in, at, in a state	about	on all sides, around
		above	in the sky, in a higher place
		around	on all sides, surrounding
		aside	on the side
		away	on the way
be-	on, around, about, to, at, make, cause to be	because	for the reason that
		belittle	to make little
		bemoan	to express grief
		beside	by the side of
		between	in the intermediate space
bi-	two	biannual	twice a year
		bicycle	two wheels
		bifocal	two focal lengths
		bimonthly	every two months or twice a month
		biped	a two-footed animal
de-	do the opposite of, take away, or reduce	deemphasize	to lessen the emphasis
		defame	to ruin the fame of
		defrost	free from ice
		dehydrate	take the water out of

Prefix	Meaning	Example Words	Meaning of Example Words
dis-	not	disappointed	hopes were not realized
		discouraged	not encouraged
		disobedient	not obedient
		disobey	not to obey
		dissatisfied	not satisfied
en-	in, within, cause to be	encase	to enclose
		encourage	inspire with courage
		ensure	to make sure
pre-	before	prepay	pay before
		pretest	test before
		preview	view before
quad-	four	quadrangle	four-sided enclosure surrounded by buildings
		quadruped	a four-footed animal
		quadruplets	four children born at one birth
quin-	five	quintet	group of five
		quintuplets	five children born at one birth
re-	again	recall	call again
		re-create	create again
		redo	do again
		redraw	draw again
		relocate	locate again
		remake	make again
		review	view again
		revisit	visit again
		rewrite	write again

Prefix	Meaning	Example Words	Meaning of Example Words
tri-	three	triangle	three angles
		tricycle	three wheels
		trimester	three terms
		tripod	three-legged stand
un-	not	unannounced	not announced
		unfair	not fair
		unhappy	not happy
		unnecessary	not necessary
		unsafe	not safe
		unsatisfied	not satisfied
		unsure	not sure

Part P

Suffixes and Word-Ending Patterns

Suffix or Word-Ending Patterns	Pronunciation	Meaning (Where Applicable)	Example Words
-able	(uh-bull)	capable of	capable laughable likable lovable manageable marketable salable verifiable
-ible	(uh-bull)	capable of	edible incredible possible terrible
-ly	(lee)	in the manner of	beautifully lovely quickly rapidly slowly

Suffix or Word-Ending Patterns	Pronunciation	Meaning (Where Applicable)	Example Words
-ily	(uh-lee)	in the manner of	angrily cheerily happily luckily merrily
-ness	(ness)	state, condition	happiness madness mindfulness sadness unhappiness
-ful	(full)	full of	beautiful fearful joyful sorrowful tearful wonderful
-age	(ij)	collection, rate, house, state	baggage dosage luggage postage
-iage	(ij)	state	carriage marriage

Suffix or Word-Ending Patterns	Pronunciation	Meaning (Where Applicable)	Example Words
-tion	(shun)	state of	action fascination imitation mention motion nation notion transportation
-ion	(yon)	act, result of an act, or a state	billion bunion million onion opinion trillion union vermilion
-sion	(shun)	state of	confusion fission fusion illusion tension
-le	(ul)		battle cattle kettle little

Suffix or Word-Ending Patterns	Pronunciation	Meaning (Where Applicable)	Example Words
-ble	(bul)		able bubble capable noble rubble sable stable trouble
-dle	(dul)		bundle candle fiddle handle huddle idle saddle
-gle	(gul)		boggle bugle goggle triangle
-al	(ul)	of the	final national rational tribal
-ance	(ince)	the action of, or state of	alliance brilliance defiance reliance

Suffix or Word-Ending Patterns	Pronunciation	Meaning (Where Applicable)	Example Words
-ence	(ince)	the action of, or state of	magnificence reference science
-ar	(er)	relating to, being	molecular particular
-iar	(yar)	relating to, being	familiar peculiar

Part Q

Root Words and Word Parts

Root Word or Word Parts	Meaning	Example Words	Meaning of Example Words
aqua	water	aqualung	apparatus to help breathe under water
		aquamarine	blue-green color like seawater
		aquarium	a tank for water plants and animals
astro	space	astronaut	one who travels in space
		astronomy	the study of space
bio	life	biography	to write the life of
		biology	the study of life
		biosphere	a globe or planet containing life

Root Word or Word Parts	Meaning	Example Words	Meaning of Example Words
cycle	wheel	bicycle	two wheels
		motorcycle	motorized wheels
		tricycle	three wheels
		unicycle	one wheel
geo	earth	geography	one who maps (writes) the earth
		geologist	one who studies the earth
		geology	the study of earth
		geothermal	heat from the earth
graph	to write	autobiography	to write one's own life
		autograph	to write one's own name
		biography	to write the life of
		seismograph	to chart earthquakes
		telegraph	to write from far away
micro	small	microchip	small chip
		microscope	to see small things
		microwave	short waves

Root Word or Word Parts	Meaning	Example Words	Meaning of Example Words
ogist or ist	one who studies	biologist	one who studies biology
		botanist	one who studies plants
		chemist	one who studies chemistry
		physicist	one who studies physics
ology	study of	biology	the study of life
		meteorology	the study of weather
		zoology	the study of animals
onomy	study of	astronomy	the study of space
ped	foot	biped	a two-footed animal
		moped	using motor and the feet
		pedal	a foot lever
		pedestal	foot of a stand
		pedestrian	one who travels by foot
		pedicure	care of the feet

Root Word or Word Parts	Meaning	Example Words	Meaning of Example Words
phone	sound	phonics	sounds of the letters
		phonograph	record player in which sound is etched into a record
		telephone	sound from far away
sphere	globe	atmosphere	air around the globe
		biosphere	a globe or planet containing life
		hemisphere	half a globe
		spherical	round like the globe
tele	far	telecommunication	to communicate from far away
		telephone	sound from far away
		telescope	to help see objects far away
		television	to see from far away
vision	to see	television	to see from far away

Part R

Checklist of Vocabulary Skills

___ Uses a dictionary and glossary to get word meaning

___ Uses context clues to get word meaning

___ Uses knowledge of word parts: roots, prefixes, suffixes to get word meaning

Part S

Checklist of Comprehension Skills

Literal:

___ States main idea

___ Identifies details

___ Identifies sequence (Time-order)

Inferential:

___ Identifies inferred main idea

___ Makes predictions

___ Makes judgments

___ Identifies cause and effect relationships

National Reading Diagnostics Institute, founded by Ricki Linksman, M.Ed., provides training for parents, teachers, and school administrators in reading instruction and using learning styles to accelerate progress. It offers workshops, seminars, college courses, consultations to school districts and parent groups. It provides diagnostic services to assess a student's reading needs and learning style and also provides individualized learning plans and materials to help students improve reading and study skills. For more information, please call or write:

National Reading Diagnostics Institute
1755 Park St., Suite 200
Naperville, IL 60563
(708) 717-4221

Index

Acceleration of reading, 88–89, 129–30, 258
Accomplishment, sense of, 239, 253–54
ADD (attention-deficit disorder), xi
  how kinesthetic learners appear restless and need more movement, 23–24, 28–29
Adults, xi, 45
Affirmations, positive, 41–48, 250–51
Aides, reading, 73–74, 81
Alphabet,
  activities to learn through learning styles, 131–36
Anticipatory reading, 255
Approval, 238, 242–43
Auditory learners. *See also learning styles, auditory.*
  comprehension, 200
  description of, 17, 21–22, 24–27, 93–95, 97–100
  games for learning vowel sounds, 139–40
  how to adapt instruction to, 112
  how to diagnose, 18–20, 93–114
  how to teach letter-sound relationships, 102, 131–32
  how to teach reading to, 102, 105–107, 114, 130–32
  how to teach vocabulary, 105–107, 181–82

Backwards, writing, 60
Basal readers, 70
BD. *See behavioral disorders.*
Behavioral disorders, xi, 63

Belonging, sense of, 238, 249–52
Bibliotherapy, 247
Blindness, 65
Body language,
  negative, 39
  positive 39, 243
Bonding between parent and child through reading, 246
Book store, 242, 245–46
Books,
  chapter books, 254
  how to select, 245–46, 259–60
  interest in, 55, 255–56, 259
  love of, 55
  picture, 254
  reading aloud, 246
  resolving emotional issues through, 247

Cause and effect. *See comprehension, cause and effect.*
Chapter I (Title I), 74, 87
Challenges, meeting, 238, 243–46, 254
College entrance examinations, preparing for, 193–94
College students, xi, 45, 65
Comfort, 238, 247–49
Compare and contrast. *See comprehension, compare and contrast.*
Comprehension, 7, 12–14, 15–16, 69, 72, 85–86, 195–228, 238, 258
  analyze, 86
  application, 86

Comprehension (*cont.*)
  cause and effect, 224–27;
    games, 224–26; strategies for
    teaching, 224–26
  compare and contrast, 86
  details, 85, 199, 209–13; games,
    212–13; strategies for
    teaching, 209–13; teaching
    the difference between main
    idea and, 214; test for
    problems in, 196–97
  diagnosing problems in,
    195–201
  evaluate, 86
  factual questions. *See
    comprehension, details.*
  how to test for and analyze
    problems in, 196–201, 207
  inference, 86, 199; games,
    221–24; inferring characters'
    feelings, 218–20; strategies for
    teaching, 218–24; test for
    problems in, 197–98
  judgment questions, 86, 199;
    test for problems in, 198
  learning style and, 200
  main idea, 85, 199, 210,
    213–15; factual, 213; games,
    215; inferential, 213; strategies
    for teaching, 213–17; teaching
    the difference between details
    and, 214; test for problems in,
    197
  memory and problems in, 200
  predictions, 86, 199, 256;
    strategies for teaching,
    217–18; test for problems in,
    198
  reading level and, 199
  relationship between problems
    in letter-sound relationships
    and comprehension, 201
  relationship between problems
    in vocabulary and
    comprehension, 176–77, 195,
    200–201
  relevance of comprehension to
    everyday life, 226–28
  remedies for problems in,
    202–28
  skimming, 207–209, 210; for
    key words, 208–209, 210
  strategies for answering
    comprehension questions,
    207–27
  teaching students how to
    comprehend, 202–206
  time order questions, 85, 199;
    games, 216–17; strategies for
    teaching, 216–17; test for
    problems in, 197
Consonants, 8
  blends, 8, 146–49, 168; games
    for, 147–49
  digraphs, 8, 153–56, 168; games
    for, 156
  irregular, 164–67
  silent, 166–67
Context clues, 10–11, 85, 174–75.
  *See also vocabulary, context
  clues.*
Contractions, 163
Curiosity, satisfying one's, 239,
  255–56

Deafness, 65
Decoding skills, 7–8
Details. *See comprehension,
  details.*
Diagnosing reading skills. *See
  diagnosis under
  comprehension, independent
  reading strategies, letter-
  sound relationships, and
  vocabulary.*
Dictionary. *See vocabulary,
  dictionary.*
Dyslexia, 56–57,

ED. *See emotional disorders.*
Educable mentally handicapped,
  63
Educable mentally retarded, 63
Elementary school students, xi, 44,
  127, 169–70

teaching through learning styles
to, 101–104
EMH. *See educable mentally
handicapped.*
Emotional disorders, xi, 45, 63
Emotional satisfaction from
reading, 238, 246–47
Empowerment, sense of, 238,
252–53
EMR. *See educable mentally
retarded.*
English classes, 87
English language, 7–8, 157
difficulties in learning the, 7–8
Evaluate. *See comprehension,
evaluate.*

Facial expressions,
negative, 38
positive, 37–38, 243
Federal assistance for reading, 74,
87

Games and activities,
activities to learn the alphabet
through learning styles,
131–36
auditory learner games for vowel
sounds, 139–40
cause and effect games, 224–26
consonant blend games, 147–49
consonant digraph games, 156
context clue games, 186–7
detail games, 212–23
dictionary games, 183–84
glossary games, 183–84
inference games, 221–24
kinesthetic learner games for
vowel sounds, 140–41
main idea games, 215
prefix games, 189
root word games, 191–92
suffix games, 190–91
tactile learner games for vowel
sounds, 140
time order games, 216–17
visual learner games for vowel
sounds, 139

Gifted, xi, 45
Global learners, 142, 216
Glossary. *See vocabulary,
glossary.*
Guidance counselor, 63
Guide words, 179–80
Gustatory learners. *See also
learning styles, gustatory.*
description of, 17
how to teach reading to, 113–14

High school students, xi, 44,
65–66, 127, 170, 246
comprehension skills and,
12–13,
preparing for college entrance
examinations, 193–94
relationship between reading
achievement and acceptance
into college or vocational
school, 252
relationship between reading
and getting a good job, 253
relationship between reading
and winning a scholarship,
252
teaching through learning styles
to, 104–10
Higher-level thinking, 88–89,
227–28
Hobbies, and reading, 239–42
Homework, 53, 67

Imagination, 256
Inclusion (REI), 75
Independent reading strategies, 7,
14–16, 69, 72, 86, 193,
229–38, 258
how to diagnose and analyze
problems in, 230–32
remedies for, 233–37
Infants, 89, 246, 255
Inference. *See comprehension,
inference.*
Interest in reading, 238–42,
255–57, 259

Judgment questions. *See
comprehension, judgment.*
Junior high school. *See middle
school.*

Kinesthetic learners. *See also
learning styles, kinesthetic.*
comprehension, 200
description of, 17, 23–25,
28–29, 93–94, 96–97, 100
games for learning vowel
sounds, 140–41
how to adapt instruction to, 113,
256
how to diagnose, 18–20, 93–114
how to teach letter-sound
relationships, 103–104,
132–33
how to teach reading to,
103–104, 109–10, 114, 130,
133–34
how to teach vocabulary,
109–10, 182

Learning disabilities, xi, 3, 28,
45–46, 56–67
definition, 56
of auditory input, 57, 59
of aural output, 57, 59–60
of visual input, 57–59, 65
of written output, 57, 60
testing for, 58–63
Learning styles, 4, 17–30, 31,
93–114
Descriptions of. *See learning
styles, types and descriptions
of.*
Diagnosing, 93–101; by
observation checklist, 94–97;
by questionnaire, 18–20, 94;
by speaking with the child,
94, 97–100; by trying
different teaching methods,
94, 100–101
How students can adapt
instruction to their own style;

111–14; auditory adaptations,
112; kinesthetic adaptations,
113, 256; tactile adaptations,
112; visual adaptations,
111–12
How to teach letter-sound
relationships according to,
130–34, 139–41; auditory
learners, 102, 131–32;
kinesthetic learners, 103–104,
133–34; tactile learners,
102–103, 132–33; visual
learners, 101, 131
How to teach reading according
to, 101–14; how to teach
auditory learners, 102,
105–107, 114, 130–32; how to
teach gustatory learners,
113–14; how to teach
kinesthetic learners, 103–104,
109–10, 114, 130, 133–34;
how to teach learners with
several preferences, 110–11,
134; how to teach olfactory
learners, 113–14; how to
teach tactile learners,
102–103, 107–109, 114,
132–33; how to teach visual
learners, 101, 104, 114, 131
Matching to instruction, 24–25,
61–62, 93
Reading problems due to
instruction in wrong style,
25–30
Types and descriptions of;
auditory, 17, 21–22, 24–27,
93–95, 97–100; gustatory, 17;
kinesthetic, 17, 23–25,
28–29, 93–94, 96–97, 100;
olfactory, 17; tactile, 17,
22–25, 27–28, 93–95, 97,
99–100; visual, 17–18, 21,
24–26, 93–95, 97–98, 100
Learning styles test, 18–20
Letter-sound relationships, 7–8,
14, 15, 69, 72, 83–85,
101–104, 122, 233, 238, 258
consonant blends. *See*

consonant blends.
consonant digraphs. *See consonant digraphs.*
consonants, irregular. *See consonants, irregular.*
consonants, silent. *See consonants, silent.*
diagnosing problems in, 115–28, 169–70; using passage reading for, 116–25, 169–70; using word lists for, 125–26, 169–70
how to remedy problems in, 129–71
irregular word patterns, 167–69
multisyllable words, 170–71
relationship between problems in letter-sound relationships and comprehension, 201
teaching to auditory learners, 102
teaching to kinesthetic learners, 103–104
teaching to tactile learners, 102–103
teaching to visual learners, 101
vowels. *See vowels, short, long, combinations, irregular patterns, and vowels followed by "l" and "r."*
Library, 15, 242, 245–46
Literature classes, 86–87
analyzing literature: character development, 87; conflict, 87; plot, 86–87; theme, 86–87; use of language and literature techniques, 87; writer's craft, 86
Love of reading. *See reading, enjoyment of.*

Magazines, and interest in reading, 240, 242
Main ideas. *See comprehension, main idea.*
Memory improvement, 182–83, 194, 257
Mental retardation, xi, 45–46, 63

Middle school students, xi, 44, 65–66, 127, 170
teaching through learning styles to, 104–10
Monitoring. *See self-monitoring.*
Motivation, 3, 49–55, 61–62
lack of, 3, 49–55
success in reading and, 49–55
Movies,
comparison between book version and, 221
to teach inference skills, 219–20, 222–24

Newspapers, 240, 242
Nonverbal communication, 3, 22–23, 37–41, 218–19, 243, 248–49
Novel or unique experiences. *See unique or novel experiences.*

Olfactory learners. *See also learning styles, olfactory.*
description of, 17
how to teach reading to, 114

Parents,
record-keeping, 7–8
training, xi
volunteers, 73–74
Parent-teacher conferences, 111–14
Parts of speech, 180
Phonics, 70, 168–69
Physical handicaps, xi
Positive statements, 41–48
Predictions. *See comprehension, predictions.*
Prefixes. *See vocabulary, prefixes.*
Preschool, 83, 89
Programmed readers, 70
Psychologist. *See school psychologist.*
Public and private schools, 62, 81, 88

Reading,
acceleration and advancement, 88–89, 129–30

Reading (*cont.*)
  enjoyment of, 238–57
  how it is learned: preschool, 83;
    elementary school, 83–86;
    middle school, 86; high
    school, 87
  independent reading strategies.
    *See independent reading
    strategies*; in the content
    areas, 87
  practice time, 144–45, 259
  shared, 246–47
Reading at
  frustration level, 121, 123–25,
    244–25, 259
  independent level, 121, 122–23,
    125, 244–45, 259
  instructional level, 121, 123, 125,
    244–45, 259
Reading diagnosis. *See diagnosis
    under comprehension,
    independent reading
    strategies, letter-sound
    relationships, and vocabulary.*
Reading problems,
  causes of, 1–67
  undiagnosed reading problems,
    258
Reading programs, 69–77
Reading rate, 119–20, 122–25
Reading specialist, 63, 75–77, 81,
    88, 90
Reading speed, increasing, 259
Reading teacher, 63, 75–77, 81
Reading-writing connection,
    135–36
Recognition, 238, 242–43
Regular education initiative (REI
    or inclusion), 75
Remedial reading class, 65–66,
    74, 87–88
Report cards, 89, 252
Reversals of letters, 57, 60
Rewards, 55
Roots. *See vocabulary, roots.*

School psychologist, 58–60,
    63–64

Security, 238, 247–49
Self-concept. *See self-esteem.*
Self-esteem, 3, 31–48, 61–62,
    127–28, 249–52
  how it develops, 32
  low, 3, 31, 33–35, 43, 127, 258
  positive, 31, 35–37, 130
  raising, 127–28, 258–59
  school achievement and, 32
Self-fulfilling prophecy, 41–42
Self-monitoring reading, 235–37
Sequential learners, 142, 216
Skills chart, 7, 71
SLD (Specific learning disability).
    See learning disability.
Social worker, 63
Special education, 58, 60, 64
Special reading class, 74
Specific learning disability. *See
    learning disability.*
Standardized tests, 61–62, 89
Strategies for independent reading.
    *See independent reading
    strategies.*
Suffixes. *See vocabulary, suffixes.*
Sustained silent reading, 123
Syllables, 170–71
  multisyllable words, 170–71

Tactile learners. *See also learning
    styles, tactile.*
  comprehension, 200
  description of, 17, 22–25,
    27–28, 93–95, 97, 99–100
  games for learning vowel
    sounds, 140
  how to adapt instruction to, 112
  how to diagnose, 18–20, 93–114
  how to teach letter-sound
    relationships, 102–103,
    132–33
  how to teach reading to,
    102–103, 107–109, 114,
    132–33
  how to teach vocabulary,
    107–109, 182
Television,
  decreasing viewing of television

and increasing reading time, 251–52
to teach inference skills, 220
Thinking skills,
developing, 129–30
Time order questions. See comprehension, time order questions.
Title I (Chapter I), 74, 87
TMH. See trainable mentally handicapped.
TMR. See trainable mentally retarded.
Toddlers, 89, 255
Tone of voice,
negative, 40–41, 248–49
positive, 39–41, 243, 249
Trainable mentally handicapped, 63
Trainable mentally retarded, 63

Unique or novel experiences, 239, 256–57
United States Department of Education Study, xi

Video games,
decreasing time used for video games and increasing reading time, 251–52
Visual learners. See also learning styles, visual.
comprehension, 200
description of, 17–18, 21, 24–26, 93–95, 97–98, 100
games for learning vowel sounds, 139
how to adapt instruction to, 111–12
how to diagnose, 18–20, 93–114
how to teach letter-sound relationships, 101, 131
how to teach reading to, 101, 104, 114, 131
how to teach vocabulary, 104–105, 181
Vocabulary, 7, 10–12, 14, 15, 69, 72, 85–86, 104–10, 172–94,

233, 238, 244, 258
college entrance examinations and, 193–94
diagnosing problems with, 172–77
how to test for and analyze problems in, 173–77
remedies for problems in, 178–194
relationship between problems in vocabulary and comprehension, 176–77, 195, 200–201
remembering, 182–83
teaching to auditory learners, 105–107, 181–82
teaching to kinesthetic learners, 109–10, 182
teaching to tactile learners, 107–109, 182
teaching to visual learners, 104–105, 181
techniques to getting meaning: context clues, 178, 184–87, 193, 234. See also context clues; games, 186–87; dictionary, 178–82, 192, 231; games, 183–84, using a, 11, 178–82; glossary, 178–82, 192, 231, using a, 11, 178–82; games, 183–84; knowledge of word parts, 175, 178, 187–92, 233; prefixes, 175, 178, 187–9, 193–4, 233, games, 189; roots, 175, 178, 187, 191–94, 233, games, 191–92; suffixes, 175, 178, 187, 190–91, 193–94, 233, games, 190–91
Vowel and Consonant Guide,
how to use, 71, 121, 125–26, 141–42, 147, 153, 157–58, 163–64, 167, 171, 183, 199
Vowel Book, 141–42, 157–58, 161, 163
Vowel sounds, 7–8, 115–16, 136–46; games for, 142–44; auditory, 139–40; kinesthetic,

Vowel sounds (*cont.*)
140–41; learning through
learning styles, 139–41;
tactile, 140; visual, 139
long, 7–8, 149–53, 168
short, 7–8, 137–46, 168
vowel combinations, 156–62,
168

vowels followed by l, 163–64
vowels followed by r, 162–63

Whole language programs, 70,
168–69
Word-attack skills, 7–8.
Word parts. *See vocabulary, word
parts.*